Children, School and Society in Nineteenth-Century England

Children, School and Society in Nineteenth-Century England

Anne Digby
and
Peter Searby

First published 1981 by
THE MACMILLAN PRESS LTD
London and Basingstoke
Associated companies in Delhi Dublin
Hong Kong Johannesburg Lagos Melbourne
New York Singapore and Tokyo

Printed in Hong Kong

British Library Cataloguing in Publication Data

Digby, Anne, *b. 1942*
　　Children, school and society in nineteenth-century England.
　　1. Educational sociology – England
　　2. Education – England – History – 19th century
　　I. Title   II. Searby, Peter
　　370.19'3'0942　　　　　LC191.8.G7

　　ISBN 0-333-24678-0
　　ISBN 0-333-24679-9 pbk

CONTENTS

PREFACE

This book originated in an undergraduate course on nineteenth-century education and society that we taught together in Cambridge for five years. We wished to exemplify and illustrate our teaching by the use of documents, but found that the focus of existing collections was too narrowly bureaucratic and legislative; it reflected a view of education from Westminster or Whitehall rather than from the home or the schoolroom. We also felt that much modern writing for students looked at educational history in a constricted way which isolated it from intellectual developments in other historical fields. Part One – Problems and Perspectives: Schools and Schooling in the Nineteenth Century – aims to provide a social and educational context within which the documents in Part Two can be interpreted. Through drawing on recent work on the history of education some leading themes within the field have been selected for discussion, and an attempt made to place them within wider changes in nineteenth-century society.

The first four sections of Part One analyse changes in literacy and contemporary developments in institutional schooling in order to provide a general educational framework for the period. Sections 5, 6 and 7 are related more specifically to Section I of the documents, Education, Religion and Morality, while Sections 8 and 9 relate to Section II, Education, Social Class and the Economy. A linking passage on the school curriculum follows in Sections 10 and 11. Sections 12 and 13 are concerned with teachers and give the context for section III of the documents, Teachers and the Classroom. Section IV of the documents on Education and Girls is introduced by the final sections, 14 and 15 of Part One.

The documents themselves have been chosen to illuminate the assumptions and attitudes which informed schools and schooling in the nineteenth century. Each documentary section is organised round a theme and outlined in a short sectional preface. It is our hope that organising the collection in this way will provide a corrective to the common but outmoded view of educational history as a dreary sequence of institutional growth.

We have both found the experience of writing with a colleague stimulating. A. D. compiled Sections II and IV, P. S. I and III. A. D. drafted those parts of the interpretative essay dealing with the elementary school, social control and the economy, and the education of girls; P. S. drafted pages dealing with literacy, religion, State intervention and secondary schooling. We offered criticisms of each other's work and revised our own in the light of them. We jointly take responsibility for the judgements made in the book.

We should like most of all to thank colleagues and students in Cambridge for their helpful comments.

ANNE DIGBY

PETER SEARBY

ACKNOWLEDGEMENTS

The publishers and editors are grateful to the following for permission to reproduce material:
Managers of Park Street School, Cambridge (doc. 39); Sheila Malmstrom (doc. 22, 41); Norfolk Record Office (doc. 72); the Castle Museum, York (docs 27, 28, 34, 58, 71); the Headmistress and School Council of Wycombe Abbey School (doc. 60); Oxford University Press (doc. 59).

Note to the Reader
A number of documents in Part Two have been reproduced facsimile from handwritten originals and for clarity each one is accompanied by a transcription in ordinary type.

PART ONE

Problems and Perspectives: Schools and Schooling in the Nineteenth Century

1. EDUCATIONAL PROVISION AND THE GROWTH OF LITERACY

To measure the precise impact of educational agencies on generations long dead is one of the hardest tasks that can face the historian, since he must assess data on the ability to read, write and calculate which for the most part have not been preserved, or indeed were not often recorded. Even when available to us, such information is often cryptic and unrevealing. This is certainly true of the material exploited to show the growth of literacy in England and Wales in the last two centuries – signatures or marks in the marriage registers kept by Anglican churches from 1754 onwards, and by other bodies after 1837.

These registers are firm evidence only of spouses' capacity to sign their own names. They do not, it is obvious, show whether it was acquired in childhood or later, or at a school or through more informal means. It has even been asserted that attestation by mark rather than signature is no proof of inability to sign, since spouses frequently concealed their ability through fear of embarrassing their partner. This contention, intrinsically open to doubt, is rendered even harder to sustain by the lack of the firm marks to be expected in such cases. At least, therefore, we can be satisfied that 'marking' reflects incapacity to write. It is harder to estimate the exact degree of literacy a signature denotes. It is usually taken to show the ability to read fluently and to write laboriously: those with the skill to write easily would be fewer in number than 'signatories', at all events before the coming of efficient mass education, and those able to read only haltingly would be greater in number, perhaps by 50 per cent.[1] This scale is consistent with the findings of Victorian surveys of literacy and with the usual pattern of elementary instruction before 1840; more were taught to read than to write. Nevertheless, it is important to remember our uncertainty about the wider meaning of signature evidence. And we have no body of evidence bearing on arithmetical skills, arguably as important an educational benefit as literacy.

After 1838 the register evidence was collated by the Registrar General and published in his annual reports. They show that 66 per cent of males signed the register in 1840, and that the percentage rose steadily thereafter, reaching 80 per cent in 1870 and 97 per cent in 1900. The signatures are of bridegrooms who had left school twelve or fifteen years previously, and so reflect the schools' performance in a delayed fashion; thus it was not until 1880 at the earliest (when the male literacy rate was 86 per cent) that signature evidence can be said to be showing the effects of the 1870 Act. Mass literacy was largely achieved by private and voluntary schools.

The rise in the percentage of signatories between 1840 and 1900 reflects the vast increase in educational provision after 1820, and is roughly equal to the rise in the five centuries before 1840. This earlier increase is singularly hard to track because before 1754 the evidence is extremely scrappy and after it is dispersed in a host of parish registers. Recently, however, the evidence from some widely different parishes has been collated and analysed.[2] Roger Schofield's work shows that fewer than 60 per cent of bridegrooms signed in 1754 and that the percentage stayed constant for the next fifty years – a remarkable plateau, which had not been suggested by the work of earlier historians. After some short-term perturbations the literacy rate rose steadily from 1805 onwards. The evidence relating to brides is rather different. Under 40 per cent signed in 1754, the percentage increasing slowly thereafter to just over 50 per cent in 1840.

It is important to have knowledge of these national trends, but of course in 1780 education was planned and administered nationally far less than in 1880, let alone today. Aggregate figures for the kingdom as a whole mask considerable variations between one area and another. The percentage of spouses 'signing' in the English counties in 1870 varied from 88 in Surrey to 60 in Staffordshire. Even county aggregates conceal heterogeneity. The signature rate in the town of Cambridge in 1866 was 87 per cent, but in the county 72 per cent. In his survey of all Bedfordshire marriages between 1754 and 1844 Roger Schofield found that in 14 parishes the male literacy rate fell by more than 10 per cent over the period, and in 24 rose by more than 10 per cent. It is difficult to relate much of this variation to underlying socio-economic differences, but some correspondences seem clear. First, market towns appear to have had a consistently good educational performance. In all such places surveyed by Schofield the literacy rate rose in the period. The more detailed evidence after 1840 suggests the same buoyancy, with market towns (for example, Ipswich and Shrewsbury) often achieving higher scores than their purely agricultural hinterlands; we see a reflection of superior educational provision and a greater proportion of middle-class inhabitants. Secondly, towns such as Leeds that were subject to industrialisation tended to perform badly, and the impact of the Industrial Revolution was sometimes catastrophic; in Ashton-under-Lyne the percentage signing fell from 48 per cent in 1823 to 9 in 1843.[3] It is not, however, convincing to imply, as one author has recently, that the crucial determinant was the factory, which lowered educational standards achieved by the outwork system.[4] In Victorian times some of the lowest literacy figures were found in Coventry, Leicester and Nottingham, where the factory came late and where the Industrial Revolution took the form of an extension of outwork. In the industrial towns, where the literacy rate was below the national average, education suffered not because of the factory but because provision was swamped by a rapid increase in population, and because industrial labour lured children from the schoolrooms.

2. PRIVATE AND PUBLIC INITIATIVES IN ELEMENTARY SCHOOLING

In spite of the economic pressures which militated against poor people finding the school pence to provide education for their children, considerable numbers of working-class parents were prepared to make the requisite financial sacrifices if the character of the available schooling was congenial to them. One perceptive study[5] points out the importance of self-financing private schools in the education of children of the poor. Lacking the regulations as to dress, appearance and attendance imposed by church schools, and without their air of charitable condescension and repressive social discipline, they were much more a part of working-class communities. They were frequently preferred by parents, although their fees were often higher. It is estimated that out of over 250,000 pupils in 1750 at least 70 per cent were in private schools – it having recently been shown that many of these were not, as had often previously been thought, 'public' charity schools.[6] Out of over 1·2 million schoolchildren in 1833 almost 60 per cent were in private schools, and in 1851 just over 30 per cent from over 2 million. The virtual demise of private elementary schooling was accomplished by the growth of increasingly subsidised (and eventually free) public education in the next half century.

The orthodox interpretation justifiably stresses the initiating and creative role of churches and other 'public' agencies. But it is necessary to redress the balance by pointing out that the rise of public provision, at least in the early decades of the century, was in part a conscious *reaction* to private schooling. 'The poor will have education', one Anglican school committee stated, 'and if our system fails the schoolmaster of sedition and infidelity is not sleeping at his post.'[7] In the eighteenth century the churches' educational achievement sprang from individual and isolated effort; early in the nineteenth century the foundation of the voluntary societies (the National Society and the British and Foreign Schools' Society) gave some central direction and aid. The churches' inability to finance their growing educational ambitions led to government grants, at first very modest ones in 1833 but rapidly increasing in size decade by decade, and also led to the foundation in 1839 of the Education Committee of the Privy Council Office to dispense them. For this department – usually called the 'Education Department' – the power of the purse quickly came to entail the right of inspection and approval too, and elementary schools receiving government grants were surrounded by a mesh of regulation and counsel. The Education Department was the largest and most powerful of the State agencies involved with education. When the others, which were chiefly concerned with secondary schools, were amalgamated with it in 1899 so as to form the Board of Education, effectively it absorbed them.

In its first ten years the Education Department grew very rapidly; by 1849 it comprised fifty civil servants of varying duties and status, and was in fact one of the largest branches of government. Yet, with some notable exceptions, historians have omitted it from consideration in the long (and now surely moribund) debate on the origins of growth in the so-called revolution in government during the Victorian period.[8] The omission, the most bizarre example of the way historians fail to give education its appropriate significance, is all the more regrettable since the Education Department shows the inadequacy of two common interpretations of the period.[9] The first sees change and the government agencies which effected it as originating in the humanitarianism that found social evils 'intolerable'; yet simple moral indignation was much more easily aroused by the cruelties of the emigrant traffic or child labour than by ignorance, where the ethical imperatives were much less obvious. The second interpretation, which stresses the influence of Benthamism, is unconvincing where elementary education is concerned because Benthamism was only one of several motives behind the early years of government intervention.

The growth and direction of the Education Department from 1839 to 1849 owed most to its Secretary, James Kay-Shuttleworth, one of the energetic civil servants who were 'statesmen in disguise'. In the 1830s, by his work as a poor-law inspector and through the men of ideas he was in touch with, Utilitarians being prominent among them, he came to believe in the civilising power of mass education, and the need for the State to be involved in it. Mass schooling was advocated as a preventive of pauperism and crime: the 'Captain Swing of tomorrow is formed in the idle and ragged urchin of today', said Thomas Wyse MP, the educational enthusiast.[10] Earlier impulses too were important in encouraging Kay-Shuttleworth to value the school as a corrective agency. From his training in the Edinburgh Medical School, and notably from the teaching of W. P. Alison, he brought a lasting sense that much human wrongdoing has its roots in evil surroundings which could be improved. Another lasting influence was the austere piety of his Congregationalist origins, which often (in contradiction to his Edinburgh lessons) led him to hold human beings responsible for their misfortunes, and contributed to his harsh dismissal of the working-class family as vicious and improvident. It was, therefore, unfit to socialise children and so, of course, was the private school that working-class parents often preferred: this is why Kay-Shuttleworth believed that the 'public' elementary school should do it instead.[11]

Nor is it fanciful to argue that his strange and complex temperament affected his political attitudes. Contemporaries like Dickens felt uneasy in his distrustful, edgy, humourless presence. The emotional aridity of his relationship with adults encouraged him to sentimentalise children, especially in the abstract. It is hard not to see deep personal compensations in his vision of the elementary school as a substitute family, where children responded to the teacher's firm guidance with affectionate industry and disciplined liveliness – a sort of symbol of what Kay-Shuttleworth wished the adult world to become.

Before compulsive overwork and inability to delegate brought breakdown and premature retirement, Kay-Shuttleworth's creative energies laid down a pattern of government involvement which lasted till the end of the century. Invaluable financial help was given to the voluntary agencies, in return for inspection and approval by the Education Department on stringent terms. The most notable initiative was the Minutes of 1846, Kay-Shuttleworth's plan to make the school an effective paternalist instrument by replacing the haphazard medley of untrained teachers and monitors with a disciplined corps of certificated assistants and trainees, and to pay teachers and schools for helping in the process. The price they paid was acceptance of detailed control by the Department over the choice of trainees and the curriculum they followed, and hence the sort of teachers they became. It was centralisation by stealth, accomplished by regulation not statute, and so largely inaccessible to parliamentary scrutiny. The Minutes also contained a sort of built-in multiplier for the government bureaucracy; as more pupil teachers were engaged, more assistants were certificated and more schools became eligible for grants, so the number of inspectors and clerks to monitor and process the flow of cash increased.

By the end of the century there were well over 5 million children in public elementary schools. Plainly it was a period of growth, of new policies enacted and problems overcome. Yet very rarely after Kay-Shuttleworth were new departures initiated by civil servants, until Morant's work at the beginning of this century. So the Education Department does not fit models of government growth which are derived from the patterns of regulation which civil servants built up for public health or the emigrant traffic.[12]

After 1849 the Education Department did not lead events; it responded to them, dotting the 'i's and crossing the 't's on plans drawn up elsewhere. Kay-Shuttleworth's successor, R. R. W. Lingen, regarded himself as a professional administrator merely; he maintained regularity and order in the Department's workings, but despite his trenchant private opinions deliberately eschewed offering counsel to his political masters as to the direction State involvement should take. In the 1850s the 'multiplier' effect of the grant system pushed up government spending on education by nearly £100,000 a year; by 1862 the education grant reached £840,000. When in 1860 the government decided on economy it was the politician Robert Lowe, Lingen's superior, who devised the principles of payment by results, introducing stringent examinations as a test of fitness for much of the annual grant; Lingen merely worked out the details of the 'Revised Code'.[13]

3. UNIVERSALITY AND COMPULSION IN ELEMENTARY EDUCATION

There was a similar abdication by the Department in the late 1860s in the debate that preceded the 1870 Act. It was generally agreed that some sort of increased State intervention was necessary to 'fill the gaps' in voluntary provision and to conciliate hostile religious interests. It was a field where the civil servants might have been expected to offer authoritative advice to government. In fact the terms of the debate were essentially set by political forces, the educational pressure groups. On one side the National Education League wished to supersede denominational schools with schools controlled by elected local authorities and financed by rates. On the other the National Education Union wanted increased State subsidy for church schools. Between these partisan extremes the 1870 Bill was a compromise, essentially devised by W. E. Forster, the political head of the Education Department, with minimal aid from the officials, and then amended in detail in parliament in a welter of pressures and divisions. So the voluntary system was to remain, indeed was able to grow though shorn of some of its privileges; local authorities, the school boards, were to be created only where gaps had to be filled.[14]

An illuminating study shows how uncreative the senior officials of the Education Department were.[15] Middle-class Oxbridge graduates chosen by patronage, they felt no quickening bond of sympathy with schools for an essentially inferior class; it would not have crossed their minds to send their own children to them. The London officials tended to devote the energies spared by a very unexacting and dull bureaucratic routine to scholarship and poetry. Her Majesty's Inspectors entered schools and examined pupils daily, yet at best as gentlemen judging players, while after the Revised Code was introduced the harsh mechanical grind of examining served to distance them further from children and teachers. Each year in the 1860s two inspectors visited Tysoe village school in Warwickshire:

> two gentlemen with a deportment of high authority, with rich voices. Each would sit at a desk and children would be called in turn to one or other. The master hovered round, calling children out as they were needed. The children could see him start with vexation as a good pupil stuck at a word in the reading-book he had been using all the year . . . . The master's anxiety was deep, for his earnings depended on the children's work. One year the atmosphere of anxiety so affected the lower standards that, one after another as they were brought to the Inspector, the boys howled and the girls whimpered. It took hours to get through them.[16]

In 1870 many educationists felt that compulsion was the only way to ensure the attendance of all children, especially the poorest children, the 'ragamuffins' and 'urchins' who provoked so much discussion. Forster himself regarded compulsion as necessary, but could not convert the Cabinet. The idea of compulsion conflicted with deeply entrenched beliefs on parental responsiblity – and with sympathy for parents who needed children's earnings and with the employers (especially farmers) who needed their labour. So the 1870 Act merely gave school boards the right to insist on attendance in their area, a right conferred on local authorities in areas without school boards by an Act of 1876. This Act originated in pressure from voluntary school managers for powers of compulsion; it was acceded to by Lord Sandon, the Conservative politician eager to benefit church education. Growing realisation by educationists that compulsion alone could guarantee attendance led them to press for action; in 1880 they made the Liberals enact legislation forcing local authorities everywhere to assume compulsion powers. Though it was possible to leave school at the age of ten in some areas (and the minimum leaving age was not raised to eleven till 1893) at least now every child had to have five years' schooling. The gradual nudging towards compulsion in the 1870s was effected by educationists and politicians; the civil servants merely transmitted messages from one side to the other.

These three groups played the same respective parts over revision of payment by results and of the fee system. The payment of fees became an issue after compulsion, and their abolition seemed increasingly to be entailed by it. It was difficult to extract fees from recalcitrant parents and some school boards gave up really trying; one estimate was that in London there was only one chance in 700 of a defaulter being prosecuted. School boards increasingly wanted fees abolished, but schools would need more help from public funds in compensation. Since this would strengthen the case for public control of the voluntary system the churches were in two minds over abolition. Salisbury tackled the question in a complicated balancing act in 1891, providing an extra grant from central government to enable fees to be ended or lowered but without reducing schools' autonomy. At least all teachers and school managers agreed in detesting the Revised Code; extensive amendments in 1871 did not satisfy them, and repeated tinkering in the next two decades left intact the central principle of payment on the results of examinations in the 'three Rs'. Radical alteration was effected by Salisbury's government in 1890, and the last vestiges of the Code were swept away by Acland, the Liberal Vice-President of the Council, from 1893 to 1895.[17]

4. SOCIAL HIERARCHY AND SECONDARY SCHOOLING

Victorians usually talked not of 'secondary' but of 'middle-class' schools – a phrase which indicates neatly that the divisions within education ran along lines of class, status and money, rather than age. Foremost in prestige among secondary schools were the seven (some said nine) 'great' or 'public' schools. These largely catered for the landed class and the uppermost sections of gentlemanly commerce and the professions, rather than the great social spectrum, ranging from army officers to small farmers, which the Victorians commonly meant by 'middle class'. For the middle class there was a multitude of often short-lived private schools,[18] some scores of 'proprietary' schools owned by shareholders, and the ancient endowed grammar schools, 700 in number early in the century, and usually founded by charitable benefaction in the sixteenth and seventeenth centuries.

This medley of schools became transformed during the century, the grammar schools being improved from the small and indolent establishments they often were in 1800, especially in the countryside and small towns. Such changes were part of a wider structural one – involving the creation of tiers of schools, with different curricula, leaving ages, staffs, fees and clienteles, for different levels of income and status and thus expectation, within the 'middle class'. It was a process of grading and differentiation which reflected one of the most widely accepted axioms of Victorian society – that education should reflect disparities of social class and should only slightly seek to transcend them. Thus Nathaniel Woodard and Joseph Brereton, who devoted their lives to founding proprietary schools, placed them in a rigid hierarchy giving only the slightest encouragement to upward mobility;[19] identical principles informed the Liverpool Collegiate School, founded in 1840 and containing three carefully separated divisions to correspond to distinct groups within the middle class.[20]

Much the most spectacular aspect of this careful articulation of a status pyramid of schools was the development by 1900 of some sixty 'public' schools which recognised each other as possessing the same superior qualities: they were fit to be placed in the same category as the 'seven'.[21] This creaming process was effected very largely by the schools themselves; they came to see that a private school like Loretto or a proprietary one like Cheltenham was worthy to be ranked with them. Many of the schools which came to possess public-school status were in fact endowed grammar schools in origin, and though their rise came partly from the efforts of men like Grignon at Felsted to attract large numbers of gentlemen's sons to their school, it also came from the activities of State agencies, deeply involved in reorganising and regrading grammar schools.

This work, though to some extent attempted by the Charity Commissioners before the Taunton Commission, really began after it reported in 1868. The Endowed Schools' Commissioners, and then their successors a renewed Charity Commission, remoulded endowments and schools, carefully articulating them into three highly differentiated grades very similar to those of the Liverpool proprietary school mentioned earlier. Free places were severely reduced in number; they were suspect because they gave a place (commonly given on grounds of local residence) to boys of an inferior social class to that predicated for the school.[22] They were replaced by a few scholarships to provide a narrow ladder of opportunity for the very gifted.[23] Endowments originally intended for the education of the poor were diverted to middle-class children – girls, it should be observed, benefited considerably from the energetic social engineering of the commissioners. Its dramatic nature may be clearly seen at Bedford, where the resources of the Harpur Trust, supporting two boys' secondary schools and three elementary schools, were reorganised so that the secondary sector received the lion's share and two middle-class girls' schools were additionally provided for from it.[24]

A significant influence on secondary education also came from the Department of Science and Art, set up in 1853 but with roots dating from 1837. From the 1850s it was encouraging the teaching of science and art by making grants to schools, at first on a modest scale but by the 1880s very extensively, so that its subsidies were of great importance, as H. G. Wells discovered at Midhurst Grammar School.[25] Many endowed grammar schools benefited. So did some schools that were nominally elementary in nature – the higher grade schools organised by school boards and occasionally by voluntary agencies after 1870.[26] These provided more advanced courses than were usual in elementary education; they were quasi-secondary schools. Another complication in the pattern of English education was the power given to new county councils in 1889 to offer aid from the rates for technical instruction; grammar schools benefited from this source too. It was this jumble of overlapping authorities and provisions that the Education Act of 1902 was intended to sort out.

In the field of secondary education central government was highly creative, transforming and founding grammar schools in the most notable piece of Victorian social engineering. The middle classes were beneficiaries of these changes. On balance the Victorian working class may have lost by them, since it is arguable that the right of free entry to unreformed grammar schools (unsuitable though the education they gave often was)[27] was of greater value than the scholarships for elementary school children that were given after the grammar schools were reformed.[28]

The extension of public elementary schooling has traditionally been regarded as a benefit to working people, and of course if education is of value at all it must be so regarded. But it is much less easy to advance the claim in an unqualified way than it was a generation ago. Recent writing[29] points to ways in which public provision 'stifled' private working-class schooling which although more expensive was nevertheless often more responsive to working-class desires. Though public agencies gave the middle classes the sort of education they wanted for their children, they never felt full sympathy for working-class values. This explains the suspicious attitude towards these agencies which working-class radicals often evinced. Thus William Lovett, in the most famous radical prescription for education, wished his 'public' schools to be controlled by local committees elected by universal suffrage, to guard against the destruction of 'local energies, experiments and improvements so desirable to be fostered for the advancement of knowledge'. The East London female Chartists called for the rejection of 'Church and State offers of education for our children, which is only calculated to debase the mind, and render it subservient to class interest'.[30] In public elementary education, the contrast between what the people wanted, and what was presumed to be for their good, was a constant source of tension.

5. DENOMINATIONAL SCHOOLING

'Give me a servant as can nayther read nor write, I say, and doesn't know the year o' the Lord as she was born in. I should like to know what good those Sunday schools have done, now.'[31] When George Eliot's Warwickshire miller voiced these sentiments, about 1830, they were decidedly old-fashioned, although they were to continue to be approved by many for a long time to come. Replacing them in conventional wisdom was the view that schooling the children of the poor was an essential Christian mission. Thus the Bishop of Chichester praised the 'spirit of zeal for the education of the Poor' that had sprung up and promised 'to produce a fruitful harvest of soul-saving knowledge to future generations'.[32]

Apart from those run for private profit, almost all elementary schools were provided by the churches before 1870, sometimes as isolated ventures by individual clergymen, but more often under the aegis of a nationwide society. Much the largest was the National Society for Promoting the Education of the Poor in the Principles of the Church of England; the British Society represented Protestant Dissenting sects, and the Wesleyans and Roman Catholics had their own groupings too.[33]

This religious dimension to Victorian elementary education is often wrongly perceived by historians. It is viewed far too exclusively in terms of 'warring sects', seen as fighting each other with equal selfishness for control of children's minds and the school system.[34] In fact the 'war' (which certainly existed) was caused far more by the Church of England than the other churches which shared responsibility for elementary schools with it. Also the conflict was as much between the Church of England and the State as between sects: it mostly took place, that is, within the governing 'Establishment'. A second misleading perception is that Victorian descriptions of education as a great spiritual endeavour are too heavily discounted, and motives of 'social control' (of course undoubtedly present) are overestimated. This genuine religious inspiration may be seen most clearly in Sunday schools, a movement which largely reflected autonomous working-class energies, and shows them to have been as vigorous in religious enterprise as in the political ones usually considered by historians.

Behind all denominational schools was the sincere belief that doctrinal differences were supremely important – a fact easily forgotten or misunderstood today; all such schools existed in part to inculcate sectarian creeds. Social tension would not have thereby arisen if denominations and their schools had been perfectly matched in location and number, and no children had been forced to suffer instruction in an alien creed. Such was not the case. The problem was caused very little by the Roman Catholic and Dissenting schools; they were built for their own confessions only, and tended not to contain others. Difficulties arose because of the number of Anglican schools and the extent of Anglican demands.

Naturally enough Anglicans took the fact of Establishment very seriously, believing that it laid upon the Church of England the duty of instructing as many of the nation's children as possible. Naturally too the Church of England regarded the Establishment as dangerously under attack after 1830, when militant Dissent was supported by liberals in parliament. The Church of England's intense educational effort in the 1830s should be seen as in part a response to threat.[35] Anglican laity were richer or more generous than others, and were spread over the country; Nonconformity was handicapped by the lack of a rural gentry. For these reasons, Anglican provision was greater than any other. It included many schools in rural areas where there were no others; the choice for non-Anglicans was often between Anglican education or no education at all. Moreover, Anglicans argued that secular instruction must always be informed by religous truth. As one Tory newspaper put it, 'It is not bigotry, on the part of Churchmen, to insist that their children shall be trained in the principles, and instructed in the doctrines which they themselves believe to be true, and to have been preserved from an admixture of error, by the watchful and apostolic care of the episcopal guardians of the Church.'[36] Such words meant in practice that Roman Catholic pupils, like those in Liverpool, would not be excused the reading of the Authorised Version.[37] For Anglican educators, the Protestant Bible was the irreducible confessional minimum; Evangelical clergy were often content to demand no more than that, since they were anxious to stress their affinity with Protestant Dissent rather than points of difference. High Churchmen (and the National Society) conscious of the Church of England's doctrinal separateness insisted also on the Anglican catechism, a policy deeply offensive to Dissenters as well as Catholics.

From the 1830s onwards the unsuitability of sectarianism as a basis for truly national education was argued by Radicals and Nonconformists, naturally dismayed by the vulnerability of their own children in Anglican 'single-school' areas. One idea played with was an interdenominational or unsectarian prescription, a sort of 'agreed syllabus' that would contain as much religious truth as could be generally accepted. 'Secularism' was another remedy – not Godlessness, but the separation of secular and religious instruction, the latter to be given by clergy of the various denominations to children desiring it. Both ideas were adopted for the government's scheme for Irish elementary education begun in 1831. Agreed passages from the Bible might be read by all pupils; denominational instruction was to be given to Roman Catholic and Protestant groups separately. The Irish plan strongly influenced liberals in Liverpool; they introduced it into the Corporation's elementary schools in 1836.

These ideas strongly influenced Lord John Russell, the Home Secretary, and James Kay-Shuttleworth, appointed secretary of the Committee of Council on Education in 1839. A government teachers' training college and a model school were to be set up, with 'general' and denominational religious instruction on the Irish plan. Though welcomed by Dissenters, it was denounced by Anglicans. Given the contemporary balance of political forces defeat of the government scheme was inevitable. Also defeated in its original form was Kay-Shuttleworth's plan to make government grants in support of schools dependent on favourable reports from Her Majesty's Inspectors. The so-called Concordat of 1840 gave to the archbishops rights of consultation over the composition and duties of the inspectorate which were more extensive than those given to the other voluntary bodies. Even so, inspection was repugnant to a small group of High Churchmen, who regarded it as the badge of Erastian dependence. They believed that grants should be given to the Established Church without strings, and refused them henceforth in noisy disgust.

Resentment at Establishment privilege was much increased in 1843, by the education clauses of Sir James Graham's Factory Bill; schools to be set up for factory children were to have Anglican teachers and religious instruction, though non-Anglicans were to have the right to withdraw their children. The clauses reflected the natural Anglican predilections of a Tory government. They aroused the opposition of Nonconformists, Roman Catholics, Liberal Churchmen, and Wesleyans traditionally reluctant to attack the Established Church. The most vehement criticism came from Radical Nonconformists already uneasy about the 'centralising' tendencies they detected in the Committee of Council and the inspectorate; they suspected that the government, worried by the Chartist disturbances in the summer of 1842, had devised the factory schools to keep the country politically quiescent.[38] Despite Graham's dropping of the hated education clauses the 'Voluntaryist' movement which had been stimulated by the 1843 Factory Bill gathered strength, especially among Congregationalists and Baptists. Voluntaryists stressed the threat to freedom in State support for schools and churches; the movement overlapped with a campaign to disestablish the Church of England. They refused government grants and sometimes even returned money given years before. They pointed to the generosity and fortitude of the people as proof that Voluntaryist schools could cope with the educational task: the movement was a correlative of self-help. The Voluntaryists indeed made immense efforts, building and sustaining several hundred day schools. But they failed to convince even most Nonconformists that it was necessary to eschew State support, or possible to contemplate mass day-school education without it; in the 1860s the Voluntaryists confessed defeat.[39]

Yet a much larger group of self-financing schools were successful. Sunday schools, in which Nonconformity was also closely involved, were largely attended, staffed, financed and (at least up to 1850) controlled by laity in the working class. The schools testify not only to the intensity of their religious culture but also to their desire for secular instruction and ability to provide it for themselves. In 1851 over 2 million were enrolled in English Sunday schools, or one-eighth of the population. In many places as in Chesterfield, pupils 'raised their youthful voices high, and made Chesterfield-street ring with Jehovah's praises'. For numerous students, many of them adults, the Sunday school was an agency as much secular as Godly – men like Adam Rushton, for whom, at his Sunday writing class 'came forth words, and sentences, and even my own name, written in large strong strokes of my quill pen'.[40]

6. VOLUNTARYISM AND THE STATE

From 1840 to 1870 the Committee of Council saw no practicable alternative to a partnership between government and the voluntary societies in elementary schooling; both agencies were necessary, and it was not feasible for the enterprise to be undertaken by either alone. The Committee of Council's aim was to persuade each voluntary society to serve the nation rather than a sect. Children were to be permitted to withdraw from religious instruction, and the clergyman's control of an individual school, especially in non-religious matters, was to be shared with a board of managers with strong lay membership. Non-Anglicans were ready enough to concede the essence of the Council's 'conscience' and 'management' clauses. So were many Churchmen, especially Evangelicals. The National Society resisted. It was forced to accept the management clauses in respect of new schools by the Council's strongest lever, the grant; on the conscience clause, implying as it did the impious separation of religious and secular instruction, the society was adamant for years.

By 1870 the Church of England was willing to accept the conscience clause as a fair price for continued State aid for its schools. On little else was there agreement, however, except on the need for increased educational provision for the poor and the inability of the voluntary agencies to supply it.[41] More State cash seemed essential, and the prevailing sympathy for localism meant that rate support was the generally favoured form. The problem was to whom should it be given? Nonconformists pressed for it to go to schools with no religious teaching, or perhaps unsectarian teaching. But given that the Established Church and its schools were powerfully entrenched it was quite unrealistic for Nonconformists to expect any parliament to push the National schools into an unsectarian solution. On the other hand, the Anglican and Roman Catholic prescription for educational advance – rate aid for their schools – was equally impracticable; the Dissenters' objections to a new State subsidy for militant sectarianism were too powerful. The terms of the 1870 Act reflect the balance of forces within the nation: voluntary schools remained, but were denied rate aid and were complemented by board schools.

On the issue of religious instruction itself the 1870 debates showed the government's desire to detach the State from controversy. Religious teaching would no longer be inspected – as the Church of England had traditionally insisted on. Nor would government contemplate an agreed form of 'unsectarian' teaching for board schools: Gladstone made clear his repugnance for a formula which would entail having 'a new sort of Pope in the Council office'[42] to interpret it. The solution that emerged from the interplay of conflicting forces in parliament meant great freedom for school boards (and their teachers) to choose whether to have religious instruction, and if so, how much and what sort; the Cowper-Temple clause merely limited – it certainly did not remove – local freedom to teach sectarian doctrine.[43] In the event about thirty small rural boards prescribed Anglican doctrinal teaching. Other boards, for example Manchester, permitted teachers to offer it, but assumed that it would be within the Protestant tradition. Most boards attempted unsectarian instruction, based on the Biblical essentials. Very few opted for 'secular' instruction; Birmingham, where Nonconformists had for years pressed this policy, found when the board applied it that the exclusion of the Bible from classrooms was unpopular.

After 1870 the Nonconformists ceased to provide 'voluntary' schools, but the Act stimulated Anglicans and Roman Catholics to prodigies of effort. Many church schools were built in the early 1870s. Between 1870 and 1902 supporters gave at least £12 million to build voluntary schools, and at the end of the period more than half the pupils were in the voluntary sector. The voluntary movement was powerful politically, and was feared by its rivals till this century. Yet in fact after 1870 it was in increasing difficulty. The board-school system was growing much more rapidly, and was on the whole better equipped and staffed. Board schools enjoyed an immense financial advantage – rates; considerable effort and ingenuity was applied by the Conservatives, the voluntary schools' parliamentary friends, to devise means of giving them extra help without being too obvious about it,[44] though the most notable piece of help, the granting of rate-aid to voluntary schools by the 1902 Act, was very obvious indeed.

1870 marks the start of decline in the significance of the voluntary societies and the credal truths they had been founded to propagate. A determined effort was made to recruit into the board schools the children of the urban lower working class – compulsion being of course an essential part of this process. This was precisely the class that organised religion (or at all events Protestantism) had since the eighteenth century increasingly failed to reach.[45] To compete with the school boards in a campaign to educate their children presented the Anglicans with acute problems. Partly they were financial, and it was certainly in financial terms that they were most often articulated: nevertheless, the psychological difficulty of confronting the churchless masses was also great. Increasingly the Church of England retreated behind barricades of class, confining its efforts to schooling the children of the upper working or even lower middle classes.[46] It was becoming merely one denomination among many.

The Church of England had been sustained in its prodigies of educational effort by the profound belief that its doctrine was truth, and that its truth would be brought to each generation by the catechistical school. It would be in the countryside, where patterns of deference and hierarchy reinforced the effects of the monopolistic Anglican school, that one would expect to find the Church of England's certitudes most deeply accepted. Yet Anglican doctrine often failed to pierce the mind of the captive audience. Among the rural poor Christian beliefs were mingled with acceptance of magic and witchcraft; in Lincolnshire animal sacrifice took place as an act of propitiation during the cattle plague of 1866.[47] In Oxfordshire in the 1880s, Flora Thompson records, the catechism was duly learned by school-children, but when they were adults, 'the majority regarded religion as something proper to extreme old age, for which they themselves had as yet no use'.[48] At the same time the educated increasingly rejected the credal message because of the thrust of 'science': the vision of a vast and impersonal cosmos was incompatible with the Biblical literalism on which doctrine reposed, and broad and liberal creeds provided no secure and permanent alternative. Church attendance and the intensity of faith diminished. The retreat from worship encouraged intersectarian co-operation: the alliance of the Anglican and Catholic voluntary societies after 1870 was the effect very largely of religion's sense of encirclement. Religious decline has accelerated this century: the 1902 Act gave the Church schools what they wanted, when it was beginning not to matter whether they had it or not. The decline had begun long before in the seventeenth century; the evangelising effort of the nineteenth, in which schooling formed so important a part, merely arrested it for a time.

7. RELIGION, FAITH AND RIGHT CONDUCT IN THE SECONDARY SCHOOL

The great struggles for religious freedom concerned elementary schools. In secondary education the problem was much less acute: in day schools instruction in an alien faith was not usually insisted on, and though in boarding schools attendance at religious worship was obligatory, 'aliens' rarely tried to enter such schools. Endowed grammar schools were almost always Anglican institutions, giving Anglican religious instruction, but in most cases the children of non-Anglicans secured without difficulty the right to absent themselves from it. Such toleration was practised even in the Liverpool College, a proprietary school founded expressly to serve the Anglican community; local Non-conformists attended in numbers, and were not constrained.[49]

The college had only a handful of boarding pupils. But though day schools might perforce feel that their function was as much secular as religious, Anglican boarding schools (the great majority even of the Victorian foundations were Anglican)[50] recruiting in any case from one confession only, attached sovereign importance to the Christian nature of their mission. They distinguished between the mere imparting of facts about religion and the inculcation of faith and right conduct. Thomas Arnold defined Christian education as 'the fashioning all the parts of our nature for the very ends which God designed for them; the teaching our understandings to know the highest truth, the teaching our affections to love the highest good'.[51]

It was common in public schools to hold obligatory chapel services twice on Sundays, and sometimes more frequently, in addition to brief workday observances. One fear constantly expressed by public-school masters was that compulsion was itself harmful to genuine religious feelings. The desire for proof of *willing* commitment always nagged at the back of their minds – hence the importance attached to Confirmation. Housemasters regarded the preparation of boys for it as their most momentous task, and communicants in many schools formed Communicants' Guilds, meeting monthly, to preserve the intensity of their witness amid the mundane concerns of school. 'Lectiones', Scripture passages for private use each day, were circulated by the Public Schools' Scripture Union. Some schools hoped to raise the corporate sense of religious dedication by enlisting the boys' support for evangelical missions which aimed 'to mitigate the forlornness of a small poor industrial district, and to supply them with a friend and a permanent link with another class'.[52]

Yet the devotional life of the school always varied enormously in richness. At one extreme are testaments of lifelong gratitude for contact, in public school, with a faith powerful enough to give purpose and direction to life. The school promoter, J. L. Brereton, recalled at the age of seventy-three the effect of Thomas Arnold on him as a boy at Rugby: 'the tenderness and humbleness of a true Christian . . . irresistibly pleaded with the boy's conscience and heart for responsive obedience and love'.[53] On the other hand Brereton's contemporary at Rugby, the anonymous author of a memoir of the 1830s, seems to have no direct and personal sense of Arnold's power and draws on Stanley's biography for an account. His memories of Rugby centre on fishing, football, fossilising and cross-country running; the peace and relaxation of Sunday are recalled with pleasure, but religion is scarcely mentioned.[54]

The contrast shows how dependent was the real awakening of the religious sense upon currents of sympathy between personalities – much less easy to stimulate and sustain than the workaday tolerance needed for classroom instruction. Some masters, religious or not, were easy to regard as unsympathetic; and increasingly after 1860 some masters did not favour or encourage religion. Colleagues at Harrow in the 1870s, for

example, were two men very different in all respects save in not fostering
the religious spirit as Arnold had understood it. John Smith was a near-
insane Fourth Form master, whose consciousness of sin was oppressive
and whose utterance often morbid and absurd. 'Once he said, with a
queer smile, to a boy standing at a second-floor window: "Jump out
dear fellow; you'll be in heaven in a minute!"' This was said to be a
'characteristic' example of his humour. Plainly schoolboy insensitivity
to the adult world protected his pupils.[55] On the other hand, W. E.
Bowen was anti-clerical, with only perfunctory piety and a reluctance
to intrude into boys' privacy, which was one of the grounds of his
penetrating attack on Thomas Arnold.[56] It is often forgotten that
public-school masters, like their pupils, varied in character and outlook,
and transmitted a medley of messages to them.

Bowen's headmaster, Welldon, saw that its emotional base often
meant that schoolboy religion was impermanent; the feeling aroused in
adolescence by chapel and sermon tended to disappear at university.[57]
Welldon was here giving a new twist to the immemorial complaint of
educationists – that the values of school and world were hostile. Equally
worrying to some was the way in which the attitudes of the world at
large, increasingly indifferent to religion towards the end of the century,
naturally penetrated the boarding schools – a process measured partly
by the increased numbers of lay assistant masters. Perhaps the most
telling explanation of the schools' devotional aridity came from W. W.
Vaughan at the end of the First World War. He argued that in fact the
values of boarding school and religion were antipathetic, since the
schools were based on principles of competition and self-assertiveness
that were 'hard to reconcile with the ideals that are upheld in the New
Testament'.[58] It was an argument that would have dismayed Arnold,
but in the eighty years since Arnold the public-school ideal had
changed vastly. In the character that he had wished the schools to
mould, physical fitness and pluck were balanced by sensitivity,
scholarship and vital religious belief. By the end of the century,
however, the balance was upset; the ideal type was dominated by the
straightforward 'manly' virtues, losing the complexity and mature
humaneness of his predecessor. In this decline from earlier subtlety and
depth the concentration on games and athletic prowess played a key
part.[59]

In the Golden Age of the public schools masters complained that
their pupils were conformist, sheep-like, unintellectual, unoriginal –
but did so in utterance that revealed, celebrated and explained the very

defects it condemned. Thus Alfred Lyttelton admitted that Eton's peculiar strength lay not in scholarship but in imparting to patricians the talent to control their intellectual superiors.[60] One Chips-like figure, giving kindly advice to schoolboys, lamented that the public schools 'turn out men all of a pattern – a good article it is true but often a sadly inadequate unimaginative article as well'; he regretted too that the unusual boy, the 'real out and out freak' did not enjoy school – 'but he is a very rare bird anyhow'.[61]

So it is not surprising that masters complain too of the formal, arid, superficial, mechanical nature of public-school religion. 'What they learn is . . . possibly very useful in examinations, but not living truth, nor permanently held.'[62] Comfort was found by some in the reflection that although faith might be transitory, it would help to create character nevertheless: 'so that men who have strayed from the paths of orthodox belief, yet hold fast the ideals of honour and duty and service which won the allegiance of youth and boyhood in the sheltered days of the life of the school'.[63] So diminished an expectation would not have satisfied Arnold. It meant that religion had ceased to be regarded as the great permanent legacy of schooling, the informing principle of life, and was relegated to the status of classics or football – to an instrumental function which might like them be forgotten after school. Education had become instruction.

8. THE SCHOOL AS AN AGENCY OF SOCIAL CONTROL

Yet instruction rather than education had been the preferred objective in schooling the working class. The transition from a rural and agrarian to an urban, industrial economy in the late eighteenth and early nineteenth centuries had produced deep strains and stresses within society. Popular disturbances – most frequent in the 1830s and 1840s – had led some individuals within the propertied classes to reflect on ways in which society could be made more peaceful and stable. Elementary instruction as a means of socialising the working class appeared to be one obvious form of remedial activity. Historians and sociologists have begun to analyse this concern to increase social order through the expansion of schooling and have applied the flexible concept of 'social control' to it. This has given a fresh theoretical perspective to well-known developments in elementary education, although it should be remembered that this is only one among several possible explanations for the increase in educational activity during this period.

In the 1780s social disturbances in the south-west of England, in the form of juvenile crowds which threatened property, led Robert Raikes to start the first Sunday schools in Gloucester as a means of imposing social discipline on the poor child. Others soon imitated his in-novation.[64] The further development of the Sunday-school movement took place in a tense political climate in which the French Revolution seemed to many to challenge traditional institutions and forms of behaviour. In this context it has become usual to see the early Sunday schools, as well as the day schools begun in the early nineteenth century by the National and British Societies, as middle-class organisations directed at social regeneration through moralising the poor and inculcating in them deferential attitudes to their betters. Evidence to support this interpretation has been drawn from analysis of tracts and reward books distributed to pupils, of the texts and magazines used in classrooms, and of the statements of intent by educators.[65] The literature commended to pupils laid emphasis on the desirability of punctuality, cleanliness, humility, order, industry and thrift. It has been suggested that the indoctrination of these 'middle-class' values into working-class children was useful to the capitalists who organised the first factories. They needed to replace the irregular patterns of labour of the domestic worker by disciplined habits in a docile and well-ordered factory labour force. Subordinate to the factory and controlled by individuals within the same social group, the large Sunday schools in northern, industrial towns appear to have had a similar organisation to the factory, with a comparable stress on punctuality and well-disciplined activity. It is claimed therefore that Sunday schools indoctrinated future workers with the 'time-thrift' necessary for the successful operation of industrial capitalism.[66]

This interpretation, which has achieved the status of a new orthodoxy among left-wing social and educational historians, has been challenged recently in the first detailed study of the Sunday-school movement. T. W. Laqueur has criticised the view that an alien middle-class culture was imposed on the working-class child in any but the early Sunday schools. He has argued persuasively that an increasing proportion of Sunday-school teachers were themselves working class, and that they retained substantial independence from middle-class school managers. He concludes that very few Sunday schools were linked to factories, and that any resemblance between the two organisations was a function of similarity in size rather than of ideological congruity. Less convincing is Laqueur's view that the predominance of religious teaching over secular instruction in the Sunday school minimised the opportunities for political and social indoctrination of the scholars, since it is arguable that the particular moral values transmitted in religious teaching had a socio-political application.

Further enquiry and polemic will no doubt be stimulated by Laqueur's opinion that the moral values communicated by the Sunday-school teacher were as characteristic of the respectable working class, as of the middle class. Different interpretations are possible here. It could be argued either that Sunday schools were not a major agency of social control through the transmission of alien values, or that the very similarity of working- and middle-class values by the mid-nineteenth century was a product of earlier indoctrination. A third persuasive interpretation is that of T. R. Tholfsen, who argues that both the middle and working classes in mid-Victorian England had common cultural roots in the Enlightenment and Evangelicalism of the eighteenth century; this led to an overlap in their ideals.[67]

The 1830s and 1840s were characterised by increased tension between social classes, as was shown by the rural 'Swing' riots of 1830–1, the mainly urban anti-poor-law agitation of 1835–7, and the Chartist movement. As Roebuck remarked when introducing the Education Bill in 1833, 'as mere matter of police, the education of the people ought to be considered as a part of the duties of government.'[68] The 1830s were similar to the 1780s in that education was seen consciously as a means of increasing social order and protecting property, and the function of schooling as a means of social control was discussed explicitly in speeches and pamphlets. The possibility of a centralised system of social control having begun to operate in the 1830s has been raised in relation to the state's incursion into elementary education.[69] The centralising, bureaucratic impact of the state was to result in a more uniform system; the elementary schools of the mid-nineteenth century may be seen as the focus of a powerful and impersonal attack on working-class values. Drawn from middle- or upper-class backgrounds the state's inspectors (whose numbers had risen from two in 1840 to sixteen by 1849), were often unsympathetic to the working-class family and tried to make the schools they visited a means of counteracting what they saw as its pernicious influence on the working-class child. The instructions to the inspectors to guide them in their work were written by Sir James Kay-

Shuttleworth, who we have seen viewed the elementary school as a means of socialising the working class and who also saw education as a means of safeguarding existing property rights.[70]

Yet it would be inappropriate to contend as some have done that the State's growing influence over elementary education involved a central conspiracy theory and that the working-class pupil was therefore indoctrinated through the transmission of a coherent value system. The inspectorate was conspicuously more independent intellectually during Kay-Shuttleworth's tenure as Secretary to the Committee of Council of Education from 1839 to 1849 than it was to become later under Lingen and his successors.[71] Effectively a denominational rather than a secular body, its power over school managers and teachers in the elementary schools was one of persuasion rather than control. But persuasion could be an effective influence, since the HMI as 'educational expert' was acting within a climate of opinion where the reluctance of working-class parents to use the increased number of school places was seen both as a symptom of their moral poverty and of the environmental squalor in which they lived. Thus HMIs urged the middle classes to intensify their educational efforts as school managers and patrons; the advice of the inspectors was usually given to an amenable audience.[72]

The most willing ears may well have been those of the teachers, whose professional status and financial advancement were influenced by the inspector's verdict on their professional prowess. The expansion and improvement of the training facilities for teachers in normal schools and training colleges in the mid-nineteenth century was an important means by which the state could influence the quality of elementary education. Richard Johnson has seen the trained teacher in the early Victorian period as a state mercenary who inculcated in his pupils the virtues of deference, piety and industry.[73] The emphasis given in training colleges in the 1840s and 1850s to the moral character of the student lends substance to this view, as does the stress given in inspectors' reports to the crucial importance of the moral influence of the teacher on his pupil. This gives a useful insight into the 'cross-cultural transformation' which may have operated within the class-room, but it is necessary to see its limitations as a complete explanation of the complexities of teacher–pupil interaction. Many teachers were unqualified and had not undergone a college training. Among the certificated teachers there was a groundswell of professional independence by the 1850s, which was indicated by the proliferation of professional organisations and journals.[74] It is salutary to reflect how very little we know at present about what went on in the Victorian schoolroom. While a local study like that on Durham mining areas increases our information, it indicates also that it is easier to show the educational intentions of those who provided schools than it is to demonstrate how effectively these purposes were translated into classroom practice. In this case R. Colls argues that the colliery owners wished to train a submissive workforce for the mines and consciously organised local schools as an attack on working-class cultural independence. But he fails to show how these desires were enforced on teachers and realised in their teaching.[75]

A pupil 'must be trained in industry, in correct moral habits, and in religion, and must be fitted to discharge the duties of its station', commented Kay-Shuttleworth on the function of the workhouse.[76] Of all educational institutions in the mid-nineteenth century workhouse schools for pauper children, industrial schools for very poor, deserted or orphaned children, and reform schools for youthful offenders displayed the most obviously society's desire to impose social control on its recalcitrant members. A utilitarian view of education was also found in elementary schools, which provoked Dickens in 1854 to denounce 'gradgrindism' in *Hard Times*. Yet the lessons of political economy which so offended the social radicalism of Dickens had earlier seemed to many propertied members of society to be a necessary antidote to a disturbed society. By the 1830s popular education was thought to be less dangerous than mass ignorance, provided that instruction was so carefully circumscribed that it inculcated conformist values rather than encouraged independent thought. As a response to this socially perceived need, lesson books began to include stories displaying the principles of political economy in a defence, and rationalisation, of the *status quo* in society. The clearest examples of these were found in the Irish National School Books, which were praised by the inspectorate and distributed widely in English elementary schools.[77]

There was a strong line of continuity between the secularised virtues of these Irish lesson books and the moral fables and tracts which had been used in the schoolrooms at the turn of the nineteenth century. In both types of publication a socially desirable model of behaviour was put before the child, although references to sin and appeals to a higher authority were replaced gradually by a more earthly concern with self-advancement as the rationale for good (that is socially desirable) behaviour in children. Both attempted to impose the values of the middle, or upper, class on the children of the poor, and in this they were aiming at the eventual cross-cultural transformation of the working class.

Cross-cultural transformation provides a more appropriate interpretation of the educational aims of the schools that were provided for the poor child in the late eighteenth and early nineteenth centuries than social control. This is an appropriate description only of specific institutions at particular points in time, and one might instance some Sunday schools in the 1780s and 1790s or workhouse schools in the late 1830s as examples of the operation of social control. Yet neither the theory of social control nor that of cross-cultural transformation gives sufficient weight to social and educational diversity. It is open to doubt whether the values of the middle and upper classes were so monolithic and different from those of other social groups as to constitute a 'gentry hegemony'. Nor was the working class such a distinct and homogeneous group as some interpretations would indicate. The classroom organisation of the Sunday, or elementary, school was unlikely to have been so single-minded in its social instrumentality, while the growing educational bureaucracy of the state cannot be explained solely by reference to an expansionist utilitarian ideology.

In drawing attention to the self-interestedness of much educational provision historians have provided recently a useful corrective to the older interpretations of disinterested religious philanthropy as the key to educational expansion at the beginning of our period. But to advance the discussion from sociological theory to historical hypothesis requires more detailed investigations of data. This would help to clarify key ambiguities in the present discussions on social control by illuminating whether it was seen most decisively at the local or central level, whether it operated mainly through personal or institutional agencies, and whether it was applied consciously or unconsciously in response to socio-economic developments. It is also illuminating for the historian to extend the period under investigation beyond the 1850s, since class differentiation in educational provision continued throughout the nineteenth century and distinct social objectives continued to operate in the education of working-class children. One example of this was the domestic instruction for girls in elementary schools which is discussed below. In this context it should be remembered that an efficient imposition of social control or of cross-cultural transformation was dependent on the development of compulsory, free, elementary education at the end of the nineteenth century.

9. EDUCATION AND THE ECONOMY

The 'social wretchedness which blights all educational promise' was referred to by Horace Mann during an analysis in 1851 of the failure of the working class to utilise fully the expanded elementary school provision of the preceding decades.[78] Earlier, educational reform had seemed to be a substitute for the more general social reforms which rapid industrialisation and urbanisation had made desirable. By the 1850s it was becoming evident that educational progress was intimately related to the social environment and that poverty in the working-class family often resulted in the sacrifice of schooling because of the need for children's earnings. School attendance was voluntary for most children until Sandon's Act of 1876 and Mundella's Act of 1880, and even after this it proved a hard task to enforce compulsion.

The similarity of the Lancasterian schoolroom to the early nineteenth-century factory has become a historical commonplace; it has been assumed that the pupil trained in the monitorial schoolroom was at the start of an assembly line ending in the factory. What perhaps needs greater emphasis is the extent to which, in an era of voluntary school attendance, the factory was in practice a substitute for the day school. Michael Sanderson has alerted us to the injurious impact of early industrialisation in Lancashire on children's day schooling.[79] Given that children in industrial or mining areas had little opportunity for formal instruction in day schools, the education available to them in Sunday schools was correspondingly more important. Laqueur's figures suggest a rapid growth in the percentage of working-class children going to Sunday schools: from 13·8 in 1801 to 49·6 in 1831 and 75·4 by 1851. While there was considerable regional variation in the extent to which the Sunday school provided the only education for the working-class child, we know that in the period from 1834 to 1843 the great majority of the children in Sunday schools in the industrial and mining areas of the midlands and north received no day schooling.[80]

Educational opportunities for many of these children were to improve with the development of the half-time system of education. Foreshadowed by Acts in 1802 and 1833, the legislation of 1845, which effectively began the system, gave children three hours daily schooling for five days per week. Starting with children in textiles factories it was gradually extended to children in a range of mills, workshops and mines. Although contemporaries were divided about its merits, the system was found to be sufficiently useful for it to last until 1918. For some contemporaries it seemed an ideal form of education for those in the lowest strata of society since a short and limited form of education was all that was required to produce an unskilled and low-paid work force. Factory owners in particular were explicit in their desire for such a half-time education to instil the right moral attitudes rather than produce a literate worker. A deferential and industrious workforce which was obedient, punctual, and had decent manners and a clean appearance was the desired outcome from half-time schooling. In spite of the inflated claims of some factory inspectors in the early Victorian period it is probable that the half-time system reinforced the class system by subordinating education to the needs of the economy.[81]

Industrialists' preference for deferential attitudes rather than skills in the factory workforce during the first Industrial Revolution came from their perception that most factory employment did not require literacy. The view of some modern economists in thinking that a 40 per cent literacy rate was a pre-condition for industrialisation was not substantiated by the experience of England in the eighteenth century. Available figures on English literacy suggest that although male literacy had reached this threshold by 1750 industrialisation was well under way before female illiteracy fell below the 60 per cent level in 1795.[82]

With the growing importance of technologically more advanced industries such as steel, chemicals, and precision engineering in the mid-nineteenth century, it was felt that increasingly complex technology required a more scientific and skilled workforce. The poor showing of Britain in the International Exhibition in Paris in 1867 suggested to perceptive contemporaries that Britain was ill-qualified to compete industrially with nations like Germany, which had not only universal elementary education but also a more efficient system of scientific and technical instruction. A compulsory period of elementary schooling for the working-class child was felt to be necessary to inculcate the skills of literacy and numeracy which would underpin a later superstructure of technical and scientific education. Forster's oft-quoted remark, as he introduced the 1870 Elementary Education Act, that 'upon the speedy provision of elementary education depends our industrial prosperity', symbolised a new determination to gear education to the needs of an industrialised economy.[83]

However, the 1870 Act failed to grapple with many of the key issues that would have achieved this – compulsory school attendance, free school places and a reformed curriculum in the elementary school.

Instead its clauses continued the mid-nineteenth century emphasis on the priority of expanding school provision. This concern for the supply of education tended to mean that the factors which influenced the demand by working-class parents for schooling were relatively neglected. Yet the problem of getting children to attend schools once places had been expanded was crucial to educational progress. Before 1870 pupils' early withdrawal and irregular attendance had hampered education in both rural and urban areas.[84] In part this was because of poverty and dependence on child earnings, but important also was working-class consumer-resistance to the kind of education that was proffered. The earlier preference of some working-class parents for uninspected private or adventure schools rather than the more efficient inspected schools run by the National or British Society suggested that there was dislike of their regimented, class nature.[85] After the Acts of 1876 and 1880 had legislated for the compulsory attendance of children until at least the age of ten, parents were pressurised to some extent by attendance committees and their officers, and ultimately by magistrates, into sending their children to school. Yet there was continued social ambivalence towards the desirability of such an extended period of schooling for the working-class child, so that the unwillingness or inability of parents to send children to school was almost equalled in many areas by the reluctance of the authorities to prosecute them. In some cases this was because those who were supposed to compel attendance, by virtue of their membership of attendance committees or seat on the bench, were reluctant to enforce the law through the nature of their interests as employers of child labour.[86] That social attitude rather than legislation was the main influence on school attendance is suggested by the minimal improvement in the number of children at school which was effected by Mundella's Act of 1880. The legislation of 1891 which made possible the creation of more free places did lead to better attendances, which suggests that family poverty had earlier been a cause of empty desks. By 1900 an estimated 87·78 per cent of those under twelve years of age were on the registers, and 72·12 in average daily attendance.[87] By this time the economic demand for child labour had decreased so that the possibility of substituting employment for schooling had diminished.

Scientific and technical education expanded slowly in response to the changing nature of the economy. The elementary school of the mid-nineteenth century usually covered science only in an unsystematic way in the teaching of object lessons on subjects such as the elephant, the mountain, or the bee. Some improvement took place after 1871 when more flexible Education Codes made it possible to teach science lessons and earn grants for the school by so doing. The bigger School Boards (for example London or Liverpool) gave encouragement to scientific teaching by issuing science syllabuses and text books, and providing visiting lecturers to Board Schools who gave demonstrations of scientific experiments to teachers and pupils. The Department of Science and Art in South Kensington had given generous grants for science classes in elementary schools from the 1850s onwards, and also in the 1890s encouraged the formation of organised science schools. In London the City and Guilds Institute helped technical education by giving money to the School Board to establish classes on manual instruction. The creation in urban areas of higher grade schools from the 1870s provided increased opportunities for more advanced instruction in mathematics and science. Yet the growing multiplicity of scientific enterprises should not conceal the underlying educational reality, which was that only a small minority of working-class children received any kind of systematic scientific instruction by the end of the nineteenth century.

Opportunities for learning science were also restricted for the middle- or upper-class child. It is likely that more middle- than working-class children availed themselves of the instruction in the higher grade schools, since the high fees charged and the postponement of employment involved put these schools out of the reach of all but the most prosperous working-class families. Higher grade schools were found only in urban areas, and in rural areas there were minimal opportunities for scientific instruction. The Technical Instruction Act of 1889 led to some improvement in the technical and scientific education available in rural grammar schools in the 1890s. Such improvement was much needed, since in a survey of 128 endowed schools in the early 1870s the Devonshire Commission on Scientific Instruction and the Advancement of Science had found that half the schools taught no science at all while nine-tenths of the institutions were without science laboratories. Expansion of scientific education was slow and this was in part because of a resource problem; money for building school laboratories was hard to find, and the increase in the number of civic universities in the 1870s and 1880s only gradually added to the number of graduates who might teach science in secondary schools. A more significant cause of this sluggish growth was a continued social prejudice against science. Schools were divided into classical and modern sides, and headmasters directed the less bright pupil to learn science in the modern side. The relatively low attainments of these boys then had a tendency to confirm the head's preconception that science was intellectually inferior to the classics. But by the end of the century there had been some advance on the position outlined in the early 1880s by the Samuelson Commission on Technical Instruction, which had found that there was a widespread failure to increase the opportunities for technical education and that scientific instruction in both elementary and secondary schools was still inadequate.

At the end of our period contemporaries were still concerned about the relationship between Britain's economic growth and the nature and extent of educational opportunity. Yet the evidence and findings of the Cross and Bryce Commissions of the 1880s and 1890s were similar to those of the Newcastle, Clarendon, and Taunton Commissions in the 1860s, in seeing educational provision in class terms. The elementary school was seen as a means of socialising working-class pupils for work within a stratified society. There was a continued fear lest too advanced an education should be given to the lower classes, and this social anxiety probably played its part in delaying the expansion of scientific and technical education in elementary, or higher grade, schools. Influential too in contemporary thinking was the division of society into 'gentlemen' and 'players', and with the corollary that the former needed a liberal (that is classical) education to fulfil their role of leadership, while it was only the mere players who required training in useful subjects such as science or technology.[88] Devoid of social prestige, science was slow therefore to attract the necessary resources for it to become a more central part of the school curriculum.

10. THE CURRICULUM IN THE ELEMENTARY SCHOOL

Instruction in the monitorial classroom at the beginning of our period was centred on the three Rs of reading, writing and arithmetic, although the achievement of basic literacy and numeracy was usually subordinated to the inculcation of a further two Rs, those of religion and respect for one's betters. Reading and writing often involved the use of religious tracts and texts, while even arithmetic was not immune from moralistic instruction. Morning and afternoon sessions in school began with scripture or learning the catechism, while singing lessons often consisted of a hymn practice.[89] By the 1840s and 1850s the curriculum was extended in many schools to include geography and grammar, while history was being taught in a progressive minority of institutions. In some cases this liberalisation might be more apparent than real since scriptural imperialism might result in sacred history (for example a chronicle of the tribes of Israel), or sacred geography (for example a study of the maps of the Holy Land or the journeys of St Paul). Girls might be excluded from geography or more advanced mathematics because of the socially perceived need for them to be instructed in plain needlework. But both girls and boys participated in object lessons, which focused on topics of general interest which were often of a scientific character.

The increased popularity of the object lesson in the mid-century was also an indication of the growth of a new form of teaching. Object lessons were taught to a whole age group, and this form of instruction was known as simultaneous or class teaching. It contrasted with the earlier form of monitorial instruction, in which the teacher had taught selected older pupils, and these monitors had then mechanically instructed small groups of younger children. The noisy inefficiency and excessive regimentation of this type of instruction in the over-large and under-equipped, monitorial schoolroom was the inevitable result of scarce resources in elementary education. By mid-century more and better teachers were coming from the training colleges; they made the adoption of class teaching more feasible. It was also facilitated by the introduction of the pupil-teacher scheme after 1846; under it teachers were given assistants who were older and better educated than monitors. However, not every school had pupil teachers, while some of them were of such poor quality that they proved a dubious asset to the hard-pressed teacher. But during our period the overall standard of teaching tended to rise, and the pupil–teacher ratio to fall, and this helped to develop more efficient and varied instruction in the elementary school.

The liberalisation of the curriculum was still at an early stage when the Revised Code of 1862 made examinations in the three Rs (together with pupil attendances), the basis of public grants to elementary schools. The fact that there was still only a restricted range of subjects taught before this new code suggests that its impact was minimal and that it did not lead to an immediate narrowing of the curriculum.[90] In the majority of elementary schools an increasing variety of subjects came much later in the century: the result of belated public recognition both that more resources should be channelled into this educational sector and that the aims of elementary education needed to be made more liberal. A progressive relaxation of the Education Codes followed from this. After 1867 it became possible under the codes for schools to earn grants from the Education Department by entering individual pupils for examination in 'specific' subjects (commonly grammar, geography and history), and after 1875 to enter groups for examination in 'class' subjects (usually English, grammar, geography, or plain needlework). By this time the three Rs were taught to a more advanced standard, so that arithmetic consisted not only of addition, subtraction and multiplication tables but for older children of mental arithmetic, algebra or Euclid; while reading and writing might include beside spelling and repetition, dictation, composition, grammar or even etymology. Schools were encouraged to include science and drawing in their curriculum by the generous grants for these subjects given by the Department of Science and Art in South Kensington. In the 1870s military drill for boys was introduced, to be succeeded in the 1880s and 1890s by Swedish drill, physical exercises or games, as the objectives of teaching physical education changed from the imposition of social discipline to that of encouraging the all-round development of the pupil.[91] Girls had ordinary, or Swedish, drill and also took an increasing range of domestic subjects. For the minority of older children who went on to the higher grade schools there was more advanced linguistic, mathematical and scientific instruction.

At the opposite end of the period of schooling, infant education initiated many of the progressive changes in teaching style which were to spread gradually throughout the elementary school. In the first half of the century the most notable of these innovations had been object lessons (which had been pioneered by Wilderspin in Smithfield and Stow in Glasgow), and the provision of a varied timetable within an attractive schoolroom (made famous by Robert Owen at New Lanark). In the second half of the century the ideas of the German educationist, Froebel, became more widely known in England so that increasingly kindergartens and infant rooms were organised where young children could develop their understanding through play.

However, the gap between the progressive ideal and the reality of the elementary-school classroom was wide. Too often the elementary-school teacher had received a professional training which was not an adequate preparation for the rigours of teaching large numbers of unruly children. There were few resources to ease the load since the basic furniture of the classroom consisted of rows of forms and tables (later replaced by desks), a blackboard, a cupboard, a clock and a stove. Although supplies of books improved, a globe or map was considered something of a luxury, while scientific apparatus was unusual. In this context it is hardly surprising that, for example, the Pestalozzian ideal of the object lesson (in which children learned through direct observation of selected objects), deteriorated within the Victorian classroom into a sterile exercise (in which the teacher 'pictured-out' in words an object which had an existence solely within the pages of his teacher's manual). Not only teaching methods but also school organisation suffered from the inadequate training and resources given to the teacher. Those school boards which built schools in which separate classrooms formed the main teaching accommodation found it difficult to recruit teachers of sufficient ability to overcome discipline problems singlehanded. The traditional arrangement of a large schoolroom, in which more experienced teachers taught alongside younger assistants, was more successful in providing much-needed support for poorly trained novices. Useful too were the numerous teachers' manuals which were produced throughout the century. In their concentration on classroom mechanics (often depicted as akin to barrack-room drill) and in their relative neglect of any psychological insight into child development these manuals revealed only too clearly the limited objectives of many elementary schools. However, the sheer variety of practice in the elementary schools is easy to underestimate as has been shown by several interesting studies.[92] As in the secondary school, however, diversity within the curriculum was limited by the perception that the kind of education that was made available must be related to the pupils' social class.

11. THE CURRICULUM IN THE SECONDARY SCHOOL

Those two great families of writers, the Greek and the Roman Classics, form the intellectual ancestors of all the cultivated minds of modern times; and we must be well acquainted with their language, their thoughts, their forms of composition, their beauties, in order that we may have our share in that inheritance by which men belong to the intellectual aristocracy of mankind.[93]

These words of the Master of Trinity reflect a common early Victorian faith in the surpassing educational power of the classics. Implying the inferiority of other studies, they suggest the reason why a classical education was regarded as the distinguishing feature of both the scholar and the gentleman. Whewell's words could well have been uttered in the sixteenth century, when the curriculum of the great colleges and endowed grammar schools was centred on the classics. But at that time Latin was frequently the language of learned discourse – a living tongue still, at least for an élite. Latin was in a moribund state by the eighteenth century since it had no liturgical use in England; Samuel Johnson's ability to speak Latin as fluently as he wrote it was a sign of his unusual erudition.

But there was no decline in reverence for the classics. Indeed, as Whewell's words suggest, the reverse was the case. The great English classicists of the late eighteenth century – Porson and others – revitalised the study of Greek and this gave it a more important place in the curriculum of the great schools. The forthright and spirited defence of the classics offered by the teachers of the early nineteenth century sprang from the self-confidence of this renaissance.[94]

In the early nineteenth century three-quarters or four-fifths of a public schoolboy's time was spent on Latin and Greek, and ancient history and geography. All other subjects – mathematics, English, modern languages – were squashed into the remainder, along with a medley of options such as fencing and music. Regular scientific instruction did not begin till 1849 – at Rugby and Eton, and then only on a modest scale. Boys were taught in classes or 'divisions', promotion from which was by a combination of seniority and talent. Whiskery dullards and bright juniors were often in the same group; one class at Rugby in 1861 varied in age from twelve to eighteen.

Classics were also prominent in early Victorian England in the curriculum of 400 endowed grammar schools. They varied greatly however in the level attained and in the proportion of pupils who took them seriously. Few sent more than a handful of boys to university and so competed with the great schools in intensive classical training; about half of the 400 schools taught Latin but no Greek.[95] Classical grammar schools tended to pay more attention to 'modern' subjects than the great schools did; but both sets of institutions neglected science. As has recently been shown, they were influenced by the eighteenth-century emphasis on subjects such as English, mathematics, and French, which were thought to be suitable for commercial and professional careers.

Innovation was however hampered by school statutes, the conservatism of trustees and teachers, and Eldon's Chancery decision (1805) in the Leeds Grammar School case.[96] Eldon had decided that although the grammar school had to continue the classical curriculum other subjects might be added to it, but later interpretations of his decision were even more restrictive. So classicality blighted fruitful change, if only often as an unachieved ambition that inhibited more practicable aims.

A tiny minority of boys with considerable innate talent gained from the classical regime a love for ancient writers which lasted throughout life; this was gained, for example, by Gladstone at Eton, and Edward White Benson at King Edward's Grammar School, Birmingham. The gain was greatest if they were taught (as Benson certainly was) by a superlative teacher who brought pupils to feel that they were touching a living tongue and literature – men like Samuel Butler and Benjamin Kennedy at Shrewsbury, or Thomas Arnold, whose novel and exciting stress on content rather than stylistic nicety in classical texts marked his creative talent quite as much as did his changes in school organisation. But most pupils, like Tom Tulliver at Mr Stelling's private school, were taught by duller men and in any case did not possess the brilliance needed to grasp the language fast enough to maintain their interest. Most classics education involved the memorising of grammatical rules and lines of verse, translation at snail's pace, and the composition of classical verse in tortuous patterns. Most boys never attained the fluent reading of literature, despite years of study, or could recall more than a few phrases shortly after leaving school. Nevertheless headmasters argued that classics provided an irreplaceable mental training, and 'a master-key to unlock all modern European tongues'.[97]

Throughout the Victorian period many were attached to the classical curriculum because of its snobbish or scholarly associations. But it was for many so boring, artificial and over-demanding that pressure for new curricula came from a desire for humane, as well as vocational, relevance. Most famous is T. H. Huxley's trenchant advocacy of science as the centre of a new liberal curriculum. More influential, at least on the public schools, was the recommendation by the Clarendon Commission (1864) and by Farrar, in his collection of essays (1867), that the classics should be reduced in impact, and supplemented by English, modern languages, science, mathematics, history and geography – subjects appealing more readily than the classics to boys' interest and curiosity. The new subjects were more manageable while possessing the classics' capacity for mental training (or 'gymnastic' as it was sometimes called).

For the endowed grammar schools, the Taunton Commission's proposals (1868) repeated arguments advanced often in the previous generation – that the schools should be reformed so as to serve the middle classes much more efficiently and closely, and that the schools should be rearranged in a threefold hierarchy, each level possessing its distinctive curriculum, leaving age, clientele and presumed occupational ambition. Third-grade schools should offer (in addition to the usual elementary school curriculum) the 'elements' of Latin or a modern language, algebra or geometry, and science; second-grade schools should offer Latin and up to two modern languages, plus science; first-grade schools should usually offer both classical languages, though some would provide more modern subjects in place of Greek. Never has a congruence between social class and the curriculum been more explicitly avowed.

The Taunton Commission's notion of a semi-classical first-grade school was influenced by the organisation of the new proprietary boarding schools of which Cheltenham, founded in 1840, was the first. These aimed at equality of status with the great schools and offered both a full classical regime and a modern one. Boys on this side took Latin but not Greek, and often aimed at the Sandhurst or Woolwich examinations and military careers.

After 1860 it became general for boarding and first-grade day schools to have modern as well as classical sides, the schools responding to the problems of organising a complexity of courses for a range of talent by placing boys in forms by age and then setting for much work, particularly mathematics. Some schools, for example Clifton, had military sides too, where extra science was studied – entry to them however tending to be delayed till boys were sixteen because of the schools' wish to emphasise language study. Modern classes commonly had three or four hours of science and drawing, twelve of Latin and modern languages, five each for mathematics and English subjects.[98]

Fundamentally, however, the élite schools changed very little, and because of their expansion there were more boys studying the classics intensively in 1900 than 1800. Eton, Winchester and Charterhouse had no modern sides; at Eton all boys did at least fifteen hours classics, and no more than two hours science – a suitably amateurish preparation for the Foreign Office clerkship or commission in an infantry regiment which the ex-Etonian might take as a career. In large schools the brightest boys took classics, not modern subjects, and the small first-grade day schools tended to be dominated still by Latin and Greek. This was for reasons of prestige and status, and because the scholarships at the two universities to which such schools most naturally aspired were very largely for classics, and indeed elementary competence in them was required for entry to Oxford and Cambridge.

The ancient tongues were defended as vigorously as ever for their unique gymnastic and civilising roles. To a nation worried about export competitiveness and turning to commercial education, classicists praised their bulwark against 'the utilitarianism which is the curse of modern education'. Classics encouraged patriotism and the martial virtues and therefore was a better spur to a balance-of-payments surplus than learning book-keeping; they had been 'the training of a nation and a class which as, it is true, achieved commercial success, but only because it steadily despised commercial ideals'.[99] Modern languages were regarded as a sort of substitute for the classics, offering the same mental training. They were taught in the same way (often of course by men trained in the classics) with stress on formal grammar and rote learning; headmasters resisted the sensible army view that future officers should be taught colloquial French and German.[100] In schools impregnated with classicist attitudes it was natural for teachers of history and science (from which so much had been expected in mid-century) to take to the practice of 'cram'. Edward Lyttelton lamented that the schools for England's élite should so persistently disregard educational theory – but unthinking adherence to old habits blighted upper-class education.[101]

The average teacher in a second-grade grammar school was perhaps just as unconscious of the value of theory, but at least was less trammelled by inert ideas. The second- and third-grade schools were revitalised after 1860. The exclusion of Greek from their curriculum prevented their aiming at Oxford and Cambridge. The grant-earning examinations of the Department of Science and Art, and the cash available from county councils after the Technical Instruction Act of 1889, led them to emphasise science within a balanced curriculum. Thus the average second-grade school in the 1890s offered to its middle years four or five hours of science, plus mathematics, the English subjects and a modern language, Latin and a second language often being alternatives.[102]

12. THE ELEMENTARY SCHOOL TEACHER

Untrained, and with a failure to succeed at alternative occupations as his most conspicuous qualification, the typical teacher in an elementary school at the beginning of our period, had low social status and poor remuneration. By the 1830s a small minority were receiving training, in the form of a brief apprenticeship in central schools run either by the British and National Societies or by diocesan authorities, but it was not until after 1839 with the creation of training colleges that a lengthier and more formal preparation for elementary school teaching was made more widely available. Upright moral character and the ability to pay the fees usually took priority over academic talent in the early recruitment of students to these denominational institutions. This meant that many students were semi-literate and needed secondary rather than higher education from the college; this generally took the form of factual cramming in a wide range of subjects. In the crowded academic timetable of the student teacher there was little time for professional training either in lectures on method, or in a practical apprenticeship in the classrooms within model schools.[103] The introduction by the state of the pupil-teacher scheme in 1846 (under which those wishing to become teachers could benefit from a five-year apprenticeship before competing for a Queen's Scholarship to take them to college), should have made it possible for the colleges to provide a more liberal and advanced training for their better educated students. Instead, a recognition of the educational shortcomings which arose from the over-pressurised lives of the pupil-teachers, led colleges to repeat, rather than extend, the instruction of the intending teacher. They repeated not only the content, but also the method of instruction, with the result that the trained teacher entered the classroom of the elementary school convinced from his own experience as pupil-teacher and student that education was a form of passive schooling rather than of active enquiry. In the second half of the nineteenth century the aridity of much teacher training could be attributed to a considerable extent to state intervention; first, through the inspectorate imposing uniform syllabuses on the colleges after 1854, and secondly, in lowering the standard of entry by ending grants to pupil-teachers and abolishing Queen's Scholarships under the Revised Code.

Recruited from working-class homes, student teachers entered narrow inward-looking institutions which regulated their lives closely in order to elevate their moral character and enable them to withstand the pressures arising from their humble vocation. Trained to adopt a middle-class frame of reference, but not yet accepted within society as belonging to that class, the elementary school teacher occupied a no-man's land in society. Social ambivalence was shown in trivial matters such as some school managers' concern for women teachers to adopt plain and decorous dress which would not rival that of their own wives. It was revealed in a more serious professional area in the continued refusal by the Education Department to promote teachers to the full inspectorate, a genteel preserve from which they were debarred until 1894 by their working-class origins. In this context it is hardly surprising that the elementary teacher's aspiration for professional status was recognised only minimally in this period; their sole success lay in the concession of pension rights in 1898.[104]

Professional sensitivities, made more intense by social isolation, preoccupied many elementary teachers in mid-century as was abundantly shown in the columns of a growing number of teachers' journals. There was emerging by this time, a professional self-awareness and self-confidence which conflicted with their enforced subservience to school managers and inspectors. However, it was not until the closing decades of the nineteenth century that the National Union of Elementary Teachers (founded in 1870) grew sufficiently strong to exert pressure either on managers who dismissed teachers summarily, or on inspectors who hindered, unjustly, the professional progress of a teacher in the annual inspections of his or her work. The lack of muscle in teachers' professional organisations reflected their diversity of status, income and interest. By 1899 certificated teachers outnumbered the uncertificated by more than two to one and could command much better salaries. But even among certificated teachers there was much variation in income and a teacher in a board school might earn half as much again as one in a church school.

A strained relationship existed between teachers in elementary schools and graduate teachers in secondary and public schools, as was shown by NUET opposition in 1879 to the College of Preceptors' abortive parliamentary Bill to establish a teachers' register which would have excluded elementary teachers. Not only did teachers in elementary schools lack high-status qualifications but they showed their social inferiority additionally by becoming increasingly a female preserve. By

1899 three-fifths of certificated teachers and four-fifths of pupil teachers in elementary schools were women.[105]

13. TEACHERS IN SECONDARY EDUCATION

Women predominated in teaching in our period both because the profession was one of the few respectable occupations open to them and because by the standard of other *female* employment it was relatively well paid. In the early nineteenth century the middle-class girl left without means of support often found employment as a governess since qualifications for the post assumed gentility and poverty rather than academic attainment. This concentration on social status rather than skills was also evident in the schoolmistresses in private schools.[106] Until the creation of Queen's, and Bedford, Colleges in the 1840s, and the opening to girls of local examinations in the 1860s, there were few opportunities for girls to obtain academic qualifications. While the first girls' high schools were staffed by some teachers who had benefited from these developments, others were cultivated women whose attainments had been acquired within the traditional confines of the home. A further expansion of girls' schooling was dependent on the growth in the number of well-qualified teachers and this was made possible by the widening opportunities for women to receive a university education in the 1870s and 1880s. The teachers in these early days of the new high, and boarding, schools for girls were dedicated women who were not discouraged either by poor marriage prospects (arising from their 'over-educated' character), or by meagre salaries.

They were conscious educational pioneers in wishing to widen the educational opportunities for their own sex, and unconscious radicals in developing a different kind of school. In borrowing what they saw as the best elements in the academic and sporting characteristics of the boys' schools, and combining them with the traditionally feminine concern for the moral character of the individual, they produced fortuitously a more humane and balanced institution. This was recognised by Edward Thring, headmaster of Uppingham, when in 1887 he told the Association of Headmistresses, 'You are fresh and enthusiastic, and comparatively untrammelled whilst we are weighed down by tradition, cast like iron in the rigid moulds of the past . . . the hope of teaching lies in you.'[107] But the foundation of organisations such as the Association of

Headmistresses in 1874, and the Association of Assistant Mistresses a decade later, suggests that women teachers were beginning to formulate distinctive professional ideals which in turn could produce institutional and pedagogic orthodoxies to rival those in boys' schools. By the 1890s the graduates who were recruited to the staffrooms of reformed girls' schools were eager to implement the meritocratic ideals of academic excellence and public service developed by the new class of professional headmistresses.[108]

Male teachers in elementary schools, like the pupils, were drawn from the working class. There was no corresponding social homogeneity in boys' secondary schools. Their masters had in common their graduate status (at all events for the great majority) and their untrained nature – both of them, of course, marking them off from elementary school teachers. Not till the 1880s did professional training for secondary masters have its hesitant beginning; not till this century did headmasters and governors cease to regard it as a wasteful irrelevance. The master's success was thought to depend on his scholarship, gentlemanly manner, and moral power; none of these attributes was believed to be enhanced by training. They derived crucially, however, from his social class and education – especially his university education. Oxford and Cambridge were regarded as intellectually and socially pre-eminent, conferring a badge of acceptability on boys of humble social origin – provided, of course, that they truly overcame it by adopting the mien and outlook of the gentleman.

One way in which lesser 'middle-class' schools strove to establish parity with their betters was by insisting on recruitment from Oxford and Cambridge. Thus in 1864 Nathaniel Woodard wrote to an associate that unless they were vigilant, 'we may get some queer characters from the London University; and it might happen that hereafter an MA of that university might be elected Provost – an event not to be desired'.[109] A similarly acute sense of social hierarchy informed the Liverpool College, whose three levels were planned to serve, with different fees, curricula, leaving ages and forms of punishment, different strata within the middle class; in the 1860s the upper school had seven Oxbridge graduates, while the middle and lower schools had, in addition to many non-graduates, respectively four graduates from Dublin and three from London.

At the top of the pyramid were the 'great schools', whose staffs largely were from the upper and professional classes and educated at public schools – often at their own school; Eton was a spectacular self-recruiter.

But far more were from humble origins or grammar schools than from 'other' universities – a graphic sign of the ability of Oxford and Cambridge to impress gentility on the talented poor scholar. Their headmasters earned at least £1000 a year and their assistants' earnings, while they might be as little as £200, were likely to be far higher; in 1862 the thirteen classical masters of Rugby earned over £1000 on average. Housemasters at Eton or Harrow, dynamic entrepreneurs within the Victorian education system, could swell their incomes to over £1500 with the profits of boarding. The great schools' headmasters might move to bishoprics or the headships of Oxford colleges, their assistants to deaneries.[110]

At the other extreme were the endowed grammar schools, whose staffs seem often to have been from the same lower-middle-class strata as many of their pupils. At the beginning of our period they were frequently products of Oxford and Cambridge, while towards the end of the century they were increasingly graduates of London and the 'civics'. Their headmasters earned less than assistant teachers at the great schools. Assistants in grammar schools earned only £105 a year at the end of the century.[111] At that time Newport (Essex) Grammar School paid its headmaster only £100 a year and a proportion of the fees, and its assistants only £70; graduates would not stay for salaries lower than elementary teachers', and Newport's masters were sometimes ex-sixth formers waiting to go to university.[112]

In one respect the experience of schools across the secondary spectrum was similar; staffs were laicised. At the beginning of the nineteenth century most schoolmasters were clergymen. As late as 1870 54 per cent of the staffs of the great schools were ordained; by 1906 only 13 per cent were. To some extent this trend reflects the steady decline in ordinations in the period; it also resulted from the increasing penetration of schools by the ethic of competition and examination success. Headships were the last positions to be held by clergymen, because of the special pastoral and moralising function which Arnold, Benson and Thring stamped on the popular conception of the headmaster. The great boarding schools were the last to appoint lay heads. In this sense the Victorian age did not end at Rugby till 1903, and at Eton till thirty years later.

14. THE EDUCATION OF GIRLS

It is a singular injustice which is often exercised towards women, first to give them a most defective education, and then to expect from them the most undeviating purity of conduct; to train them in such a manner as shall lay them open to the most dangerous faults, and then to censure them for not proving faultless.[113]

Hannah More's trenchant comment was made at the very end of the eighteenth century, yet it touched on issues which were to remain the main debating points on education for middle- and upper-class girls for the century which followed. Schooling for these girls was not seen primarily as the development of academic abilities but rather as the training of moral character to fit them for their future role as paragons within the home. Much discussion on female education in our period was to refine, rather than to challenge, accepted social assumptions about women's domestic vocation. The debate on the schooling of girls from working-class families was conducted separately, since education was seen in segregated class terms, although similar conclusions were reached. Poor girls were thought to need domestic training in their schooling which would fit them for their future as domestic servants or working men's wives. So it is arguable that sexism was as powerful an influence as social class in contemporary attitudes to girls' education since irrespective of the position occupied in the social hierarchy a girl's education was seen as being different from that of a boy.

It is easy to underestimate the differences which existed between the education of working-class girls and boys because they attended the same school and might be thought to share the same curriculum. But not only was there a substantial provision made for domestic subjects in the girls' curriculum which precluded them from studying the same range of academic subjects as boys; a hidden curriculum operated even within the academic subjects that were taken by girls. Plain sewing was seen as an essential training for girls in the charity schools and schools of industry in the eighteenth century and this was imitated in the schools of the National and British Societies founded in 1811 and 1814. While girls sewed, boys did geography or more advanced mathematics. Under the Education Department's Codes for elementary schools which started in 1862, needlework became an obligatory subject for girls, and in compensation for this they were permitted a lower standard in the annual arithmetic examinations. With the growth in the range of subjects which could earn grants from the government for a school, girls tended to spend a growing proportion of their time on domestic subjects. It was possible to take plain needlework from 1875, cookery from 1882, laundry work from 1890, and domestic economy from 1894, as 'class' subjects in which the inspector assessed the whole class for grant-earning purposes. For older girls in the higher standards of the elementary school one of two optional 'specific' subjects, in which they could be examined individually after 1875, was domestic economy. In 1878 the Education Department made this a mandatory subject for girls, so that their choice of academic 'specific' subjects was curtailed severely. The emphasis on domestic training did not end there since even if a girl took an academic subject, the hidden curriculum operated to slant the instruction towards domesticity; there is a revealing example of this occurring in science lessons under the London School Board.[114]

Comparatively few girls stayed on into the higher standards and were able to take advantage of more advanced instruction. Schooling was thought to be less necessary for the working-class girl than for her male counterpart: some school boards demanded a lower leaving standard for girls than boys, and girls' school attendance was enforced less rigorously because of the recognition that girls' help at home was frequently necessary, and, indeed, desirable. Working-class girls were educated primarily for a domestic future, although discussion by their 'betters' is often revealingly ambivalent as to whether their schooling was designed to turn out well-trained domestic servants for middle-class households, or efficient wives and mothers whose well-ordered home would keep their husbands from the public house and their children from delinquency.[115] In either context it is possible to see elementary schools as agents of social control – (when this is defined as cross-cultural transformation) – since bourgeois aspirations and middle-class ideas of domestic respectability were presented to the working-class schoolgirls in their elementary-school domestic instruction.

While the contemporary literature on the instruction of working-class girls was explicit on the need to train them for their confined domestic future, a parallel concern not to over-educate middle- and upper-class girls was expressed obliquely through a concern to retain accomplishments as an important element in their schooling. Gentle trills on the piano, a little conversational French, a charming song or two, sketches of picturesque ruins and some delicate tapestry work, all figured largely among the attainments which it was thought that a middle- or upper-class girl of the early or mid-nineteenth century should have acquired from a governess or private school, before she ventured into the marriage market. That parents placed such importance on social graces forced the new academic high schools, established in the second half of the nineteenth century, to retain drawing and music in their curriculum. Some early educational reformers were conciliatory towards this social preference and developed more serious studies on the basis of subjects which had previously served only as superficial accomplishments.[116]

As public opinion became more favourable towards women having a less ornamental existence in society, so reformers in the 1860s were emboldened to attack the time spent on accomplishments rather than on formal schooling. Maria Grey argued that in stressing accomplishments girls were being educated not to be wives but to get husbands.[117] However, an education for a future role as wife and mother was not disputed and the fact that those wishing to develop schooling for girls of the middle and upper classes did so in these moderate terms, resulted less from a perceived need to conciliate a dominant social viewpoint than from a shared perspective on the distinctive role of women in society. Throughout the nineteenth century arguments for developing middle- and upper-class girls' education rested squarely on the need for an elevated moral character in prospective wives. What was new was the way in which reformers extended this conservative rationale so as to suggest the necessity for growth in girls' education. They argued that the development of the intellect was a necessary precondition for moral understanding in a Christian woman and also that better schooling would avoid premature, foolish marriages.[118] As the view of a desirable marriage changed gradually from one in which the wife was an inferior dependent to one where she was an equal partner and friend, so it became possible to argue that showy accomplishments were less important than solid academic attainments. The latter were widely acknowledged to be essential for the growing numbers of single women; concern for a more efficient education that would enable them to earn their livelihood was an important reason for the development of new types of girls' schools in the middle of our period. This was inaugurated by the establishment of the North London Collegiate School in 1850 and Cheltenham Ladies College in 1853, and came of age with the establishment of proprietary and endowed girls' high schools in the 1870s.

An academic education for girls was only possible if it could be shown that they had an intellect which was sufficiently strong for them to benefit from it. A major obstacle to the development of a formal education for middle- and upper-class girls was the general view that moral superiority in the female was balanced by a corresponding intellectual infirmity. It was held that woman was inferior to man in intellectual understanding, judgement, and will-power although possessing good powers of intuition, imagination and memory.[119] Progressives argued that this was the result of girls receiving an inferior education, and authoritative support for this view was given by the Taunton Commission in 1868.[120] The 1860s and 1870s marked a peak of liberal optimism, since it was assumed that the establishment of girls' high schools, with more rigorous study within a balanced curriculum, would vindicate in practice the theoretical assertions about the potential strength of girls' intellect. But by the 1880s there was a conservative backlash and instruction in the reformed girls' schools was attacked because its academic aridity would manufacture female pedants who would be unfitted for their future domestic role. Instruction in depth, as in the teaching of grammar, was condemned as 'intellectual vivisection' and it was argued that girls needed a broader curriculum, and one which was different from that in boys' schools.[121] Conservative social attitudes were buttressed by physiological work on the brain, which indicated that a woman's brain weighed five ounces less than that of a man. When this finding was related to Darwinistic thinking it seemed obvious that, as G. J. Romanes wrote in 1887, 'it must take many centuries for heredity to produce the necessary five ounces of the female brain'.[122] Once this was accepted then it followed that educational differences did not cause mental inferiority in girls and women and that the female should not seek to rival the male in intellectual matters.

'I was always hearing that girls would be turned into boys by study-ing the same subjects', commented Dorothea Beale in 1888, after thirty years as headmistress of Cheltenham Ladies College.[123] The assertion that girls would unsex themselves if they pursued an academic education or entered a profession that had been occupied traditionally by men grew in intensity as the openings for girls widened during the second half of the nineteenth century. What were to become the two main emphases in debate were found as early as 1868 in Eliza Lynn Linton's notorious article 'The Girl of the Period'. She argued firstly that the modern English girl, 'bold in bearing and masculine in mind', paid a heavy price in claiming equality since she either scared men from marriage or proved a cold mother to her children. Equally insistent was her view that in seeking to rival men the modern girl 'pleases them as little as she elevates them', and hence, by implication, that the growth of feminine intellect necessarily atrophied the traditional moral adornments of English womanhood.[124] It was held that one faculty could not be developed without loss to another, a view corroborated by the medical opinion that human energy was finite. A woman doctor argued in 1899 that, 'One cannot possess all the delicately evolved qualities of womanhood together with the muscular and mental energies of man', and argued vigorously against girls' cycling for this reason.[125] Such views reveal the way in which social ideology influenced medical pronouncements in making them applicable only to middle- and upper-class women and ignored conveniently the harsh physical toil of working-class women which took place without medical concern for its toll on motherhood.

The finite nature of energy, as a rationale for women inhabiting a confined social mould, was a useful, because flexible, argument for conservatives since it could suggest that any emancipated activity would involve the loss of womanhood. Social Darwinism was applied to girls' schooling first in the United States because its integrated co-educational pattern of education aroused an early concern about overstrain in girl pupils. The view of John Thorburn, Professor of Obstetric Medicine at the Victoria University of Manchester and a notable opponent of educational integration, suggested how prevalent Social Darwinism had become in Britain by the 1880s. He thought that 'future healthy mothers of our race' needed an intermittent and restricted education and advised doctors to tell parents that regular work in school for girls over twelve, without rest and relaxation during menstruation, might entail 'the unsexing of the girl'.[126] Anxiety about the diseases which would be developed specifically in girls as a result of over-intensive schooling merged into a more generalised concern during the 1880s about overpressure in both boys and girls as a result of too much brain work. This uneasiness had originated in elementary education with wild assertions about overpressure leading to an amazing range of illnesses, from insanity to elephantiasis, but had also led to an allegation on the ill effects of cramming in girls' schools.[127]

The development of girls' schooling was influenced, but not dominated, by these conservative ideas and assumptions, so that the practice of the new girls' high schools and boarding schools resembled that of the boys' endowed, and proprietary, schools in some respects although differing in others. Recognition both of the physical frailty of girls and of the social undesirability of their prolonged absence from home led to many high schools imitating the pioneering North London

Collegiate School in having a school day which lasted only for the morning. The curriculum was varied, since those wishing to expand the opportunities for girls had been encouraged by the argument of the Taunton Commission that girls' brains and bodies benefited from greater mental and physical exertion than had been customary in the private day or boarding schools of the early and mid-nineteenth century. The academic curriculum of girls' schools avoided the heavy classical bias of many boys' schools, and gave more weight to a wide range of subjects, which included the humanities, ancient and modern languages, mathematics, and science. (The expansion of higher educational opportunities for women tended to offset an early difficulty in the new girls' schools of recruiting able teachers who could give instruction in these areas). In the mid-nineteenth century there was some disagreement between 'hard' and 'soft' line reformers as to the suitability of 'masculine' subjects like mathematics or classics for the female mind, and whether it was seemly for girls to compete with boys in the local examinations, which were first opened to girls in 1865. Hardliners were heartened both by the girls' success in these public examinations, and by the example set by the achievements of women pioneers like Mary Somerville. The influence of Social Darwinism in the 1870s and 1880s led teachers in the high schools to emphasise to the public that good pastoral care and a careful control of homework avoided any overstrain in girls arising from a wide curriculum.[128]

Discussion on the alleged frailties of the female constitution contributed to a growing concern in girls' high schools for the all-round development of the pupils. School medical inspections (the first of which was held in 1882) produced startling evidence of the stunted physical development of high-school girls. This speeded the transition from callisthenics to gymnastics or Swedish exercises, which made possible a more scientifically controlled development of physique. Although games playing was instituted in many schools in the last quarter of the century, the athleticism of the late-Victorian boys' public school was seldom repeated. Even at St Leonard's (the first of the new public boarding schools for upper-class girls), where physical activities had formed an unusually important element in the curriculum since it was opened in 1877, girls were forbidden to play games for more than four half afternoons a week.[129] Games were seen in the new girls' schools as contributing to the all-round development of the girl; they gave spontaneity and joy to offset her conscientiousness in the classroom, and developed moral and corporate virtues.[130] The objective of the new

type of girls' school was expressed by Miss Dove, the second headmistress of St Leonard's, when at a prizegiving she told the girls that the
school's aim was that 'you may be sent forth to your life's work . . . with
as healthy a body, trained intellect and sustained character as may be
possible'.[131]

Although substantial progress was made in expanding girls' schooling the early pace of development was slow. Conservative social
attitudes were of crucial importance in limiting the financial resources
made available to establish the first reformed girls' schools; this made it
difficult to refute social prejudices, by showing that girls' abilities were
much more evident in practice than they were usually considered to be.
Public indifference to girls' schooling was only eroded slowly – by 1900
still only one third of middle-class girls attending schools were to be
found in these reformed educational institutions. Many of these new
schools were financed on the proprietary principle, but gave a poor
return to their shareholders. This was because high schools felt able to
charge only low fees since sons had first claim on the family income for
school bills. Low fees also meant serious economies were made in the
salaries of teachers, on buildings, and on equipment. Gradually more
support was given to the creation of high schools, which derived from a
belated public recognition of their success in turning out a new sort of
girl. By the end of the century there were about a hundred proprietary
high schools, the majority organised either by the non-denominational
Girls' Public Day School Company (founded in 1872), or the Anglican
Church Company (founded in 1882). Of equal importance to the
proprietary schools numerically, and complementary geographically to
them, were the endowed schools which were created under the
Endowed Schools Act of 1869. This legislation had resulted from the
Taunton Commission's findings on the meagre amount of educational
endowments which were devoted to girls' schooling. An enterprising
start in reducing this inequality was made by the Endowed Schools
Commissioners with one in four of their schemes concerned with girls'
education, but the pace slackened to only one in seven schemes under
the Charity Commissioners, who had replaced them in 1874. By the
time that the Bryce Commission reported in 1894 some eighty girls'
schools had been endowed: a useful addition yet one which left
substantial gaps to be filled after the 1902 Act by local authority
secondary schools. In their finance from the rates, in their broader social
composition, and in being organised more frequently on co-educational
lines, these schools marked a new era in secondary education.

15. COEDUCATION

The extension of coeducation to middle- or upper-class children in the closing decades of the nineteenth century reveals both the substantial progress which had been taking place in girls' education and the limited social acceptance of these developments. Coeducation was not in any sense a novel practice in Britain and had been found most notably in parochial schools in Scotland and in schools for the poorer classes in England. The extension of the coeducation principle to middle- and upper-class pupils in English secondary schools at the end of our period aroused contemporary concern about the advisability of educating boys and girls together after puberty, and discussion highlighted the extent to which ideas on the traditional social roles of men and women had remained unchanged.

The fullest expression of coeducational ideals was found in the private sector of middle-class education, where enthusiasts could organise a common curriculum for boys and girls. At the Lady Barn Preparatory School (established in 1873) all pupils took the same lessons, and both boys and girls played cricket and lacrosse, while at the King Alfred School, Hampstead (founded in 1897) there was a similar pattern, although girls were debarred from playing football. Bedales (founded in 1893) opened its doors to girls in 1899 and was the first school to extend coeducation to a full school age-range up to eighteen years of age.[132] The headmaster, J. H. Badley, stated in 1900 that 'the aims and methods here put in practice are equally suitable and equally necessary for both sexes'. While girls at Bedales had their own boarding house they took the same academic lessons, shared in the same recreations, and mixed freely with the boys. In the first years differences consisted in girls doing sewing, housework or dairying rather than heavy farmwork, and in playing hockey or lacrosse instead of football. But by 1914 Badley commented 'that by education together I don't mean identical education, either in classroom or playing field', and thought that a different education for girls and boys was necessary after the age of fifteen, in order to prevent overstrain in future mothers.[133] By this time there was a greater awareness that the pace of development was unequal between girls and boys. This gave useful ammunition to those social Darwinists who wished to restrict a girl's education after puberty, since if she competed against boys she might be over-strained and harm the interests of the race.

In the private sector coeducation was adopted through conviction that the principle was right, whereas in the public sector expediency often determined the composition of new secondary schools. In rural areas, particularly, scarce resources led to the establishment of mixed schools. The apparently rapid acceptance of the coeducational ideal at the turn of the twentieth century is misleading, since in practice coeducational schools ranged from a few that were fully integrated through a pattern of common instruction in rigidly demarcated classrooms (as was practised in many board schools), to a dual system in which the education of girls and boys was organised separately but took place under a common roof. The small number of fully coeducational schools which was established suggests continuing public anxiety about educating girls and boys together, since it was thought that pupils would develop a precocious interest in the opposite sex, that boys would become effeminate and girls immodest, and that common instruction would overtax the limited physical and mental capacity of the girls.[134]

REFERENCES

1. R. S. Schofield, 'The Measurement of Literacy in Pre-Industrial England', in J. Goody (ed.), *Literacy in Traditional Societies* (1968) p. 324.
2. Most notably the survey of 274 parishes by R. S. Schofield of the Cambridge Population Group; preliminary results are detailed in R. S. Schofield, 'Dimensions of Illiteracy, 1750–1850', *Explorations in Economic History*, x (1972–3) 437–54.
3. W. B. Stephens, 'Illiteracy and Schooling in the Provincial Towns, 1640–1870', in D. Reeder (ed.), *Urban Education in the Nineteenth Century* (1977) p. 31.
4. Michael Sanderson, 'Social Change and Elementary Education in Industrial Lancashire, 1780–1840', *Northern History*, III (1968) 131–54.
5. Thomas W. Laqueur, 'Working-Class Demand and the Growth of English Elementary Education, 1750–1850', in Lawrence Stone (ed.), *Schooling and Society. Studies in the History of Education* (1976) pp. 192–205.
6. J. Simon, 'Was There a Charity School Movement? The Leicestershire Evidence', in B. Simon (ed.), *Education in Leicestershire, 1540–1940* (1968) pp. 55–100.
7. Quoted in Stone (ed.), *Schooling and Society*, p. 198.
8. For example, the Education Department is not mentioned in O. MacDonagh, *Early Victorian Government, 1830–1870* (1977).
9. The best survey of the debate is J. Hart, 'Nineteenth-Century Social Reform: A Tory Interpretation of History', *Past and Present*, XXXI (1965) 39–61.
10. Quoted in R. Parkin, *The Central Society of Education, 1836–40* (Museum of the History of Education, University of Leeds, Monograph no. 3, 1975) p. 5.
11. This paragraph owes much to R. Johnson's unpublished Cambridge Ph.D. thesis, 'The Education Department, 1839–1864. A Study in Social Policy and the Growth of Government' (1968) chs 1–6.
12. O. MacDonagh, *A Pattern of Government Growth: The Passenger Acts and Their Enforcement, 1800–60* (1961); R. Lambert, *Sir John Simon (1816–1904) and English Social Administration* (1963).
13. Johnson, 'The Education Department, 1839–1864', ch. 8, and 'Administrators in Education before 1870: Patronage, Social Position and Role', in Gillian Sutherland (ed.), *Studies in the Growth of Nineteenth-Century Government* (1972) pp. 134–6; J. Winter, *Robert Lowe* (1976) pp. 173–6.

14. D. Roland, 'The Struggle for the Elementary Education Act and its Implementation . . . 1870–73' (unpublished Oxford B. Litt. thesis, 1959).

15. G. Sutherland, *Policy-Making in Elementary Education, 1870–1895* (1973) pp. 33–80.

16. M. K. Ashby, *Joseph Ashby of Tysoe, 1859–1919* (1961) p. 18.

17. Sutherland, *Policy-Making*, pp. 115–328.

18. Their nature in one county has been graphically sketched in Simon, 'Private Schools in Leicester and the County, 1780–1840', in *Education in Leicestershire*, pp. 103–29.

19. B. Heeney, *Mission to the Middle Classes* (1969) pp. 21–47, 87–125; P. Searby, 'Joseph Lloyd Brereton and the Education of the Victorian Middle Class', *Journal of Educational Administration and History*, xi, 1 (1979).

20. *Schools' Inquiry Commission*, vol. xvii, *Parliamentary Papers* (hereafter cited as *P.P.* (1867–8) xxviii, Part xiv, pp. 574–87.

21. J. Honey, *Tom Brown's Universe* (1977) pp. 238–95. Sometimes as many as 100 schools were regarded as 'public'.

22. The plight of one such unfortunate local boy in Harrow School is described in Anthony Trollope, *Autobiography* (1883) World's Classics edn, pp. 10–12.

23. F. E. Balls, 'The Endowed Schols Act, 1869, and the Development of the English Grammar Schools in the Nineteenth Century', *Durham Research Review*, v (1967–8) 207–29.

24. J. Godber, *The Harpur Trust, 1552–1973* (1973) pp. 83–129.

25. H. G. Wells, *An Experiment in Autobiography*, vol. 1 (1934) p. 173.

26. A. B. Evans, *The Cambridge Grammar School for Boys, 1871–1971* (1971) pp. 9–16.

27. P. Searby, Weavers and Freemen in Coventry, 1838–1860', *Social History*, ii no. 3 (1977) 783.

28. Brian Simon, *Studies in the History of Education, 1780–1870* (1960) pp. 323–36; Balls, 'The Endowed Schools Act, 1869', pp. 219–29.

29. See the work of Frith and Laqueur, noted elsewhere, and also E. G. West, *Education and the State* (1965), and *Education and the Industrial Revolution* (1975), though many of West's arguments have not been accepted by historians.

30. Michael Cullen, 'The Chartists and Education', *New Zealand Journal of History*, x no. 2 (1976) 170–1.

31. George Eliot, *Janet's Repentance* (1858) ch. 1.

32. John Buckner in 1812, quoted in R. A. Soloway, *Prelates and People. Ecclesiastical Social Thought in England, 1783–1852* (1969) p. 376.

33. James Murphy, *Church, State and Schools in Britain, 1800–1870* (1971) pp. 1–9.

34. This view was summarised neatly in the *Punch* Cartoon of 2 July 1870.

35. A good account of Anglican zeal in one area is M. Sanderson, 'The

National and British School Societies in Lancashire, 1803–1839', in T. G. Cook (ed.), *Local Studies and the History of Education* (1972).

36. *Coventry Standard* (19 February 1841).

37. J. Murphy, *The Religious Problem in English Education: The Crucial Experiment* (1959) pp. 244–57.

38. See, for example, J. Gordon, *Ought the Government to Educate the People? The Question of National Education Considered in a Letter to a Friend* (1843).

39. The extreme Voluntaryism of the 1840s and 1850s is to be distinguished from the 'voluntary' enterprise after 1870 which did not eschew government grants.

40. Thomas W. Laqueur, *Religion and Respectability. Sunday Schools and Working Class Culture, 1780–1850* (1976) esp. pp. 154, 168. S. Frith, 'Socialization and Rational Schooling: Elementary Education in Leeds before 1870', in P. McCann (ed.), *Popular Education and Socialization in the Nineteenth Century* (1977) pp. 80–5.

41. The debate that led up to the 1870 Act is surveyed by A. Briggs in his Introduction to the 1972 reprint of F. Adams, *History of the Elementary School Contest in England* (1882).

42. J. Murphy, *Church, State and Schools in Britain, 1800–1970* (1971) p. 58.

43. On the 1870 debates convenient guides are J. Murphy, *The Education Act, 1870* (1972), and the articles in the commemorative issue of the *British Journal of Educational Studies* (1970). The fullest account is Roland, 'The Struggle for the Elementary Education Act'.

44. P. Smith, *Disraelian Conservatism and Social Reform* (1967) pp. 242–57; Sutherland, *Policy-Making*, pp. 263–312.

45. H. McLeod, *Class and Religion in the Late Victorian City* (1974) pp. 23–131; E. R. Wickham, *Church and People in an Industrial City* (1957) pp. 58–165.

46. W. E. Marsden, 'Social Environment, School Attendance and Educational Achievement in a Merseyside Town, 1870–1900', in McCann (ed.), *Popular Education and Socialization*, pp. 207–8.

47. James Obelkevitch, *Religion and Rural Society: South Lindsey, 1825–1875* (1976) p. 281.

48. Flora Thompson, *Lark Rise to Candleford* (1945) chs XI and XIV.

49. *Schools' Inquiry Commission*, vol. I, *P.P.* (1867–8) XXVIII, part I, pp. 140–1.

50. In 1900 about seventeen were Nonconformist, and a handful Roman Catholic; see the essays by Abbot Gasquet and N. G. B. James in *The Public Schools from Within* (1906).

51. Quoted in T. W. Bamford (ed.), *Thomas Arnold on Education* (1970) p. 68.

52. James M. Wilson, *Autobiography, 1836–1931* (1932) p. 141. Wilson was headmaster of Clifton, and writes of the school's Bristol mission, which acquired a substantial church and became the nucleus of a new parish.

53. J. L. Brereton, 'Dr. Arnold of Rugby', *Lynn Advertiser* (9 November 1893).

54. *Recollections of Rugby, by an old Rugbaean* (1848).

55. E. D. Rendall and G. H. Rendall, *Recollections and Impressions of the Rev. John Smith, M. A.* (1914) p. 26.
56. W. E Bowen, *Edward Bowen. A Memoir* (1902). His essay on Arnold – 'Arnoldides Chiffers' is reprinted there, pp. 369–75.
57. J. E. C. Welldon, 'The Religious Education of Boys', in *Thirteen Essays on Education by Members of the* XIII (1891) p. 61.
58. W. W. Vaughan, 'Religion at School', in A. C. Benson (ed.), *Cambridge Essays in Education* (1919) p. 57.
59. D. Newsome, *Godliness and Good Learning* (1961) pp. 28–91, 195–239.
60. Alfred Lyttelton, 'Eton College: as a School', in *Great Public Schools . . . by Various Authors* (c. 1890) pp. 41–2.
61. 'B. K.', *The First Term. Letters to a Schoolboy* (1923) pp. 16, 84–5.
62. E. Lyttelton, *Memories and Hopes* (1925) p. 208.
63. 'An Ex-Headmaster', 'The Religious Element', *The Public Schools from Within*, pp. 140–1.
64. *Gentleman's Magazine* I (1784) 410–12; A. P. Wadswoth, 'The First Manchester Sunday Schools', in M. W. Flinn and T. C. Smout (eds.), *Essays in Social History* (1974) pp. 100–5.
65. Flinn and Smout, *Essays in Social History*, p. 107; J. M. Goldstrom, *The Social Content of Education, 1808–1870* (1972) pp. 28–33, 41–5; R. Johnson, 'Notes on the Schooling of the English Working Class, 1780–1850', in R. Dale (ed.), *Schooling and Capitalism* (1976) p. 478.
66. S. Pollard, 'Factory Discipline in the Industrial Revolution', *Economic History Review*, 2nd ser., XVI (1963) 268–70; E. P. Thompson, 'Time, Work-Discipline and Industrial Capitalism', *Past and Present* XXXVIII (1967) 84–5.
67. Laqueur, *Religion and Respectability*, pp. 78, 92–3, 192–3, 203–9, 216–18, 223, 239; T. R. Tholfsen, *Working-Class Radicalism in Mid-Victorian England* (1976) pp. 17–18, 28–9.
68. *Hansard's Parliamentary Debates*, 3rd ser., XX (1833) 148.
69. R. Johnson, 'Educational Policy and Social Control in Early Victorian England', *Past and Present*, XLIX (1970) 119.
70. R. Johnson, 'Administrators in Education before 1870', in Sutherland (ed.), *Studies in the Growth of Nineteenth-Century Government*, pp. 116–21, 132–3.
71. J. E. Dunford, 'Robert Lowe and Inspectors' Reports', *British Journal of Educational Studies*, XXV (1977) 167; N. Ball, *Her Majesty's Inspectorate, 1839–1849* (1963) pp. 206–9.
72. R. Johnson, 'Educating the Educators: "Experts" and the State, 1833–9', in A. P. Donajgrodski (ed.), *Social Control in Nineteenth-Century Britain* (1977) pp. 87–92; M. J. Cullen, *The Statistical Movement in Early Victorian Britain* (1975) pp. 68–9.
73. Johnson, 'Educational Policy and Social Control', 115–16, 119.

74. A. Tropp, *The School Teachers* (1957) pp. 36–43, 50–7.
75. R. Colls, ' "Oh Happy English Children!" Coal, Class and Education in the North-East', *Past and Present*, LXXIII (1976) 75–6.
76. *Fourth Report of Poor Law Commissioners, P.P.* (1837–8) XXVIII p. 290.
77. J. M. Goldstrom, 'The Content of Education and the Socialization of the Working-Class Child, 1830–1860', in McCann (ed.), *Popular Education*, pp. 101–2.
78. *Census. Education, P.P.* (1852–3) XC, p. XC.
79. M. Sanderson, 'Literacy and Social Mobility in the Industrial Revolution', *Past and Present*, LVI (1972) 78–80; 'Social Change and Elementary Education', 131–42.
80. Laqueur, *Religion and Respectability*, pp. 49, 99–100.
81. H. Silver, 'Ideology and the Factory Child: Attitudes to Half-Time Education', in McCann (ed.), *Popular Education*, pp. 141–5, 152–4, 159–60; M. Sanderson, 'Education and the Factory in Industrial Lancashire, 1780–1840', *Economic History Review*, 2nd ser., XX (1967) 267–71, 279.
82. Schofield, 'Dimensions of Illiteracy, 1750–1850', 453.
83. *Hansard's Parliamentary Debates*, 3rd ser., CXCIX (1870) p. 465.
84. N. Ball, 'Elementary School Attendance and Voluntary Effort before 1870', *History of Education*, II (1973) 20–6.
85. Laqueur, 'Working-Class Demand', 196–202.
86. D. Rubinstein, *School Attendance in London, 1870–1904* (1969) pp. 59–64, 98–103.
87. A. C. O. Ellis, 'Influences on School Attendance in Victorian England', *British Journal of Educational Studies*, XXI (1973) 314–15, 317–19.
88. D. C. Coleman, 'Gentlemen and Players', *Economic History Review*, 2nd ser., XXVI (1973) 101.
89. Goldstrom, *The Social Content of Education, 1808–70*, ch. 1 *passim*.
90. The interpretation of J. Hurt in *Education in Evolution* (1972) ch. 7, is more soundly based in emphasising continuities before and after the Revised Code than is the earlier view of M. Sturt in *The Education of the People* (1967) ch. 13.
91. J. S. Hurt, 'Drill, Discipline and the Elementary School Ethos', in McCann (ed.), *Popular Education*, pp. 187–9.
92. For example, P. and H. Silver, *The Education of the Poor* (1974); M. Johnson, *Derbyshire Village Schools in the Nineteenth Century* (1968); R. R. Sellman, *Devon Village Schools in the Nineteenth Century* (1968).
93. William Whewell, *Of a Liberal Education in General . . .* , 2nd edn (1850) pp. 79–80.
94. M. L. Clarke, *Classical Education in Britain, 1500–1900* (1959) pp. 75–6.
95. In addition more than 300 other grammar schools had dropped classics altogether by the 1860s.

96. R. S. Tompson, *Classics or Charity? The Dilemma of the 18th-Century Grammar School* (1971) pp. 115–24.

97. H. Sidgwick, 'The Theory of Classical Education', in F. W. Farrar (ed.), *Essays on a Liberal Education* (1867) p. 101. The book is a sustained criticism of the classics' dominance in the curriculum.

98. P. A. Barnett (ed.), *Teaching and Organisation with Special Reference to Secondary Schools* (1897) p. 30.

99. Rev. Thomas Field, 'In Behalf of Greek', in *Thirteen Essays* (1891) pp. 240–2. Field was the headmaster of King's School, Canterbury.

100. G. G. Coulton, *Public Schools and Public Needs* (1901) pp. 74–94.

101. E. Lyttelton, 'Principles and Practice', in *Thirteen Essays* (1891), and *Schoolboys and School Work* (1909) pp. 61–105.

102. Barnett (ed.), *Teaching and Organisation*, pp. 23–33.

103. R. W. Rich, *The Training of Teachers in England and Wales during the Nineteenth Century* (1933) ch. IV *passim*.

104. Tropp, *The School Teachers*, chs 3, 8 *passim*.

105. Ibid., pp. 117–18, 120–3, 133.

106. W. F. Neff, *Victorian Working Women* (1966) ch. V *passim*; M. Jeanne Peterson, 'The Victorian Governess: Status Incongruence in Family and Society', *Victorian Studies*, XIV (1970) 7–25; J. S. Pedersen, 'Schoolmistresses and Headmistresses: Elites and Education in Nineteenth-Century England', *Journal of British Studies*, XV (1975) 192–3.

107. Quoted in N. Glenday and M. Price, *Reluctant Revolutionaries, 1874–1914* (1974) p. 21.

108. Pedersen, 'Schoolmistresses and Headmistresses', 152, 156, 158–61.

109. Heeney, *Mission to the Middle Classes*, p. 112.

110. T. W. Bamford, *The Rise of the Public Schools* (1967) pp. 116–36, and 'Public School Masters: A Nineteenth-Century Profession', in T. G. Cook (ed.), *Education and the Professions* (1973) pp. 29–47.

111. *Secondary Education Commission*, vol. IV, *P.P.* (1895) XLVI, p. 539.

112. F. Thompson, *Newport Grammar School, Essex* (1974) p. 83.

113. H. More, *Strictures on the Modern System of Female Education* (1799) vol. I, p. ix.

114. C. Dyhouse, 'Good Wives and Little Mothers: Social Anxieties and the Schoolgirl's Curriculum, 1890–1920', *Oxford Review of Education*, III (1977) 21–2; T. A. Spalding, *The Work of the London School Board* (1900) pp. 209–13.

115. C. Morley, *Studies in Board Schools* (1897) pp. 122–4.

116. M. Wollstonecroft, *Thoughts on the Education of Daughters* (1788) pp. 15–18.

117. M. Grey, *On the Special Requirements for Improving the Education of Girls* (1871) pp. 6, 25.

118. E. Shirreff, *Intellectual Education and Its Influence on the Character and Happiness of Women* (1858) p. 31, and *The Work of the National Union*, 2nd edn (1873)

pp. 13–14; 'A Utopian' (D. Beale), 'On the Education of Girls', *Frazer's Magazine*, LXXIV (1866) 510.

119. More, *Strictures*, II, 26; G. J. Romanes, 'Mental Differences between Men and Women', *Nineteenth Century*, XXI (1887) 655–9.

120. J. E. Butler (ed.), *Woman's Work and Woman's Culture* (1869) pp. xxvii, 293; E. Simcox, 'The Capacity of Women', *Nineteenth Century*, XXII (1887) 391–402; *Schools Inquiry Commission*, vol. I, *P.P.* (1867–8) XXVIII, part I, pp. 553–4.

121. E. Sewell, 'The Reign of Pedantry in Girls' Schools', *Nineteenth Century*, XXIII (1888) 216–38.

122. Romanes, 'Mental Differences', 666.

123. D. Beale, 'Girls' Schools Past and Present', *Nineteenth Century*, XXIII (1888) 54.

124. E. L. Linton, *The Girl of the Period and Other Social Essays* (1883) vol. I, p. x.

125. A. Kenealy, 'Woman as Athlete', *Nineteenth Century*, CCLXIII (1899) 644.

126. J. Thorburn, *A Practical Treatise on the Diseases of Women* (1885) p. 102.

127. T. S. Clouston, *Female Education from a Medical Point of View* (1882) pp. 26–9; A. B. Robertson, 'Children, Teachers and Society. The Over-Pressure Controversy, 1880–1886', *British Journal of Educational Studies*, XX (1972).

128. S. Bryant, *Over-Work from the Teacher's Point of View* (1885).

129. J. M. Grant, K. H. McCutcheon, E. F. Sanders, *St. Leonard's School, 1877–1927* (1927) p. 89.

130. D. Beale, L. H. M. Soulsby, J. F. Dove, *Work and Play in Girls' Schools* (1898) pp. 399–402.

131. E. Bowerman, *Stands There a School* (1966) p. 56.

132. A. Woods (ed.), *Co-education* (1903).

133. J. H. Badley, *Bedales School* (1900) p. 7; J. H. Badley, *Co-education in Practice* (1914) p. 20.

134. Ibid., pp. 18, 22–5.

PART TWO

Documents

SOURCES

Working of the Elementary Education Acts, P.P. (1887) XXIX, pp. 759, 1023–4, evidence of J. Hanson of Bradford School Board.

Minnie Bulmer's Home and School Lesson Book (1877–8), St. Maurice's Elementary School, York (Castle Museum, York). Transcription, 'The flesh of the rhinocerous', Composition, 'Wisdom Rewarded', Analysis of poem, 'We are Seven'

I. EDUCATION, RELIGION AND MORALITY

Religion had a place in almost every nineteenth-century schoolroom, although its purpose and intensity varied. For the first half of the century it was, at least in elementary schools, the most essential subject, as [1] and [2] indicate.* Religion gave point and meaning to the entire curriculum and inculcated the social acquiescence which, as much as piety, it was the function of the school to generate. Even issues susceptible of interpretation in non-religious terms attracted from teachers answers in religious currency, as [3] reveals. Churchmen, especially Anglicans and Roman Catholics, believed that the education their schools provided would be emptied of meaning if it lost its distinctive credal message [4]. Hostility to other churches informed much of their teaching, and [5] illustrates the anti-Popery which strongly marked Evangelical Protestantism. Relations between the voluntary religious agencies were therefore often rancorous.

Churches and the State agreed that the elementary school was a necessary instrument for the moral elevation of the poor. [6] expresses the belief in the State as a moral agent which was a foundation for government collectivism. [6] also reveals the conviction that the churches were inadequate to undertake the task of elementary education on their own – and a vast distrust of the working-class parent; indeed redeeming the children of the poor from their evil background was, in the mind of many educationists, a chief purpose of the school. [10], with its earnest zeal for moral improvement, helps us to see how narrow and partial such views were, and to appreciate the considerable movement for private schooling characteristic of the early Victorian working class, though the superior financial resources of the State eventually stifled these initiatives. [7] shows the hostility to government intervention that marked some Nonconformists at a time when it was reasonable to fear that State influence would be exerted on behalf of the Established Church. Most churches, even Dissenting churches, never

---

* The numbers in square brackets refer to the document numbers throughout Part Two.

ceased to rely on State assistance in a partnership that became increasingly unequal, as the new departures for government intervention made possible by the 1870 Act bore witness.

In other respects too 1870 is a watershed. Facing the superior resources of the school boards, and society's growing indifference towards religion, the voluntary agencies increasingly stressed the links between them, rather than the causes of conflict. There was much to annoy them in the sort of religious instruction common in board schools [8]. Bradford's careful prescriptions are halfway between the secularism propagated by Holyoake [9] and sectarian indoctrination. They provide a basic interdenominational Protestantism, representing a departure from doctrinal certitudes that is impossible where creed is taken seriously; it thus reflects the decline of religion in society. Impossible to proffer in the classroom, sectarian religious instruction becomes regarded in [8] as pre-eminently a parental duty – a sign that the earlier distrust of the home was being replaced by a sense of partnership later in the century.

It is a modern commonplace that a Victorian middle-class upbringing was sometimes stern and harsh. How authoritarian and cruel it could be at its worst, when natural faults of character in the parent were aggravated by religious fervour and self-righteousness, is shown by [11]. This reflects a view of the infant personality as highly plastic and innately sinful – an attitude most characteristic of Evangelical homes, but not confined to them. We often think of upper- and middle-class schools as offering, like the elementary school, a more enthusiastic religious education than the home: an opinion sustained by generalisations from Arnold's Rugby, with its intensity of religious life. But juxtaposition of [11] and [12] suggests the limitations of this view; the tepidity of institutional worship at Eton contrasts with domestic fervour, and Eton's freedom for the private self shines brightly against the deforming controls of the fanatical home.

In [13] many of the diverse lines of argument inherent in this debate over home and school are drawn together, and the educational issues are stated or implied. Lyttelton seems aware that faith is declining, and places upon the parent the primary duty of religious education. While he believes that the enforced gregariousness and common activities of the boarding school are salutary and inevitable, they also entail equally unavoidable disadvantages, such as 'impurity' and gracelessness, which it is above all a parental function to repair. Moral training cannot be left to the schoolteacher.

[1] Piety and Social Subordination in a Charity School

William Roberts, *Memoirs of Hannah More*, 2nd edn (1834) III, pp. 133–53, letters to Dr Beadon, Bishop of Bath and Wells, and W. Wilberforce, 1801. Hannah More was an Anglican educationist and prolific writer of tracts and pamphlets.

But to return to my schools. When I settled in this country thirteen years ago, I found the poor in many of the villages sunk in a deplorable state of ignorance and vice. There were, I think, no Sunday schools in the whole district, except one in my own parish, which had been established by our respectable rector, and another in the adjoining parish of Churchill. This drew me to the more neglected villages, which being distant, made it very laborious. Not one school here did I ever attempt to establish without the hearty concurrence of the clergyman of the parish. My plan of instruction is extremely simple and limited. They learn, on week-days, such coarse works as may fit them for servants. I allow of no writing for the poor. My object is not to make fanatics, but to train up the lower classes in habits of industry and piety. I knew no way of teaching morals but by teaching principles; and of inculcating Christian principles without a good knowledge of scripture. I own I have laboured this point diligently. My sisters and I always teach them ourselves every Sunday, except during our absence in the winter. By being out about thirteen hours, we have generally contrived to visit two schools the sáme day, and carry them to their respective churches. When we had more schools we commonly visited them on a Sunday. The only books we use in teaching are two little tracts called 'Questions for the Mendip Schools,' (to be had of Hatchard.) 'The Church Catechism,' (these are framed, and half-a-dozen hung up in the room.) The Catechism, broken into short questions, Spelling Books, Psalter, Common Prayer, Testament, Bible. The little ones repeat 'Watts's Hymns.' The Collect is learned every Sunday. They generally learn the Sermon on the Mount, with many other chapters and Psalms. Finding that what the children learned at school they commonly lost at home by the profaneness and ignorance of their parents, it occurred to me in some of the larger parishes to invite the latter to come at six on the Sunday evening, for an hour, to the school, together with the elder scholars. A plain printed sermon and a printed prayer is read to them, and a psalm is sung. I am not bribed by my taste, for, unluckily, I do not delight in music, but observing that singing is a help to devotion in others, I thought it right to allow the practice.

For many years I have given away annually, nearly two hundred Bibles, Common Prayer Books, and Testaments. To teach the poor to read without providing them with *safe* books, has always appeared to me an improper measure, and this consideration induced me to enter upon the laborious undertaking of the Cheap Repository Tracts. . . .

In the morning I open school with one of the Sunday School Prayers, from the Cheap Repository Tract. I have a Bible class – Testament class – Psalter class. Those who cannot read at all, are questioned out of the first little question book for the Mendip schools. In instructing the Bible or Testament class, I always begin with the Parables, which we explain to them in the most familiar manner, one at a time, till they understand that one so perfectly, that they are able to give me back the full sense of it.

We begin with the three parables in the fifteenth chapter of St. Luke, first fixing in their minds the literal sense, and then teaching them to make the practical application. When their understandings are a little exercised, we dwell for a long time on the three first chapters of Genesis, endeavouring from these to establish them in the doctrine of the fall of man. We keep them a good while close to the same subject, making them read the same parts so often, that the most important texts shall adhere to their memories; because upon this knowledge only can I ground my general conversation with them so as to be intelligible. I also encourage them by little bribes of a penny a chapter, to get by heart certain fundamental parts of Scripture, for instance, the promises, and prophecies, and confession of sin – such as the 9th of Isaiah, 53rd of Isaiah, and 51st Psalm – the beatitudes, and indeed the whole sermon on the Mount – together with the most striking parts of our Saviour's discourses in the gospel of St. John. It is my grand endeavour to make every thing as entertaining as I can, and to try to engage their affections; to excite in them the love of God; and particularly to awaken their gratitude to their Redeemer.

When they seem to get a little tired, we change the scene; and by standing up, and singing a hymn, their attention is relieved.

I have never tried the system of terror, because I have found that kindness produces a better end by better means.

About five o'clock we dismiss the little ones with a prayer and a hymn. It would be an excellent method (and has been practised with success,) to invite the grown-up children and their parents, to come to the school at six o'clock, and get some kind lady (which answers better than a teacher,) to read a little sermon to them – 'Burder's Village Sermons' are very proper.

Those who attend four Sundays, without intermission, and come in time for morning prayer, receive a penny every fourth Sunday; but if they fail once, the other three Sundays go for nothing, and they must begin again. Once in every six or eight weeks I give a little gingerbread. Once a year I distribute little books according to merit – those who deserve most, get a Bible – a second rate merit gets a prayer-book – the rest, Cheap Repository Tracts.

Once a year, also, each scholar receives some one article of dress; the boy, a hat, shirt, or pair of shoes, according to their wants – the big girls, a calico apron and cap – the little ones, a cap, and a tippet of calico.

[2] Religion Permeates 'British' Schools

Minutes of the Committee of Council (1846) Joseph Fletcher's report, *P.P.* (1847) XLV, pp. 287, 299–300. Fletcher was HMI from 1844 to 1852, and editor of the *Statistical Journal*.

The *present* purpose of a Christian education, as contemplated by the ablest supporters of the schools which I have been commissioned to inspect, appears to be, to make its recipients *good*; to make them *wise* (wise unto salvation and therefore unto virtue), as a *means*; and *great*, as a *consequence*, so long as 'righteousness exalteth a nation, and sin is a reproach to any people.' Such an education does not contemplate merely the development of *physical* strength and *intellectual* vigour, and their combined application to *arts*, enabling men to contend with the elements of nature and society for an individual subsistence on the earth; but it likewise has regard to their *passions* and their *affections*, under the conviction, that, overborne by the intoxication of the former, amidst the wiles to which our inborn pride exposes us, they will never refrain from doing evil that fancied, selfish, illusory good may come of it, unless nurtured, in affections as well as in principles, in habits as well as in words, to aspire, with the blessing of the Holy Spirit, to that glorious career of growing purity and peace promised by their Creator and opened by their Redeemer to every contrite and believing heart. Education, in this, its highest sense (embracing physical, intellectual, industrial, moral and religious education), they are well aware is not the work of the school only, but likewise of the church, the Sunday-school, the home, the play-ground, the street, the workshop, the field, the mine, the tavern, and the court-house. They are equally aware that no sane individual, in any conceivable state of society, can escape education in every branch, either to truth or error, to good or evil; that the choice to be made for them is not between 'education' and 'no education,' but between 'good' and 'bad' education. Distrusting, and with reason, the education which is given to the poor by the 'world,' – by the unregulated influences which bear upon them in the scenes of their daily life, – their conception of a school for the children of the poor, is, that it should be a little artificial world of virtuous exertion, in which, with God's blessing, every available influence of good should be brought to bear upon them for as many hours as possible, to nerve them, under the armour of humility, against the present, the future, the inevitable dangers and temptations which daily attend their 'going out' and their 'coming in.' . . .

The 'classics' of the poor in a Protestant country must ever, indeed, be the Scriptures: they contain the most useful of all knowledge; and so far from being foreign to the daily experiences of life, they especially and pre-eminently demand that acquaintance with the moral and physical elements surrounding them, which it is the purpose of our best modern school-books of 'useful knowledge' to convey, in constant connexion with and reference to the Word of God. Those who best know the intellectual lifelessness of the homes of the poor, or the trashy fictions and . criminal narratives which form the favourite reading of the majority of the vagrant minds which use their capacity to read, will not hesitate, as some yet do, to require as much as possible of this severer mental discipline. For after all, the children of the more educated classes, living in an atmosphere of comparative mental excitement, will acquire as much of this knowledge unconsciously, even in their amusements, as the children of the top classes in the schools of the poor will ever acquire in all their lessons. And to implant some acquaintance with sober truth in the mind of the workman's child, will be to him the dawn of a cheerful world, with which he will endeavour to keep up a humanizing and a useful acquaintance under all the depressing circumstances of his laborious life. Unwearied attention to the religious instruction of the children of the poor in the day-school, is, for the same reason, in the defectiveness of the home influences, more essential even than to that of the children of the more educated classes. And whether it be divine or human wisdom that is conveyed, the lessons for children, whose schooling is to terminate so soon, should, as much as possible, be so selected that they will admit of immediate application to the experience, feelings, and conduct of the pupil; a course which must conduce to those habits of practical wisdom, which are the best antidote to self-deception, and to the delusions of the visionary, at the same time that they are among the most characteristic features of the Christian character. The very few ardent minds which nature scatters in every class will thus be placed in a position for heathful effort, while all would be nerved for the necessities of their station. It is the children of the wealthier classes only, that, extending the period of education to half a life, can expressly be trained as scholars and men of science; but much may be done to bring up the children of the poor to be good servants, good parents, good neighbours, good subjects, and, if it please God, good members of Christ's church.

[3] Young Teachers' Views on Moral Education

Minutes of the Committee of Council (1846), E. C. Tufnell's report, answers to examination questions, by students of the Home and Colonial Infant and Juvenile School Society, *P.P.* (1847) XLV, pp. 579–81. Tufnell was a friend of Kay-Shuttleworth, and an Assistant Poor Law Commissioner from 1835 to 1847. The Home and Colonial Society's college was in the Gray's Inn Road, and specialised in training for infant teaching.

7. Write a sketch of a lesson to be given to infants on the death of Abel.

7th Question, as answered by No. 4. [aged 18]

Point. – To lead the children to see the awful consequence of giving way to bad temper.

First. – Examination of the print. A man standing looking very angry; another laid down upon the ground exceedingly pale, his eyes closed, and some marks of blood on his clothes. Ask, why they think he looks so? The reason of the blood? Lead them to infer from the trees and sheep represented that they are in a field. Having thus excited their curiosity, then

Secondly, relate to them the story. – The men are brothers; give the names of each, and tell their characters; how God showed his approbation of Abel by accepting his offering, and his disapprobation of Cain by rejecting his; here simply describe the manner of offering a sacrifice, and the reasons for offering them; Cain's anger, his sin; ask for a commandment which forbids murder.

Thirdly. – Application. To guard against anger. How this may be done. When struck not to strike again; when called bad names, not to call names in return. In whose sight would such a spirit be pleasing?

8. Write a sketch of a lesson to be given to infants on any part of the history of Joseph.

8th Question, as answered by No. 12. [aged 21]

Sketch of a lesson on the duty of forgiveness. My point in this lesson is to lead the children to see the duty of forgiveness. First. I will hold up to the children the example of Joseph's forgiveness to his brethren, and, supposing them to be acquainted with his previous history, read or relate that portion of the narrative which contains an account of his forgiveness; then question the children, getting them to mention the different ways in which Joseph had been injured by his brethren. What feelings led them to be so unkind? In what they manifested this unkind disposition? How Joseph treated them at first? What we may suppose to have been his motive for being harsh and severe at first. When he discovered that they had repented of their former wicked conduct how he acted? Leading the children to see how fully and freely he forgave, and how he attempted to console them.

Secondly. – Endeavour to get the children to make the application to themselves, by asking which of the parties they would most like to resemble. How they can imitate the example of Joseph? And then, supposing some circumstances in which they might exercise forgiveness, ask what would be their conduct; if, for instance, their brothers or sisters were to deprive them of anything which belonged to them. What they would do if their brother refused to share his toys or to play with them; getting them to repeat the text, 'Be ye kind one to another, tender-hearted, forgiving one another.'

20. Mention some of the feelings of children, and the means by which they may be developed and cultivated, with a view to moral training.

20th Question, as answered by No. 5. [aged 17]

The feeling of *love of approbation*, which is generally very strong in little children, is too often abused by being directed entirely to man. The love of the approbation of man is too often the stimulus by which their conduct is regulated. It is the work of teachers and parents to direct this feeling in a proper course. The love of man's approbation should be transferred for the love of God's approbation, and if rightly directed, this feeling may be of great use in the moral training of our children.

The feeling of *hope* may be cultivated by a promise being made to the children of something that will afford pleasure, and by the fulfilment of that promise; so when the children get older, they should be led to see the promise God has made of eternal life to those who love and serve him, and to hope for the fulfilment of that promise. Thus the feeling of hope may be cultivated with a view to moral training.

The feeling of *fear* is too often exclusively cultivated by parents and teachers, making it the sole means of discipline. This is an abuse of it. Instead of this, teachers and parents should endeavour to transfer the fear the children may have of man to the fear of Him who has said, 'The fear of the Lord is the beginning of wisdom.' In this sense, the feeling of fear, when properly directed, may be made very useful in the moral training of our children. If we endeavour.to implant in our children's minds a fear to offend God and of breaking his laws, we shall find this feeling a great blessing to them, when on the other hand it would prove a curse.

[4] A Moderate Anglican View of the Church's Educational Duties, *c.* 1840

W. R. W. Stephens, *The Life and Letters of Walter Farquhar Hook* (1880) I, pp. 457-60. At the time of this letter Hook was Vicar of Leeds.

LETTER TO THE SECRETARY OF THE NATIONAL SOCIETY

Reverend Sir, – I have the honour to acknowledge the receipt of your letter, dated the 11th instant, in which you desire me to give my opinion with regard to the working of the Factory Act, so far as those provisions are concerned which respect the education of the poor. . . .

You inform me further that it has been recommended, in order to remove a difficulty, which does not at present exist, that 'so far as concerns any child whose parents or guardians specially request that it should not be taught the Church Catechism, the managers of schools should not be required to enforce instruction in that formulary.'

I presume that no circumstances can arise which will justify the National Society in acting upon this recommendation. If I understand rightly the object of the National Society, it is *not* to provide for the general education of the people, but to provide a *particular kind of education*. . . .

But if, on the other hand, the National Society professes to be a Church Society, and to conduct the education of the people on the principles of the Church, it is utterly impossible for it to accede to the measure proposed without ceasing to be what it professes to be. We might just as well entertain a proposition for filling our churches by suspending the use of the forms of morning and evening prayer, as accede to a proposal that we should abandon the Catechism when instructing the young. The same Church which has imposed upon us a formulary for morning and evening prayer, has appointed a formulary to be used by us when instructing the youth of our flock; we are as much bound by that formulary as we are bound to observe the Liturgy when conducting the morning sacrifice of prayer and praise. It ought to be clearly understood that the Society is recommended to give up a fundamental principle, for if the use of the Catechism may under any circumstances be suspended, we have only to make out a strong case of expediency, and it may be suspended under *all* circumstances. And if the Society thus concedes a principle, it will not only offend the conscience of many pious Churchmen, but convert into its most decided opponents some persons who are now its warm supporters.

You observe in conclusion that 'the chief question to be considered is, whether the Society, by refusing the concession called for, would, as is confidently asserted, forego the opportunity to give full instruction on Church principles to many thousand children whose parents and guardians are willing they should receive it.'

On this passage I remark that it is not to the *words* but to the *doctrine* of the Catechism, that is, to the doctrine of the Church, as briefly stated in the Catechism, that the parents and guardians are supposed to be hostile.

If, then, the concession be made, the Society will be virtually pledged, and in honour bound to abstain from giving to the children of such parents or guardians *any* instruction in Church principles; the Society will therefore be pledged to educate them in the principles of Dissent, (for you teach error, if you abstain from teaching truth) or else in principles disconnected with religion of any kind. And in the West Riding of Yorkshire, where the Dissenters are very numerous, and where a vast number of professing Churchmen, who are willing for political purposes to uphold an Establishment, are vehemently opposed to the use of the Catechism, especially to that part of it which asserts with such peculiar force the doctrine of the Sacraments, I have no hesitation in giving it as my opinion that more than three-fourths of the parents and guardians will apply for the exemption, so that the Society will be doing, in fact, what in theory it condemns:– it will be giving a non-religious education.

It is, I am well aware, stated that an attempt is to be made to compel the masters of factories to provide schools, as well as to afford time for the education of the children employed in their factories. Until this be the law of the land, there can be no reason why the National Society should legislate on the subject. But even if it *were* the law of the land, I would rather propose to the manufacturer to erect his schoolrooms so as to admit of two departments, one for the education of Churchmen, in which a master might be provided by the National Society; another for the education of Dissenters, than recommend the Society to give up one of its fundamental principles.

[5] Anti-Popery in a School Textbook

Near Home; or, the Countries of Europe Described with Anecdotes and Numerous Illustrations (1870) p. 228.

ROME

This is the capital of Italy, and once it was the capital of the world. It was a wicked city *then*, full of idols and cruelty – and it is a wicked city *now*. Here the Pope lives. He is the chief of all the priests of the Roman Catholic religion. You see why that religion is called Roman. The Pope lives at Rome. He pretends that all he says is right. He says he is like Peter the Apostle; but Peter obeyed the word of God, and the Pope does not. When one Pope dies, another Pope is chosen.

The Pope has a great church. It is the largest in the world. It is called St. Peter's. Inside there is a large black statue of Peter. A great many people kiss its foot. How much grieved the holy Apostle Peter would have been had he known that people would worship him! . . .

There is another still more foolish ceremony performed on Good

Friday. There is a staircase which people say was once in Pontius Pilate's house, and that our Saviour trod upon it. The Pope promises to forgive the sins of any one who goes up these stairs on his knees. A great many climb up – though it is very hard to get up these stairs – but still they try.

Three hundred years ago a young man was climbing up these stairs, when suddenly he remembered the words, 'The just shall live by faith.' Then he felt that it was by faith in Christ, and not by climbing stairs, that his sins must be blotted out. He felt ashamed of what he had done, and never climbed the stairs again. Who was this young man? Martin Luther. Did you ever hear of him? It was he who persuaded many kings and their people to read the Bible, and to become Protestants. England is a Protestant country, and Wales, and Scotland, and Sweden, and Norway, and Lapland, and Iceland, and Denmark, and Holland, and Prussia, and part of Germany, and part of Switzerland.

[6] The State as a Moral Agent in the Education of the Poor

Sir James Kay-Shuttleworth, *Public Education as Affected by the Minutes of the Committee of Council* (1853) pp. 276–81.

The resources derived for public education from subscriptions, collections, and School pence, have in other respects a common character of uncertainty. They are liable to be affected, by those crises in manufacturing and agricultural prosperity, which, while they compel the capitalist to retrench and to limit his charities, render the condition of the labourer full of anxiety, if not of suffering. Such crises are attended with the failure of firms, the breaking up of manufacturing establishments, diminution of employment, reduction of wages, or complete destitution of work. They sweep away like a flood the result of years of labour and anxiety. The School perishes like the manufactory, and can only be again restored by slow and painful efforts.

Even in the fairest periods of prosperity, the School income derived from these sources is precarious. Dr. Hook graphically describes the humiliating course of canvassing for subscriptions, which has become the most harassing, but unavoidable, duty of the clergy. The inspectors report the undue sacrifices made by parochial ministers, from small stipends, to support schools in rural districts. Even many laymen who are most earnest in promoting, by large subscriptions and personal exertions, the education of their poorer neighbours, feel that it is an evil that this charge should fall on themselves alone; for, by exhausting their charitable resources, it limits within a narrow circle that influence, which might otherwise be wide in its sphere like the light. Every statesman is conscious that, to tax the benevolent only, is the worst form of inequality, in the incidence of public burthens. One earnest man often thus bears the charge of a whole parish. A generous landed proprietor supports the School, which educates all the children of a purely manufacturing population, none of whom are his tenants or dependents. Or, an enlightened mining or mill proprietor may found and support Schools, in which the children of the occupiers of farms and the labourers in the same parish are educated, without any adequate contribution from the owners of the soil. These inequalities ought not to exist. It is not sufficient to answer, that they will cease when all men are actuated by a sense of the duties of their station, as members of a Christian commonwealth. Such a form of society has great collective duties. A Christian government cannot permit its citizens to be cradled in ignorance; nurtured by bad example in barbarous manners; brought up without faith and without hope: rude and miserable, the support of sedition, the prey of demagogues, the element of popular tumults, the food of the gaol, the convict ship, and the gallows. A Christian commonwealth cannot wait till the indigent are in comfort; till the Arabs of our great cities are settled and at rest; till the corrupted and ignorant are so far weaned from gross sensual indulgence, as not to waste the School pence of their children on beer, spirits, and tobacco. Nor can it postpone its aid until the physical condition of every part of our labouring population is such, as to enable them to provide for the instruction of their children without suffering. If the recklessness of the desperate; the sensuality which is the characteristic of a rude material life; the ignorance which no school has corrected; the apathy never disturbed by faith; the dark despair never penetrated by a ray of spiritual hope, are not fruitful sources for School-income; are the wretched to be denied the remedy for these evils, because of some barren speculation as to the province of the State in Education? Is society to continue to pay upwards of two millions, annually, for the repression of crime, and five millions for the relief of indigence; because, though this outlay is derived from compulsory assessments, the consciences of a minority would be afflicted, if a remedy for these chronic social distempers were purchased by the same means?

It is the distinction of arbitrary governments that, when directed by a powerful intelligence, they afford prompt and efficacious means for the execution of the measures which a provident wisdom dictates. Nothing would so certainly discredit representative institutions, as that popular minorities should obtain a collective power, to obstruct the civilisation which they are incompetent to establish. Yet the question of National Education in the United Kingdom has exhibited the lamentable spectacle, hitherto, of such minorities triumphant over the collective will of the nation as represented in Parliament. Are we then to be governed by minorities, or by the three Estates of the Realm? A wise government cannot permit the education of the people to pass entirely from its influence, into whatever hands are ready to attempt to mould the youth of this country to their own ideal. Shall the priests of Johanna Southcote, at Ashton-under-Line, and the Mormonites, throughout our manufacturing and mining districts, be free to build and maintain Schools, and the government of a Christian state be excluded from every form of interference? Yet such is the doctrine of the purely voluntary party. According to them, Christendom itself, could it be organised into one great empire, ought to have no collective power to rescue the ignorant heathen of its peoples, from the brutish sensuality which is without God.

If we may analyse such a formula, these are its elements: All remedial agencies by which the condition of mankind may be improved, through the medium of their intelligence or moral nature, are so inseparable from the relations of conscience to the spiritual world, that they can only be the acts of individuals, or of voluntary associations. Therefore, Government, because it may not interfere with conscience, is excluded from all action, excepting that of the repression of crime and the relief of suffering. The State has not only no collective religious character, but, inasmuch as the true basis of all morality is religion, it has no essentially moral character. It protects persons and property, and upholds the national security for economical or prudential, as distinguished from moral, reasons. It is the soldier, the policeman, the bailiff, the sheriff's officer of the national will, and that will is directed by whatever morality and religion exist in the nation. But the State has no morality, just as it has no religion. It is not even a moral agent, but only the agent of a moral nation. The Government may not, therefore, employ any moral machinery. Colleges and Schools are institutions, which develope the intelligence, and so 'mould the mind of the nation,' and because of this power, they are instruments of tyranny, when promoted or supported even partially by the State. Education is, therefore, the function solely of individuals and voluntary associations. This is the doctrine of the voluntary party. . . .

Does not the absurdity of such conclusions awaken a suspicion of the soundness of the theory. Is Government, then, in no sense a moral agent? May it incarcerate criminals, and separate itself, as an impassive spectator, from all the festering moral pollution of the common wards of the old prison, and the terrible agonies of the separate cell? Has it no message of peace and redemption entrusted to it by Him, who said to the penitent thief upon the cross 'To-day shalt thou be with me in paradise.' Are the Howards and the Frys alone to convey this message? Or is the workhouse merely a pauper farm, where certain human animals are fed at the least cost to the parish, till, nailed between rough boards, their bodies are buried like dogs by the sexton and the beadle? Is this a Christian household, or a pauper *barracoon?* Can the State separate itself from certain grave and high responsibilities, as to the spiritual future of these unfortunates? Are the children to remain ignorant and rude; the adults, servile or disaffected helots; the aged, torpid expectants of a grave without hope? Are the Army and the Navy to be disciplined in the terrible array of war, for the destruction of human life, with every animal energy centupled in force, by death-like engines, by organiza-tion, and the maddening sympathy of numbers? But is no still small voice to whisper 'Blessed are the meek: for they shall inherit the earth. Blessed are the merciful: for they shall obtain mercy. Blessed are the peacemakers: for they shall be called the children of God'?

[7] Necessary Limits to the State's Concern with Morality and Education

Edward Baines, jun., *Letters to the Right Hon. Lord John Russell on State Education* (1846) pp. 12–15. Baines, of a Leeds manufacturing family, was a noted Congregationalist, free trader and Liberal.

I believe that the well-meant interference of the civil power under imperial Rome, in support of Christianity, was the source of the manifold evils which have resulted to mankind from Papal tyranny, and from every form of compulsory and State religion. The motive to that interference was pious; the inducement was strong; practical men would have scoffed at the scruples which should have opposed it. But such deviations from the straight course, out of regard to expediency, are like By-path Meadow in Bunyan's inimitable allegory, smooth, green, and pleasant to the feet of weary pilgrims, and appearing to run exactly alongside of the king's highway, but imperceptibly leading off from it, till the traveller finds himself involved in manifest transgression and danger. I would take the part of Hopeful, and warn my Christian friends to resist the soft seduction, to stand fast in the way of truth, though it be sometimes hard and stony, and to be assured that it is the path of wisdom, as well as of duty. . . .

In all countries Government has gone beyond its province, and especially in the matters I have referred to. This is very natural in unenlightened times. Much of the business of civilization is to undo the follies of former ages. Legislation is a power so mighty, and men are naturally so fond of the use of power, that there has always been a tendency to *over-legislate*. The temptation is irresistible. An imprudent legislature is like a boy with his first knife, who, in his impatience to use it, notches his mother's tables and chairs. The hardest lesson for Government or urchin to learn is, what it ought *not* do. It is perhaps the highest attainment of a constitutional Government, *to confide in the People*.

I have said that I think it is not the province of the Government to train the mind of the people. What are the duties of Government? Generally speaking, to maintain the frame of society; and for this end to restrain violence and crime, – to protect person and property, – to enact and administer the laws needful for the maintenance of peace, order, and justice, – to sanction public works called for by the general convenience, as docks, harbours, canals, railways, &c., – to conduct the relations of society with other communities, – to provide for the public safety against external attack, – to appoint the officers, raise the taxes, pass the laws, construct the buildings, &c., requisite for these purposes.

On the other hand, it is *not*, I conceive, the duty of Government to interfere with the free action of the subject beyond what is necessary for these protective and defensive objects. It is *not* the duty of the Government to feed the people, to clothe them, to build houses for them, to direct their industry or their commerce, to superintend their families, to cultivate their minds, to shape their opinions, or to supply them with religious teachers, physicians, schoolmasters, books, or newspapers.

These are things which the people can and ought to do for themselves, and which it is not the province of Government to do for them. In all these things Governments have interfered, and I believe in all with mischievous effect. The natural faculties, instincts, and reason of men, together with the powerful stimulus of self-interest, the sense of individual responsibility to God, and the revelation of truth and love given by our Divine Lawgiver and Saviour, are sufficient to stimulate and to guide them in these matters. . . .

I am aware that there are questions of nicety as to the limits of the duties of Government. One has reference to a national provision for the poor. Partly to protect society from the evils of mendicancy and crime, and partly out of humanity, a legal provision is made for the destitute. Admitting that there seems a paramount necessity for such a provision, it must be observed that this is found in practice to be one of the most difficult and delicate duties a Government has to discharge. Only within a few years, abuses existed in the administration of the Poor Law which seemed to be eating like a cancer into society, cutting the sinews of industry, and pauperizing the labouring class. When a system was adopted to reform these abuses, it became odious from the centralized and arbitrary power created. The liability to abuse in any poor-law system, local or central, is extreme.

It is doubtless a fair question, whether Government is not called upon to provide *education* for the children of the pauper class, as it provides them with food. Some advocate a state provision for education on this ground, to operate as a kind of *preventive-police*.

Let me, then, point out, that the analogy would justify nothing whatever beyond a provision for the education of the *pauper class*. It would justify no scheme of State Education for the working classes generally, still less for the whole country. It would be strictly limited by the necessity of the case, and would be an exception to the great rule. This, therefore, would not countenance in the slightest degree the extensive projects propounded by Dr. Hook, and supposed to be contemplated by yourself; which clearly go on the principle that Government ought to provide for and superintend the education of *the country at large*. It would not countenance any kind of interference with schools, but would rather look to a weekly parochial allowance to pauper families for the payment of school pence, leaving the parents at liberty to choose the schools. This would be a totally different thing from any proposal hitherto made. It would be excessively open to fraud and abuse. The changing residences of the pauper population, and the very uncertain continuance of their dependence on the parish, would make such a plan difficult to administer. And it would require the most cautious examination whether the plan would tend to encourage pauperism or to prolong its duration.

My opinion is decidedly *against* the attempt of Government to provide education for the children of *out-door* paupers. The existing educational societies – possibly with some addition to their plans – would do it better than the Government. It is in entire accordance with their principles and with their present operations.

There can be no difference of opinion as to the propriety of educating the children in the workhouses. They are for the most part orphans, thrown absolutely on public support, and shut up in the parochial building. The parish is to them in the relation of parents, and it is its duty to supply them with education, as it does with food, clothing, and lodging, – though this ought to be done on the most liberal plan, and not on the principle on which Dr. Hook has acted in the Leeds Workhouse in regard to religious instruction, where he has contrived to exclude all the Dissenting and Wesleyan Ministers, the Town Missionaries, and Sunday School Teachers, who had given religious instruction there with great regularity for years, and has monopolised the place for himself and his clerical coadjutors.

But I repeat, there is nothing in the circumstances of the pauper class to justify a plan of State Education.

[8] 'Non-Sectarian' Christian Teaching in Board Schools

Second Report of the Royal Commission Appointed to Inquire into the Working of the Elementary Education Acts, P. P. (1887) XXIX, pp. 759, 1023-4, evidence of J. Hanson of Bradford School Board.

Q. 35,785. (*Rev. Dr. Rigg.*) I think I understood you to say just now, in answer to a question that was put to you by Canon Gregory, that you think that when the nation is undertaking to provide education it should provide equally for all according to their beliefs? – No; my notion is that the State should not recognise their beliefs.

Q. 35,786. Then you meant without respect to their beliefs? – Yes, they should provide for the education that we all want in common.

Q. 35,787. (*Chairman.*) Supposing that my theory is that you cannot have education without religion, how do you provide for me? – I do not think that it is desirable to have education without religion.

Q. 35,788. You say that everybody must be provided for; supposing that I and a great number of other people think that you cannot have education without religion, and that you cannot separate the two, how would you provide for me and that particular class? – I say that the State should provide that which you all want in common.

Q. 35,789. Then you would neglect me (I speak of myself as an individual) and you would neglect those who think that education and religion cannot be separated? – No.

Q. 35,790. What would you do for them? – The best part of the religious education is that which is given by the parents.

Q. 35,791. I will take the instance of a Roman Catholic. The Roman Catholics believe that it is wrong to separate religious education from any other education, and therefore they will not willingly send their children to board schools; how are you going to provide for that class? – We provide a certain amount of religious education in our board schools, and they are not brought up without it. It may not be such as they desire, but if what they want is in excess of, or different from ours, they ought to provide it for themselves. If a man wants luxuries you know he cannot get them from the State.

Q. 35,792. (Rev. Dr. Rigg.) I understood you to say in answer to Canon Gregory that the nation in undertaking to provide education should provide equally for all according to their beliefs? – I do not think that I said anything of the kind; I never thought of anything of the kind. I do not mean the State to recognise their religious beliefs, but to treat them as citizens.

Q. 35,793. May I ask whether, in refusing to recognise the conscientious religious beliefs of citizens who happen to have a distinct religious belief, the State is providing equally for all? – I do not know that I could enter into that; I think that my own principle clears away all difficulties of that kind.

Q. 35,794. As I understand your recent answer, you regard the specific beliefs of citizens as luxuries? – No; I never said anything of the kind. I said that if persons wanted luxuries they must provide them for themselves.

Q. 35,795. Then what I want to know is, what did the term luxuries refer to, if it was not to specific beliefs? – I say this again. Taking the case of a Roman Catholic, the State provides education in those subjects that all alike need, whether they are Catholic or Protestant, or whatever they may be, all the elements of education are provided for, and those points that they differ upon, those definite religious beliefs, I am anxious that they should be provided with, and I think that every parent thinks it his duty to provide them, but they cannot be provided by the State.

Q. 35,796. Those definite religious beliefs which are not provided for by the State you spoke of as luxuries? – You may say so. I do not see that the State can base education on the religious beliefs of its citizens. I think that it is an unwise attempt to carry legislation out of its own sphere, which must fail, and always has failed.

Q. 35,797. Therefore, under those circumstances, would you maintain that the State is providing education equally for all? – It is provided for all on equal conditions if they will take it; and if they do not choose to take it, or if they cannot take it because they have a particular and special view, that is a luxury.

Q. 35,798. Is not that religious tyranny under the name of liberalism? – Not at all.

*   *   *

SCHEME OF THE BRADFORD SCHOOL BOARD FOR RELIGIOUS
OBSERVANCES AND INSTRUCTION

Handed in by Mr. J. Hanson, Member of the Bradford School Board and Chairman of the School Management Committee

1. The board attach very great importance to the religious instruction in their schools. Their intention is that it shall be carefully and regularly given, in order that the knowledge imparted to the children about the facts and principles of Holy Scripture may be comprehensive and thorough.

2. The order for opening the morning school must *invariably* be a hymn, the Lord's Prayer, and Bible lesson; and for closing the afternoon school, a hymn and the Lord's Prayer. These observances shall take place in the principal room, in the presence of all the teachers and scholars, and shall be conducted only by the head teacher, except as provided for by Rule 4.

3. The course of scriptural instruction shall commence at the beginning of the twelfth month of the school year and terminate in the eleventh month of the following school year.

4. In schools with an average attendance exceeding 150, the school management committee may, on application from the head teacher, allow the assistant teachers to read *without comment* to *classes selected by the head teacher*, the portions of scripture laid down in the scheme. The explanation on the passages read to these classes must be afterwards given by the head teacher.

5. In upper departments it is recommended that the scholars repeat the more important passages simultaneously after the teacher. This will not only secure the attention of the children, but will also familiarise them with Bible phraseology.

6. The subjects selected for infants' departments are those most generally illustrated by pictures, and head teachers are advised to use these in the daily Bible lessons.

7. Monday mornings shall be reserved for oral questions on the work of the previous week and instruction in sacred geography.

8. In the explanations and instruction given the provisions of the Elementary Education Act, in sections 7 and 14, shall be strictly observed both in letter and spirit, and no attempt shall be made to attach children to any particular denomination. Head teachers shall give such information on geographical and historical subjects as will enable the children to understand the passages of scripture in which persons, places, and events are mentioned, or in which allusions are made to the institutions or circumstances in the life of the Jews or other ancient peoples. . . .

12. Any parent may object to his or her child being present during the time of religious teaching, or religious observance; and any children withdrawn from such teaching or observance shall receive instruction in secular subjects in a separate room by an assistant teacher. . . .

INFANTS' DEPARTMENTS

Old Testament
(Tuesday and Thursday)

The Creation	Gen. i. ii.
Death of Abel	Gen. iv. 2–15
The Flood and Noah's sacrifice	Gen. vi. vii. viii. ix. 1–20
Tower of Babel	Gen. xi. 1–9
Offering of Isaac	Gen. xxii. 1–19
Jacob's Dream	Gen. xxvii. xxviii. 6–22
Joseph in the Pit	Gen. xxxvii.
Visit of Joseph's Brethren	Gen. xlii. to xlv.
Birth of Moses	Exod. ii.
Passage of the Red Sea	Exod. xiv. xv.
Manna	Exod. xvi.
Giving of the Law	Exod. xix. xx.
Brazen Serpent	Numb. xxi. 4–9.
Call of Samuel	I. Saml. i. to iii.
David and Goliath	I. Saml. xvii.
Elijah }	I. Kings xvii. xviii. xix.
Elisha mocked by the children }	II. Kings i. ii.
Elisha and the Oil, &c.	II. Kings iv.
Naaman	II. Kings v.
Daniel in the Lion's Den	Daniel vi.

New Testament
(Wednesday and Friday)

Birth of Christ	{ Matt. i. 18–25
	{ Luke i. 25–56
The Shepherds	Luke ii. 1–20
Wise Men and Flight into Egypt	Matt. ii. 1–23
Christ in the Temple at twelve years of age	Luke ii. 40–52
Preaching of John the Baptist	{ Matt. iii.
Baptism of Christ	{ Mark i. 1–13
	{ Luke iii. 1–22
Cleansing of the Temple	John ii.
Woman of Samaria	John iv.
Healing Sick of the Palsy	{ Mark ii.
	{ Luke v. 16–39
Widow's Son at Nain	Luke vii.
Calming the Storm	Luke viii. 22–25
Feeding 5,000	{ Mark vi. 30–44
	{ John vi. 1–13
Christ walking on the Sea	Matt. xiv. 22–36
Healing the Man born Blind	John ix.
The Good Shepherd	John x. 1–18
Raising of Lazarus	John xi.
The Good Samaritan	Luke x. 25–37
Prodigal Son	Luke xv. 11–32
Pharisee and Publican	Luke xviii. 9–14
Christ blessing the Children	Mark x. 13–16
Entry into Jerusalem	Luke xix. 28–48
Widow's Mite	Mark xii. 41–44
Agony and Betrayal	Matt. xxvi. 36–56
Trial ⎫	
Crucifixion ⎪	John xviii. 28–40, xix. xx
Burial ⎬	
Resurrection ⎪	Acts i. 9–11
Ascension ⎭	

[9] A Call for Secularism

George Jacob Holyoake, 'In What Respect the Educational
Conference at Manchester was not National', *The Reasoner*, x (1851)
6. Holyoake was the leading propagandist of militant atheism.

At the Educational Conference, held in Manchester the week before
last, I represented three places. The meeting at the Miles Platting
Mechanics' Institution, which elected me in conjunction with
Mr. Winstanley, Sir Benjamin Heywood's agent, did so in consideration of efforts made in the way of Instructional Reform; but the Literary
and Scientific Institution, of John Street, Fitzroy Square, London, and
the Socialists of the Garratt Road Institution, (late St. Patrick's Hall)
Manchester, appointed me in order that I might have the opportunity
of representing a party to which, in neither Lay nor Clerical Conference
has any generous representation ever yet been vouchsafed. . . .

At this Conference many speeches were delivered on the desirability
of providing schools where the children of all religions might be taught
in common fellowship – but no word was said of schools where children
of *no religion* might meet. Many clergymen were loud in demanding
equal education for all sects, but no one had a word to say for those of *no
sect*. . . .

If I could have spoken, I should have said –

'Gentleman, – Your secretary, the Rev. Mr. McKerrow, has laid it
down that they who have a right to speak here "are those who have
travelled far to be with you, and are friendly to your objects." I have
both these qualifications. Moreover I can give you an assurance, which
you all profess to need, with which to answer your enemies, and which
no one else among you can give. I observe you only propose to extend
the great benefit of public instruction to the religious sects among you.
Although you exclude my friends, I yet rejoice that fraternity is so far
developed among you to enable you to do justice to each other. Though
you may not give education to us, yet I will help you to give it to
yourselves. You all fear infidelity. You have all said so. Yet I do not fear
Religion; and though, if we should propose to make national instruction
atheistic, you would have none of it, yet, if you even propose to make it
religious, yet would we accept it; for we value knowledge so much, and
have so much confidence in the instruction of the intellect, that we will
pay any price for it, even that of all your creeds, if they must be mixed
up with it. So much for my friendliness to this cause of national
instruction. And here let me say, that if all infidelity, as you confidently
believe, originates in *antagonism*, how know you that were you generous
enough to concede schools in which the child of the atheist could be
taught, that you might not one day boast temples in which the child of
the atheist might worship? My assurance is this, that your fears are
utterly, ridiculously groundless that *secular* instruction will be infidel.
When I think of the public progress, I wish instruction to be secular;
when I think of the present progress of my party, I pray that it may be
still mixed up with religion. I have looked where the majority of our
converts come from, and I find that they are furnished from the ranks of
religious teaching. If any man among you will be the friend of infidel
progress, give us religion in abundance mixed up with scholastic
teaching. When I hear the religious standing up contending for Biblical
and Credal teaching in all our common schools, I rejoice over his folly,
so far as defeating him is concerned. One whom you call your master
told you to render to Cæsar the things which are Cæsar's, and to God the

things which are God's; but you seize upon the undeveloped soul of the young child, and mix up before him the things of the world with the things of heaven, till he does not know which is which, and he grows up in disregard of both. His perceptions blunted, his taste destroyed, he grows up *indifferent* to things sacred or secular. He is of no good to the church, of no good to progress – he is a blot upon society, and a scandal to his teachers. Yet this man I can win, though he is hard to restore to duty and life, because he is *accessible*. The purely religious man is exclusive, and he will *not hear*; but the indifferent can be reached, and those we can reach we can win. You make the indifferent by your mixed teaching, and thus you help us. The wisest and the fairest of modern Christians has told you that the Soul is that side of our nature which comes in contact with the infinite. But this can only be developed by *pure* cultivation. In political economy you have a division of labour, and you know its advantages; in your colleges, you have adopted an independent study of philosophy, and you know the profit thereof. When will you act as wisely with regard to religion? Every professor tells you, you cannot learn two things at once; yet you will persist in teaching *two* things at once. What is the consequence? You tell us that God is the name of that ineffable Being who sits on his throne of Stars, the Mighty Arbiter of human destiny. Yet you prostitute that great name to common purposes. You spout it on platforms, you parade it in lectures; it is the word of the hour in every newspaper; it is the catch-word of every tract; every man hastens to hoist it as the badge of his respectability; it is abandoned to the mob; it is the war-cry of factions, the shuttlecock of parties, and, that it may nowhere escape the contempt which familiarity ever breeds, you condemn it to be the *task word* of your schools. Then you come down with the cry that the people have *no reverence*, and that the atheist has taken it away. When the atheist is religious, he will have a religion which he can trust. When he believes in God, he will not treat him so. Accept, therefore, the disinterested warning of one you consider an enemy, and make instruction *secular* if you wish to save yourselves.'

[10] A Respectable Working-Class View

T. Shipton, 'The Responsibility of Parents to their Children', *Working Man's Friend and Family Instructor* (February 1851) Supplementary Number. T. Shipton was a printer's apprentice in Devizes.

The question may and ought to be asked, by every parent, whether rich or poor, Why is it that there is so much vice and idleness among the *youth* of our land, so much poverty and wickedness in the world? Is it not almost entirely the result of parents not being alive to their responsibilities – of parents almost entirely neglecting the improvement of those committed to their care? There are schools, institutions, and societies of various kinds, but how few of our young people give their minds to them, compared with the crowds who go in the way of vice and misery! What a vast amount of good would they confer on our land and the world at large, were they stirred up to activity and benevolence! Is it not home education and training that prepare and fit the young for society? and is it not generally the case, that as the youth is brought up so will he be in after-days? Parents, think of your accountability to God, and see if some of your children have not gone astray through your neglect.

How many young people walk the streets of our towns and cities with pipes and cigars in their mouths, and choose rather to keep the company of the wicked than that of the good and virtuous! And how many go from bad company to drunkenness and vice, which at last destroy both their body and soul! And how is it there are so few striving for the spread of knowledge among the ignorant and oppressed? I fear there are many infidels in our land through the neglect of parents, and many drunkards ruined and lost, cursing their parents for not training them up in the way they should go.

Parents! see that you suffer not your children to go astray, but urge and help them to seek knowledge where it is to be found, for your conduct in relation to them will be felt through all generations. Let them not have to lament over your neglect and carelessness towards them.

Parents! your responsibilities are in proportion to your privileges and influence, both as regards your children, the church, the world, and society at large. You are responsible for their education, their training, and habits; for as you provide homes for them, so they provide for themselves; and as you influence them, so they influence others. I would say to those who have hitherto neglected this great and responsible work, neglect it no longer, but with affection and diligence carry it out.

There is ample encouragement for the diligent and faithful parent. Your teaching, training, and influence of affection shall not be lost, but shall be blessed in its fruits to you and the whole world. It is like the little leaven that leaveneth the whole lump, and shall at length prevail against all error; and when you are sowing the seeds of truth and leading your young in the path of rectitude, do it with faith, for you shall ultimately obtain the blessing, though you may not see it now.

[11] An Evangelical Infancy

H. O. Wyon, *Bright Light in Early Dawn, or a Mother's Recollections of a Little One whom Jesus Loved* (1856) *passim*.

It is a joyful yet solemn moment when a babe is first placed in its parent's arms; to feel that the little helpless creature is a young immortal, – that the life just given can never end, and must be spent in endless bliss or woe; the thought at times is overwhelming: and I have always felt, that I would willingly part with my little ones in infancy or early childhood, when I know that through the merits of a precious Saviour's blood, they would be safe for ever; rather than that they should rise up to live without God, to dishonour Him here, and perish eternally. But it is our blessed privilege to be permitted to devote our loved ones to Him who gives them; and it is delightful to know that He graciously accepts our heart's sacrifice; and if our first desire for our children be, that they should be wholly and only his, He will doubtless fulfil the desire, and seal them his for ever. . . .

I may mention a very pleasing proof of his willing obedience to the command, 'Remember the Sabbath day, to keep it holy.' A new wheelbarrow had been promised him for nearly three weeks, and when it at length arrived, it was on a Saturday evening. As the custom was, however, he very willingly put it away before Sunday came; and although he was too unwell that day to go to church as usual, he did not wish to have it out, but, on the contrary, was very much shocked at his baby brother insisting upon getting some toys out, and said to him, 'O, naughty baby, musn't play on Sunday;' and baby going to sleep soon afterwards, he went and put away everything he had been playing with, and did not wish to have his new toy, although so much delighted with it.

On other days than the Sabbath, he would often suddenly stop when going to say or do anything, to inquire, 'Is it Sunday?' evidently with the fear lest he should do what he ought not to do on God's holy day. . . .

Although I have related much that was pleasing and attractive in our little Arthur, I do not wish to make it appear that he was faultless – far from it; the seeds of an evil and corrupt nature budded in him, in common with other children. Born in sin and shapen in iniquity, he needed with all others the renewing and sanctifying work of the Holy Spirit on his heart, to control and subdue that which was evil, and to produce the good fruit of holiness; and, blessed be God, the seed of instruction that was sown, was so richly watered by the dew of heavenly grace, that it sprang up and bore fruit abundantly to his glory. And by his Spirit's sanctifying power, that which was evil in him was effectually subdued and overcome, and by his quickening energy was his soul transformed and 'renewed in knowledge after the image of Him who created him.'

In watching the growth of our children's minds, we cannot too carefully check each budding of evil as it appears, and nip it in the bud; and see to it that we do not allow sin in them, any more than in ourselves, taking particular care to impress upon them, that although God is a loving God, yet He is also a holy and a jealous God, who cannot look upon sin, neither will allow it to go unpunished. It is the province of the mother especially to do this, and the work cannot be begun too early; and it should be her constant employment to watch as the ill weeds of sin make their appearance, and to endeavour to root them out by grave, serious, yet loving rebuke. Natural affection will lead us, perhaps, too quickly to appreciate whatever is pleasing in our children; but the Christian mother should look for, and find out whatever inclines in them to evil, ever keeping on the watch that she may check and reprove it. . . .

At the age of two years, in common with all other children, he manifested much wilful temper. His strong affection for me had to be controlled, and although such affection for a mother is very interesting and is most delightful to the parent's heart, yet even this must be kept within proper limits, else it becomes irksome and annoying to friends, if not to the parent. I well remember my first contest with this dear child was upon this very point. As much temper and passion accompanied this demonstration of his will in wishing to stay with me when I had desired the servant to take him up stairs, I felt it my duty to inflict a slight chastisement upon him. Since his removal I have wept, and I do as I write to remember I did so; but upon cool reflection I believe I did what was right in this particular, and by it he learned obedience and submission; but nevertheless loved me yet more for the correction which a sense of love and duty prompted.

Owing to a peculiar excitability of brain and a delicate constitution, our dear Arthur, when suffering from trifling causes, such as hunger, cold, or fatigue, was disposed to irritability more than some children; particularly sensitive in every respect, he felt keenly and painfully when suffering from the little discomforts of life; but here also the power and grace of God were displayed in him, and also his own desire to please Him; for when I reminded him that when he was naughty God saw him and would be angry, he would control himself and try to be good, and often succeeded, I believe, by the help of God; for on one occasion when he had been naughty, and I spoke to him afterwards about it, he looked at me very inquiringly, and said, 'Did God make me good boy?' Yes, doubtless He did so, for He knows the desire of them that fear Him, and will save them. He had shown some little temper at dinner, and had refused to say, 'Please, mamma;' for this I had sent him out of the room. The poor little fellow was broken-hearted, and said to his nurse, 'I will be good boy; I will say, P'ease, mamma;' and coming back, he kissed me with deep shame, and did all that was required. During the afternoon he talked very much to his little sister, saying to her, 'When I c'ied did God see me?' 'Was God ang'y with me?' He then kept saying at different times all through the rest of the day, 'Ar. won't be naughty boy;' 'Ar. will be good boy. When Ar. wake up in morning, Ar. will say, P'ease, mamma, give me some more.' His resolution now was made, and firmly he kept it. He was never naughty again. This was the last time I had to correct him, and the servant remarked to me that he had not been naughty since that correction.

His nurse has frequently observed to me how he would in the nursery endeavour to subdue rising temper, and has told me of his resolution not to give way to fretfulness, and of his determination to be good under his little troubles.

The cold salt water bath which he had every morning was quite a trial to him, but before having it it had become a rule with him to say to his nurse, 'Ar. won't c'y, Jane,' and he would bite his lips, and hold his breath, while he strove to keep his promise; and then when the little trouble was over and he had maintained his resolution, with much exultation and delight he would say, 'I didn't c'y;' 'Ar. was a good boy, Jane.' And when his brothers or sisters came into the nursery, he would tell them how he 'didn't c'y,' so pleased to have been able to gain a victory over himself.

When he had shown any inclination to obstinacy or disobedience during the day, I taught him to confess his fault to God in his evening prayer, and tell Him he had been naughty, and ask Him to make him a better boy, and to take away his naughty heart. These simple petitions he understood, and they made a deep impression upon him; and when he went up to bed he would tell his nurse how he had been naughty, and that he had been praying to God to make him good.

Latterly he would try to persuade his baby brother to be good, and would talk so prettily to him; and when he cried he would say to his nurse, 'Oh, isn't baby naughty boy; won't God be ang'y with him?' . . .

[Arthur died at the age of three.] Oh, how bitter, in that world, where there is blackness and darkness for ever, will the reproaches of those children be against those parents who, instead of having trained their offspring for a holy and a better world, have taught them to walk in the way of death; who instead of leading them in the path of life, and teaching them to 'strive to enter in at the strait gate,' have introduced them into the pleasures and vanities of the world, teaching them to seek happiness in those things which only draw the soul away from God, instead of endeavouring to lead them to Him, who is the only Fountain of true bliss and unfading joy. May we all as mothers seek to be faithful to the high and holy trust committed to us. Let us cry mightily to God on behalf of those we love, and wait upon the Lord, and give Him no rest, until we have good evidence that our children are born again, and are the children of God by faith in Christ Jesus; and as Christian mothers, let us travail in birth again for them, until we see 'Christ formed in them the hope of glory.'

[12] Tepid Christianity in a Public School

Arthur Duke Coleridge, *Eton in the Forties* (1896) pp. 87–100. Coleridge was a Chancery official in the Midland circuit.

The religious teaching in my schooldays was not a strong point, either in or outside Eton Chapel. Sermons so inaudibly delivered as to be, in some instances, little more than dumb-show, a hebdomadal dose of Secker in school, varied with the meagre commentaries of Burton and Valpy on the Greek Testament in pupil-room, were a spiritual diet not robust enough for intended divines, or Christian heroes *in posse*. Eton was near enough to Oxford to be affected by mutterings of the great Church upheaval, and the phases of the Oxford movement were absorbing topics of interest to more than one of the assistant masters. Hodgson, our Provost, formerly Archdeacon of Derby, a high and dry

divine, with no taste for controversy or faction, whether dominated by
Newman or Arnold, kept rigorously aloof from the vexed questions
which agitated many at Oxford and some few at Cambridge; and our
headmaster, Dr. Hawtrey, a man of letters, and the friend of literary
men, was indifferent as Gallio to the '*Credo in Newmanum*' watchword,
which awoke the suspicion of some alarmed Protestants in the cloisters
of Eton. We boys had no Goulburn or Vaughan, still less a Lightfoot or
Westcott, to keep us straight. Plain expositions and lectures on the
Greek Testament would have been a more wholesome study for some of
us than Archdeacon Manning's sermons, which were too frequently
substituted, in my tutor's pupil-room, for the ordinary subjects of
private business. These sermons, with all their beauty of style and
language, veiled but imperfectly the restless and dissatisfied mind of
their author, and I am persuaded that, at a time when the '*Tendimus in
Latium*' cry was at its loudest, they were perilous reading for boys of an
emotional turn. We attached a dangerous importance to them, and
when the Archdeacon 'went over,' his flag followers saw their mistake.
The future Cardinal bought up the four volumes, which had made the
Chichester Cathedral pulpit so justly famous, and we were taught too
late to discover the elements of slow poison in teaching for some time
warranted sound by our guides and instructors. . . .

For one year, during which time the chapel was closed for
restoration, we attended service in a wooden tabernacle, which was run
up in a field adjoining Barnes' Pool. It was said to have been originally
intended for a missionary building, to be used in the Colonies; I am
afraid it added more to our amusement than our edification. The
tabernacle was a fragile, unsubstantial structure, with boards and
benches so loosely put together that they were constantly giving way. In
the summer-time the wasps, finding out the weak points built a nest in
the interstices of the building, and this was a matter of great discomfort
to Plumptre, the Fellow of Eton who happened to be in residence during
the summer half when we first worshipped in our temporary chapel. I
should like to have compared notes with the Rev. James Lonsdale,
whose biography – the joint work of two of my contemporaries, Russell
Duckworth and the Hon. G. C. Brodrick – has won the gratitude of all
loyal Etonians. I could have added considerably to his *répertoire* of
subjects chosen for sermons, though I believe that he had a large stock,
compiled from memories of his old Eton days, long before the
tabernacle discourses. He remembered the old Fellow, that ancient
ecclesiastic, whose monosyllabic texts were famous. 'Shout!' was one of

them. Another text, declaimed by one of Plumptre's colleagues, made a
lasting impression on my friend and schoolfellow, the late Sir James
Fitzjames Stephen, who records the fact in his diary: 'It rings in my ears
after the lapse of more than forty years.' The text was this: 'The subject
of my discourse this morning, my brethren, will be the duties of the
married state.'

In the pulpit, Plumptre always held his glasses an inch or two in front
of his face. When the wasp interrupted a full view of his manuscript, or
playfully seemed disposed to settle on the preacher's nose, and leave his
mark there, the old gentleman appeared to be playing a miniature
game of racquets, back-handing, and volleying with his tormentor.
There was a huge cushion on the pulpit, and Plumptre's first idea, after
planting his cap upon it, was to turn up each end of the cushion, and
peep under it, as if he expected to find some lurking foe; then he planted
his head in his cap and glared with his swivel eye at the congregation.
His text on one occasion was, 'Whether it be to the King as supreme.'
He accented the last syllable of 'supreme,' and pronounced the word
'shu-præm;' and we had sermons from him twice at least on the same
theme. The popular opinion was, that the Provost remonstrated with
him, as he proposed taking the same text for the remainder of his course,
and that as he refused to give in, he was not allowed to preach the other
two sermons; but I fancy there would have been a row in the chapel, if
he had been forcibly prohibited from giving us the rest of his
lucubrations. The sermon itself was a 'cento' of Biblical phrases, which
the preacher adapted as describing the happiness of the English people
under Queen Victoria. 'And the land is at peace, and every man sits in
his own garden of cucumbers.' He called the Queen 'a mother in Israel,'
and made some passing allusion to the Society of Friends. Anxious that
the school should understand the allusion, he paused, and broke the
universal silence with an ejaculatory jerk pitchforked at us – 'The
Quakers' (it sounded like 'The Quakersh'). We had a very memorable
discourse on the Sunday after the Queen had been shot at. Plumptre's
indignation at the attempt made on her Majesty's life found vent in his
sermon, in which he gave a *précis* of the transaction. 'After the shot had
been fired,' said he, 'who should appear upon the scene but pedestrian
Peck? Pedestrian Peck seized the assassin, and handed him over to a Life
Guardsman.' Peck's promptitude and courage seemed to have impressed the preacher greatly, for he laid strong emphasis on 'pedesh-
trian Peck,' and evidently considered him as a protagonist in the scene.
Owing to his grotesque mannerisms and Spurgeonisms, we were highly

delighted whenever Plumptre ascended the tribune. When Long Chamber was broken up into cubicles, I doubt if Plumptre half liked the alteration, but he made an occasion of it, and we enjoyed his text: 'And Elisha said, Let every man take unto himself a beam, for the place we have made is too strait for us.' I have heard quoted, as one of his pulpit gems, the sentence: 'Your hearts are like gooseberry-tart without sugar,' but I doubt the genuineness of this story, which is probably the invention of some imaginative fourth-form boy. . . .

The Fellows of Eton, judged as a corporate body, were kindly men, conspicuous for watching the interests of their relatives and dependents; is it a libel on their memory, or the simple truth, to say that, with two exceptions, they were useless and superannuated, as preachers not only ineffective, but at times very ridiculous in the 'wood'? They contributed in a full measure to the poverty-stricken services which were then unhappily the fashion in Eton Chapel.

On Sunday morning we had no music; in the afternoon, and on Saints' days, the college borrowed the choir of St. George's Chapel, and we had a mongrel performance, miserably inferior to that in the Royal Chapel itself. It was said of our organist that he was an eminently charitable man, 'for his right hand knoweth not what his left hand doeth'; and the contrast between the two players was so humiliating, that not a few of us were frequent worshippers in St. George's, where we were sure of services and anthems in the grand style.

[13] Late Victorian Headmaster's Morality: Faith, Purity and Kindness to Animals

Rev. the Hon. E. Lyttelton, *Mothers and Sons or Problems in the Home Training of Boys* (1892) pp. 30–124. At this time Lyttelton was headmaster of Haileybury. He later became headmaster of Eton.

If, in short, he sees that his mother has no living belief in the unseen, – if nothing that she says or does in his presence recalls those truths of which he has been told, – then surely his belief in God will share the fate of his belief in fairies; and if, on the other hand, the mother's look, words, and actions, as well as his other surroundings, remind him of those truths, can any one say that his belief in them would not have a good chance of surviving? . . .

Now the results in boyhood, I should say, tally to a considerable extent with this hypothesis. It is true that a good and careful home training, even if it be largely blended with spiritual influences, will sometimes turn out a boy who, at sixteen, is apparently irreligious. But then between the home and that age six or seven years of school life have intervened; and, as things are now, no matter what care may be taken by the masters, the influence of the other boys is quite strong enough to drive the religious feelings – not away – but, for a while at any rate, under the surface. This is not meant as an indictment against schools, but simply as another way of saying that at an extremely shy and sensitive age, when young boys copy in their demeanour not the highest, but the most powerful and prevailing fashion, it is inconceivable that in English schools the expression of the religious instinct should be anything but rare. I have known some thoroughly religious school-masters affirm that this reserve, so far from being regrettable, is a sign of healthy moral and spiritual growth in boyhood, even in cases where there has previously been a thorough spiritual leavening of the child's life. During the dark period of growth, from fourteen to eighteen, there must be, and there practically always is, reticence. Possibly the state of things with French boys is different, but you and I have quite enough to do to investigate the young of one nation at a time.

But though driven for a time under the surface, the religious feeling certainly does not die. The cases of its reappearance in early manhood, and subsequent development, are too common and too plainly the outcome of the home influences to allow of any such supposition. Indeed, it could, I think, be shown that some few boys have taken pains to conceal their deepest feelings during school life, while at home there has not been any temporary access of reserve between son and mother. On the theory, then, that the instinct can be fostered in childhood, let us consider some few leading principles.

Beyond any question, of all human influences the spiritual conviction of the mother must be the strongest. It would be absurd to say that it is stronger than all others put together, because it is not; but it is stronger than any other taken singly. My impression is that its force is often weakened by shyness. If a mother is really living in communion with God, a little less formality in talking with her children, a little less of confining her influence to stated hours of prayer or lesson, would tend to produce a naturalness in religion, which is an exceedingly beautiful thing, and not at all alien to children. Remember how strangely strong is the probability that your son will grow up to restrict his religion to Sundays, and therefore do your utmost for the first nine years of his life at least to spread it over each week and every day. Take all pains to make him observe Sunday as he ought, but be on your guard against the hebdomadal piety of the Saxon. . . .

What is wanted is that boys should early be introduced to the great dogmas about the being and attributes of God contained in the Creeds; that they should know why Creeds were ever drawn up, and at what time a Church in England was first heard of, what sort of worship was carried on, whence it came, and how long it has lasted. Further, they would be interested in learning the reasons in outline of the growth of the Roman power, and the protests made in England against its encroachments; the meaning of Baptism, Confirmation, and Ordination, and the difference between Church and Dissent. On this last point, whatever view may be taken, the facts should be clearly put, and nothing said in an uncharitable spirit. And facts should also be pointed out to show that our Church dates from before Henry VIII., since error on that subject is exceedingly difficult to expel from older heads. Be concrete; be consecutive; make your history alive by visits to the village church, or to the nearest cathedral. . . .

We have much yet to learn. If we are in earnest, anxiety and love will find out the way. Stories will be told to the child emphasising the joy of renunciation. No opportunity will be lost for giving special praise at the very faintest indication of unselfishness. As soon as the boy is old enough, take him into consultation over cases of distress, though his suggestions will be poor and useless. At prayer-time in the evening take care to review the events of the day, and see if some incipient self-denial has found a place. A day without it will be felt to be incomplete.

In the same way cruelty to animals will be prevented by simple teaching of fact. A diminutive infant will maul the housefly from a wish to possess and investigate, and from failure to understand that the insect is alive. Little boys sin from ignorance. Enlighten them, therefore, as to the animal's sensitiveness by a sharp infliction of (if possible) similar pain to that which they have been giving. Inflict it without a trace of anger, merely as a means of instruction. And encourage meantime the keeping of pets, and even of toads, after the manner of Kingsley's children, and the voluntary tending of something like a lame dog or a chicken with a broken wing.

Lastly, let the small renunciations that are made take *visible* effect. The giving up of money should be thus rewarded. Delicacies should be spared, or a comfortable chair relinquished, not for the benefit of a remote hospital or of a mission in the other hemisphere, but for use in a convalescent home close by, or for the enjoyment of some indigent cottager whom the young almsgiver can personally visit, so that he may be certain that his diminutive self-denial is doing something. The nightmare of misdirected charity need not haunt him for the present. And only very gently, far on in his teens, should he be warned of the apparent fruitlessness of much voluntary renunciation. Keep these things from him for a time as carefully as you would the *Police News*. But as his imagination and his knowledge of geography grow, so his doles may be distributed farther afield; and let him, as soon as he is ready, have a voice in his mother's deliberations as to what claims upon her kindness she must heed, in the hope that he will be trained in all ways to be a cheerful, constant, and orderly distributor of this world's goods. . . .

At the present day it is demanded of a boy that he should master his appetites in so far as one temptation is concerned, that of impurity. In fact, this demand on his powers of self-discipline is made with much urgency. To anticipate a little what I shall say later on, this danger is not common to all boys by any means, but the evil is sufficiently prevalent in extent and startling in its results to have inspired a very widespread alarm among parents and masters. An immense amount of care is taken against it. . . .

And it is a great point that the boy, when the trial comes, should know that those whom he loves are aware of it. Many a school-boy has been led into evil because he believes what is generally told him by the baser sort among his companions, that 'these are things your mother and sisters know nothing of.' The temptation is worse by far when combined with a feeling of loneliness.

When your boy is entering into public school life there should be an increase of vigilance on your part, and now and then a question, to ascertain the character of the new state of life. It may be laid down as axiomatic that the assistance which can be rendered to a headmaster by plain speaking on the part of parents *who are sure of their facts*, is of priceless value. I believe the days are for ever passed away when school-masters would resent such openness as an insult to their establishments. . . .

We will suppose, then, the first year or so of school life safely passed through, and the boy's thoughts and energies freely occupied in all sorts of wholesome pursuits. It is doubtful if the mother can take any further useful action. For some boys about fourteen or fifteen a warning is most advisable. This would, however, be best given by the father or by a doctor. Again, a boy nearing the age of twenty, needs a few words of caution from the father; and, failing that, he could be given some of the publications of the White Cross Army, or be talked to by a doctor whose opinions are thoroughly sound. . . .

The conviction, however, has been forcing itself upon me ever since I had to do with boys, that the mother's work in guarding her son against this evil – and indeed all others – is of paramount importance, and if it is to be successful, must begin in the earlier years. All habits of self-control and rectitude that you implant are good; but those which have to do with the discipline of the appetites are absolutely indispensable. This simple truth is certainly far too little considered. It is true that in certain cases the facts seem to point to an inherited taint, some strain in the blood reverting back to an almost forgotten ancestry, and that against such all precautions are unavailing. But this only happens very occasionally. . . .

In conclusion, may I appeal for an effort to be made, where possible, towards kindling boys with the love of some such pursuit as gardening? When I consider the wholesomeness, the discipline, the encouragement of observation, the lessons of tenderness and patience which it gives, and when I reflect that the power of gratifying this most refined taste lingers far into old age, and outlives the shrinking of muscle and the stiffening of the knee, I assure you that, in spite of a strong, almost fanatical love of ball games, I sometimes feel doubtful if cricket and football do as much for a man's whole life as the love and tending of plants and flowers. For the somewhat artificial conditions of school life these great games are indispensable. We have to face problems arising from the presence of boys in the mass, of whom some have rude shapeless instincts, and are strangely inclined to spend their leisure in lounging, or violence, or vapid talk, and pampering of the appetites. Some are anti-social, and prefer solitary novel-reading, or aimless unconvivial dreaming, to the life that calls for a sense of citizenship and unity; others – indeed a good many – are likely to turn out grave and useful members of society, but have at present a feeble linguistic sense and slowly maturing brains, and are apparently resting for a while in the solidifying bovine stage, harmless, but inert and ready for deterioration. For all of these and many more, athleticism is a sovereign safeguard. It catches the moody and the turbulent, the anæmic and the boisterous, in its ample stream, and sweeps along good and bad alike, by dint of a powerful common interest quite social and wholesome in tone. But it is needless for me to wax eloquent on this theme. What I wish to insist on is that, however necessary at school, athletics do not require special stimulus at home. They need not be snubbed, but they ought to be tempered and supplemented.

II. EDUCATION, SOCIAL CLASS AND THE ECONOMY

Schooling as a filter for a stratified labour market, with pupils being trained for their prospective station in life, was a typical objective in educating poor children at the beginning of our period [14]. As implemented in the schoolroom it resulted in children learning their pence table with the aid of a rhyming list of virtues [15], learning to read by perusing moralising stories [16], and being introduced to traditional stories only in an 'improved' form with the addition of an appropriately utilitarian moral [17].

A functional view of education, which saw the elementary school as a preventative of contemporary disorders and crime, was increasingly influential by the 1830s [18]. The system of pauper education set up after the Poor Law Amendment Act of 1834 embodied a highly developed form of this educational utilitarianism [19]. One alleged advantage of these pauper district schools was the separation of children from feckless, pauper parents. That educationists' hostility to parental influences on working-class children, was not confined to the pauper educational sector, was revealed by an elementary-school inspector's views in [20].

A more enlightened viewpoint attributed the disappointingly slow advances in elementary education during the mid-nineteenth century to the poverty and environmental squalor in which many working-class families lived [21]. Even after school attendance was made compulsory, considerable numbers of working-class families continued to see children's education as a luxury commodity; they preferred the certain economic rewards from child labour to the low risks of prosecution and fine [22]. When children from very impoverished families *were* found in school, their torpid state made it obvious that feeding their minds was a less important social priority than nourishing their half-starved bodies [23].

It was not only in elementary education that a functional perspective equated schooling with social status. In the proprietary schools of the mid-nineteenth century a hierarchy of practical, commercial, and liberal, educational provision was matched to gradations within society as at the Liverpool College, which was founded in 1840 [24]. In spite of the educational expansion of these years the middle ranks in society still found educational opportunities too limited [25]. Where the established public schools were concerned a consciously élitist defence acknowledged their educational shortcomings, but felt their central function was to act as social agencies for transforming upper-class boys into English gentlemen [26].

By the second half of the nineteenth century it was not gentlemen, but businessmen, scientists and skilled artisans for whom England had the greatest need. Private academies were the earliest educational institutions to respond to market forces and ensure that their vocationally orientated curriculum would prepare their middle-class pupils for commercial employment [27, 28]. In contrast, public schools were sluggish in recognising the need to provide scientific education for their upper-class clientele, although Rugby's timetable by the 1890s was less dominated by classics than it had been over thirty years earlier [29]. An explanation of the small allocation of time for science in the public schools was given in [30]. At the other end of the institutional spectrum, board schools made equally small provision for science, commerce or technology [31]. Unless parents were sufficiently well-off to prolong children's schooling until they reached a Higher Grade, or Organised Science, School working-class pupils received an academic education rather than a vocational training [32]. This lack of industrial training in the elementary school ultimately caused widespread concern as [33] suggests. For by the 1880s the pressures of an advanced industrial society could hardly be ignored [34].

[14] Education for One's Station in Life

Mrs Trimmer, *Reflections upon the Education of Children in Charity Schools* (1792) pp. 7–12. Sarah Trimmer supported the education of the poor and wrote copiously for children.

Sunday Schools and Schools of Industry . . . afford instruction to unlimited numbers of children, who could not be admitted into *Charity Schools*, on account of the expense attending them; neither could such multitudes be trained up as *Charity Children* are, without great injury to society: for, however desirable it may be to rescue the lower kinds of people from that deplorable state of ignorance in which the greatest part of them were for a long time suffered to remain, it cannot be right to train them *all* in a way which will most probably raise their ideas above the very lowest occupations of life, and disqualify them for those servile offices which must be filled by some of the members of the community, and in which they may be equally happy with the highest, if they will do their duty.

*   *   *

In CHARITY SCHOOLS a comprehensive plan of tuition holds forth advantages proper for the *first degree* among the lower orders, who in these seminaries might be qualified for teachers in schools supported by charity, for apprentices to common trades, and for domestic servants in respectable families.

DAY SCHOOLS OF INDUSTRY, by mixing labour with learning, are particularly eligible for such children as are afterwards to be employed in manufactures, and other inferior offices in life, as well as for training those who are usually called *common servants*.

And SUNDAY SCHOOLS, while they hold out religious instruction suitable to all degrees of poor children, furnish a sufficient portion of learning for such as cannot be spared on week-days from the labours of the plough, or other occupations by which they contribute to the support of families.

Sunday Schools may also serve (as was before hinted) as probationary schools to try the capacities of children previously to their admission into *Charity Schools*.

[15] Virtuous Arithmetic: The Pence Table

The Archer Alphabet (n.d.).

> Twenty pence are one and eight pence,
>   Wash your face and comb your hair.
> Thirty pence are two and sixpence,
>   Every day to school repair.
> Forty pence are three and fourpence,
>   Learn to read while you are young.
> Fifty pence are four and twopence.
>   Never use a lying tongue.
> Sixty pence are five shillings,
>   Honour both your Father and Mother.
> Seventy pence are five and tenpence,
>   Love your sister and your brother.
> Eighty pence are six and eightpence,
>   Mind what you are taught at school.
> Ninety pence are seven and sixpence,
>   Never call your brother a fool.
> Hundred pence are eight and fourpence,
>   Never learn to cheat or swear.
> Hundred and ten pence are nine and twopence,
>   With bad companions take no share.
> Hundred and twenty pence are ten shillings
>   Learn to be both meek and mild.
> Hundred and thirty pence are ten and tenpence,
>   God never loves a wicked child.
> Hundred and forty pence are eleven and eightpence,
>   Learn this table at your school.
> Hundred and forty-four pence are twelve shillings,
>   Never forget the golden rule.

[16] 'Old Ann Lee'

First Reading Book, Society for Promoting Christian Knowledge (n.d.).

Old Ann Lee is well now. I saw her to-day. She is quite blind. But she can walk, and knit and spin.

Shall we go and see her?

Yes. We will go by the field.

There she is. She sits by the door of her cot, and spins.

How do you do, Ann Lee?

I am well, my dear. Thank God! I am now quite blind. But I can spin
and knit, and walk to Church.

How do you find your way to Church?

My son Tom leads me there.

Good-bye, Ann Lee. We will take care to call on you now and then. And
send to us if we can serve you.

Thank you. Good-bye, my dears.

Now then we will go home. Do you know Tom Lee?

Yes. I see him when he leads old Ann to Church.

He is a good boy. He is so kind to her.

How old is he?

He is but ten years old.

Does he work at the mill?

Yes. He works hard at the mill. And he takes home all he gets for his
work to poor Ann.

He is a good son. And if he goes on so he will be a good man.

Does Tom Lee like play?

O yes. He likes play as well as Dick Bell does.

But I do not see him at play.

No. He has no time for play. He works hard all day.

And when he goes home he reads to old Ann.

[17] The Trusty Dog

Mrs Trimmer, *The Ladder to Learning*, 19th edn (1856) pp. 159–
60.

THE

LADDER TO LEARNING:

A

COLLECTION OF FABLES;

ARRANGED PROGRESSIVELY IN

WORDS OF ONE, TWO, AND THREE SYLLABLES;

WITH ORIGINAL MORALS.

EDITED AND IMPROVED

BY MRS. TRIMMER.

FABLE VI

The Trusty Dog A lurking Thief had thrown a crust of bread to an honest Mastiff, hoping to bribe him to silence by the bait. 'Hark ye, friend,' said the Mastiff, 'what! you want to stop my tongue, I suppose, and to keep me from barking for the service of my master: but you are greatly mistaken, I assure you; for this sudden kindness will only put me the more upon my guard.'

Moral This fable affords a good lesson to servants, never to suffer themselves to be bribed to do any thing contrary to their duty to their masters or mistresses.

[18] Education to Secure Property and Order

'Causes and Cure of Disturbances and Pauperism', *Edinburgh Review*, LIII (1831) 611-12.

The outrages of the agriculturists may be repressed and put down with comparatively little difficulty; but were such a spirit to arise among the manufacturers of Lancashire as has recently prevailed in the southern counties, national bankruptcy and ruin would be the result. Let no man think that, if the spirit of discontent and outrage should once insinuate itself into the manufacturing districts, it could be suppressed or kept down by force. So mighty a mass cannot be dragooned and coerced into obedience. If we would prolong that *security* which has been the principal foundation of our prosperity, we must show the labourers that they are interested in its support; and that whatever has any tendency to weaken it, is even more injurious to them than to any other class. For this reason, we are deeply impressed with the conviction that Parliament ought to lose no time in setting about the organization of a really useful system of public education. *The safety of the empire depends wholly on the conduct of the multitude*; and such being the case, can any one doubt the paramount importance of the diffusion of sound instruction?

This is not a subject that ought any longer to be trifled with, or left to individuals or societies. The astounding exhibition of ignorance made at the late trials for rioting, shows how wretchedly the agricultural population is educated. A larger proportion of the manufacturing population can read and write; but a knowledge of these arts is not enough. Besides being instructed in them, and in the duties and obligations enjoined by religion and morality, the poor ought to be made acquainted with those circumstances which principally determine their condition in life. They ought, above all, to be instructed in the plain and elementary doctrines respecting population and wages; in the advantages derived from the institution of private property, and the introduction and improvement of machinery; and in the causes which give rise to that gradation of ranks, and inequality of fortunes, that are as natural to society as heat to fire, and cold to ice. The interests of the poor are identified with the support of all those great principles, the maintenance of which is essential to the welfare of the other classes. And, were they made fully aware that such is the fact, it would be a contradiction and an absurdity to suppose, that the securities for peace and good order would not be immeasurably increased. Those revolutionary and anti-social doctrines, now so copiously distributed, would be rejected at once by an instructed population. But it is not easy to estimate what may be their influence in a period of political excitement and public distress, when addressed to those whose education has been entirely neglected, and whose judgment is, in consequence, guided by prejudice, and not by principle.

We hope that the attention of Parliament and the country will be speedily called to this most important subject. The foundations of real security are beyond and above the law. They depend on the knowledge and morals of the people. Nor can there be a doubt, that rulers who neglect to provide their subjects with the means of procuring cheap and really useful instruction, are justly chargeable with the neglect of a most essential duty.

[19] A Utilitarian View of Workhouse Education

Sir James Kay-Shuttleworth, 'On the Establishment of County or District Schools, for the Training of the Pauper Children Maintained in Union Workhouses', *Journal of the Royal Statistical Society*, 1 (1838) 16, 20–3.

The following Table shews the state of the instruction of the children in the workhouses, even after some improvements had been effected in the schools; and an idea of the state of the children before these improvements were in progress, may possibly be in some degree realised from an attentive consideration of these facts.

	Youths from 9 to 16	*Boys from 2 to 9*	*Girls from 9 to 16*	*Girls from 2 to 9*	*Total*
Number who can Read well	206	70	173	30	479
Number who can Read imperfectly	217	149	207	186	759
Number who cannot Read	62	267	38	225	592
Number who can Write well	122	6	47	1	176
Number who can Write imperfectly	138	56	97	33	324
Number who cannot Write	211	398	262	407	1278

There are some slight inaccuracies in this Table, which do not, however, impair the general statement.

It is difficult to perceive how the dependence of the orphan, bastard, and deserted children, and the children of idiots, helpless cripples, and of widows relieved in the Union Workhouses, could cease, if no exertion were made to prepare them to earn their livelihood by skilful labour, and to fit them to discharge their social duties by training them in correct moral habits, and giving them knowledge suited to their station in life. . . .

The number of children maintained and educated in the workhouses of Norfolk and Suffolk is considerably less than in some other parts of England. Thus I am aware that the workhouse schools in the county of Kent contain a much greater number of children in proportion to the population; but on the other hand, in the north of England a smaller number of children will probably be found to be dependent on the ratepayers.

If the children maintained in the workhouses of the rest of England be admitted to bear the same proportion to the population as in Norfolk and Suffolk, the workhouses of England contain 49,556 children between the ages of 2 and 16, of whom 48,022 are more permanently resident in the workhouses.

If the want of classification and the absence of correct discipline which prevailed in the old workhouses continued in the new, a great number of these latter children would acquire the habits of hereditary paupers, or even of felons, and *if only one-tenth of them (which would by no means be improbable,) became dependent during six months of each year*, with families of the ordinary size, they would occasion a burden of 112,353*l.* per annum. . . .

The establishment of two County Schools of Industry in each of the counties of Norfolk and Suffolk appears to be rendered desirable by various important considerations. . . .

The industrial training of the children who have no natural guardians, and who are therefore altogether dependent on the Board of Guardians for instruction in the practical duties of life, is thus impaired by two circumstances, which would cease to exist provided such children were sent to a county-school.

The classification of the children separately from the adults (excepting their parents) is preserved with care in the workhouses of Norfolk and Suffolk, but cannot be rendered perfect in any workhouse as at present regulated. The adult paupers maintained in workhouses are generally persons of confirmed pauper habits, from whose society the children could acquire nothing but evil.

Children should not be taught to consider themselves paupers; and this result can scarcely be avoided if those who have lost their natural guardians are trained in a workhouse, under the same roof, and in unavoidable contact, with paupers. This stigma, and the consequent loss of self-esteem, would be entirely removed if the children were taught at a central school, with other children not received from the workhouses, nor the offspring of pauper parents. . . .

The great object to be kept in view in regulating any school for the instruction of the children of the labouring class, is the rearing of hardy and intelligent working men, whose character and habits shall afford the largest amount of security to the property and order of the community. Not only has the training of the children of labourers hitherto been defective, both in the methods of instruction pursued, and because it has been confined within the most meagre limits, but because it has failed to inculcate the great practical lesson for those whose sole dependence for their living is on the labour of their hands, by early habituating them to patient and skilful industry.

[20] An Inspector's Views on Parental Influence

Minutes of the Committee of Council, Rev. F. Watkin's report on the Northern District, 1846, *P.P.* (1847)XLV, pp. 238–9. Watkins was HMI from 1844 to 1873.

HINDRANCES FROM THE HOME

But the hindrances to elementary education are not only in the school itself – in the paucity or non-efficiency of its teachers – in the want of books and slates, and other apparatus; nor again in other circumstances of the child's life, such as its too early labour frequently interrupting, and ere long bringing to a hasty close, the hours of its employment at school. These hindrances operate chiefly against its right instruction and intellectual development; the loss which they cause to the child is in its advancement in life, and well-doing in the world. But the chief impediment to the higher part of education, to moral and religious training, arises elsewhere – not in the school from the inefficiency or thoughtlessness of the master, but at the home from the carelessness or godlessness of the parent. I have, my Lords, in previous Reports, written at some length on this point. But I should think myself shrinking from my duty, if either from mistaken feelings of delicacy, or fear of telling a twice-told tale, I should omit to mention such things as are too often visible in the manufacturing districts. It will hardly be credible that on two occasions, at different localities in Lancashire, one near to the town of Colne, the other to that of Burnley, I have seen in broad daylight, at 9 in the morning and 4 in the afternoon, men, one in the prime of youth, the other past middle age, running races or rather matches against time, on the public high road, *quite naked.* In the first case, the naked man was loudly cheered by a crowd of his companions on his arrival at the goal, and carried away in triumph on their shoulders; in the other, a large crowd was awaiting his arrival. Amongst them, and along the road on which this shameless race was run, were women of all ages – mothers, factory girls, young children: the runner seemed to excite great interest; but I could observe nothing like a trace of shame on any of the many eager faces collected there. . . .

I have mentioned, my Lords, some – and surely they are sufficient – of the most striking instances, which came under my own observation, of the shamelessness and filthy habits, the want of chastity, the ignorance and carelessness with regard to religion, the neglect of public worship, the brutality, recklessness, and almost animal state in which some of the labouring classes, both manufacturing and agricultural, of the county of Lancaster live, and to which their children must be inured from their earliest years. I do not mean to assert, nor wish it to be supposed, that the cases which I have mentioned are general, or that, in their worst form, they are common. But of this I am convinced more fully every time that I walk in any of the back streets in the larger towns, or visit any of the out-of-the-way villages, and listen to the conversation of their inhabitants, and observe something of their conduct, that there is an amount of ignorance and vice and degradation amongst them which it is difficult to imagine and hardly possible to describe in plain language. And these people are the parents of many of our school-children, and the cellars or the garrets or the cabins are their homes. It is, indeed, a sad and evil necessity, if the first lesson which they learn at school is to beware of their own parents, and to look with disgust, if not with horror, at the filthiness and abominations of their own homes. What a confusion must arise in their minds between the rules and training of the school and the language and practice of the home! I know well that even very wicked parents will scruple to bring up their children wickedly, and will, as they say, 'never teach them wickedness' but *by example*. But how easy this method of teaching is, and how difficult to counteract by any school-education, many a master of our elementary schools can witness. It is no unusual thing for them to say, in answer to some remark of the Inspector, 'That was a steady boy, sir, and was getting on well; but he has been at home for some time, and he's no better for it.'

It is no uncommon charge against elementary education for the poorer classes, especially against that given in infant-schools, that it takes children away too much from the influences of home, and interrupts the natural relation between them and their parents. It is with much reluctance, my Lords, that I state my opinion that at present, under existing circumstances, this separation of intercourse between children and parents is in the majority of families highly beneficial to the former, if not absolutely necessary. It is good for them that they should not take their parents for their examples. It is very important that they should have other views and other motives suggested to them than those which the ignorance and vice both of fathers and mothers unceasingly and practically supply to them at home.

I must not omit to mention the frequent indifference of the parents to the education of their children, even where it may be obtained at the lowest rate, and without any trouble or inconvenience to themselves. In almost every large town numbers of children of the age at which they ought to be in the elementary school are to be found in the smaller streets at play during the school-hours. On inquiry one finds that they do not go to any school and never have been under instruction except on Sunday.

[21] Social Reform a Precondition of Educational Advance

Census Education, P.P. (1852–3) xc, pp. lxxxix–xci.

It may, however, be permitted to reiterate a doubt respecting the success of any schemes to elevate the masses of the population by mere elementary instruction while the social circumstances of the multitude continue so unfriendly to their intellectual and moral progress. For the real educational calamity at present is – not that the children do not go to school, but that they stay at school for such a limited period; and this results directly from the want of adequate inducement to prolong their education in the face of opportunities for early labour. Doubtless many thousands of children would be kept at school, who are now at a very early age removed, if any great advantages from education were discernible by parents, as procuring either physical or intellectual enjoyment for the after-life. But must it not be, though reluctantly, allowed that they have only too much reason for their apathy? 'Of what avail' – they may, and not unreasonably, ask – 'can education be to those who must, of sad necessity, reside in these impure and miserable homes, from which, if it were possible, ourselves would be the first to flee? Or what delight can education yield to those who, on emerging from the school, where taste has been acquired and appetite excited, find that both the treasures and the sweets of literature are far beyond their reach?' Such, really if not in words, are the much-too-reasonable questions by which parents, of the humbler ranks excuse their inattention to their children's education: they imagine they are doing just enough to fit them for their future and unalterable lot, and that all beyond would be at best but superfluity: What then is wanted to ensure a greater measure of success to present efforts? Surely, the creation of a more benignant *atmosphere*. However carefully the tree of knowledge may be planted, and however diligently tended, it can never grow to fruitfulness or beauty in an uncongenial air. Concurrently with all direct attempts to cultivate the popular intelligence, there needs to be a vigorous endeavour to alleviate, if not remove, that social wretchedness which blights all educational promise, and to shed around the growing popular mind an affluence of wholesome light on which the half-developed plant may feed and thrive.

Whatever restrictions, therefore, may by a proper delicacy be imposed upon the expression here of any opinion on the more immediate means to be adopted for promoting elementary instruction, it will not be out of place to advocate those indirect yet influential means which – whether they be movements on behalf of temperance, health, cleanliness, and better dwellings, or for public lectures, libraries, and cheap and wholesome literature – must, by raising the position of the people and by bringing within their reach the *fruits* of intellectual toil, inevitably tend to render education much more valued, and therefore much more sought. Apart from their own special objects, all these movements have a potent favourable action upon primary education; for the social elevation of the parents makes the adequate instruction of their offspring needful to their proper pride, while the cheap diffusion of information greatly multiplies the inducements to learning by multiplying greatly its rewards. However long may last the difficulties which now hinder any equitable scheme of *national* instruction, *here* at least there is ample and common ground for effort upon which both the public and the Legislature have appropriate parts to play. And if upon the cultivation of this wide and open field a greater amount of labour be expended, who shall say it is impossible that, in the course of some few years, before the Gordian knot which now perplexes statesmen and philanthropists could be untied, the people may themselves have severed it?

[22] Attendance Problems Caused by Rural Poverty

Log book of Harlton School, Cambridgeshire, March–June 1878. The reference in the passage to '150 times' refers to 150 half-day attendances at school during the year.

Monday afternoon [18 March 1878]. It is a rule of this school (made by the Rector) that all children must bring their money on Monday morning. If not they are to be sent home by the Principal Teacher. This afternoon I sent home nine children. Five still refuse to pay the money. It is very difficult indeed to get children to come to school at all. Several mothers go out to work and keep children 7 and 8 at home to mind the house or baby. Boys are employed by the farmers at the age of 8, 9 and 10 who have not even made 150 times. Come in school just two months before the Examination. No one here forces the children to come. Six children are kept at home this week because their parents can't pay the school fee – one penny. . . .

April 2nd. This morning I sent home Albert Fuller for his money. His father opened the school door – pushed the child in and threw the money at my feet – and said I might pick it up. Rev. O. Fisher visited this morning. Told him about Fuller's behaviour. The man came and beg my pardon this afternoon. . . .

Friday May/78. The children of the (upper part) of the school attend very badly. Several times I have only one child to take in the 3rd [Standard]. Standard IV and V St[andard] children are generally away. The children are generally away. The children are very young indeed and I have sent the teachers after them and even called myself. It has no effect. . . .

June 3rd. The children in Standard III to VI very seldom come. In fact the standard work of the school has gone down two Standards lower this year. The parents send children to work. A farmer employs them. Several girls are kept at home to mind *babies* while the mothers go in the field to work. Mrs Prime asked to have her child at home for a week or two. . . . The Rector said the child must stop at home to mind the baby, as the woman was so very poor. This week Elizabeth Willmot age 10 has gone to service and Esther Muncey too. Emma Muncey is kept at home to mind her brother. As soon as the children in this village can earn a penny they are sent out to work. I have answered all letters from School Attendance Officer. Heard nothing. Wrote again the 2nd time. Have had no reply. Also gave the Rector the names of the children who come to School badly. And that has had no effect. I send after the children. It is no good. The parents are determined to keep them from school. The children are very young indeed who do come. The eldest being only 9 years who is at school [this] morning.

[23] Do Hungry Cockney Children Need Bread More than Brain-Polish?

Report on Alleged Overpressure of Work, P.P. (1884) LXI, p. 267.

In one school visited, the head-mistress assured me that to her certain knowledge as many as 8 per cent. of the girls came to school without breakfast in the depth of winter; in another school I conversed with 6 boys in a standard of 66, with 14 boys in a standard of 80, and with 6 in a standard of 56, who had had no breakfast that morning, and there was a dreadful monotony in the way in which, in reply to my queries as to the cause of their abstinence, the changes were rung on these answers: 'Father out of work;' 'Father in the hospital;' 'No bread in the house;' 'Mother lays abed.' The last of these answers I came to understand was often a childish euphemism for drunkenness, or for the morning stupor that follows a night's debauch. In still another school in which starvation abounded, I learned that it was no uncommon thing for a poverty-stricken mother, perhaps a charwoman or a flower seller, who had had to send her child to school without food, because there was neither food, money, nor money's worth in the house, to arrive at the school-house in the forenoon, after she had been out and had earned a few pence, and ask to be allowed to hand in a piece of bread to her starving child.

Many children in London who are never actually without food are still partially starved, for what they get to eat is innutritious, or insufficient in amount. The loaf is sometimes the utmost that the family resources can compass, and where there are a number of mouths there is but a small bit for each. Bread and weak tea form the sole sustenance of many children for prolonged periods. Other children are left wholly unprovided by their parents, and have to forage as best they can for themselves. I found one lad immersed in geography who had had no breakfast, and whose dinner had consisted of two rotten oranges thrown away from a huckster's stall. And there is much partial or occasional starvation amongst children not of the lowest class. The children of poor clerks who come neatly dressed to school have often a lean and hungry look that speaks volumes; and those of artizans, not rarely by a sudden failure of intellect and languor of manner, intimate to the discerning teacher, without any words, that their fathers are out of work, or prostrated by illness.

To look at these half-starved children in London schools is to be 'full of sorrow.' Very touching is it to think of the quiet heroism with which, when hunger is gnawing within and the dull misery of want overflows them, they sit uncomplaining at their little desks, toiling at their allotted tasks, wondering, no doubt, sometimes what it all means, but bearing their burdens patiently. Very pathetic is it to hear them sing in thin quavering voices, some perhaps almost with the dews of death settling upon their brows,

'Happy little sunbeams,
Happy are we.'

Sunbeams! one feels inclined to exclaim, motes in the sunbeams! germs of disease!

These children want blood, and we offer them a little brain-polish; they ask for bread, and receive a problem; for milk, and the tonic-sol-fa system is introduced to them.

[24] A Hierarchical Pattern of Schooling for Different Social Classes

Schools' Inquiry Commission, vol. XVII, *P.P.* (1867–8) XXVIII, part XIV, pp. 574–84.

THE LIVERPOOL COLLEGE

Date of Establishment. – Foundation stone laid 22 October 1840, by the Earl of Derby. . . .

Objects.–For the education of commercial, trading, and working classes; to provide for inhabitants of Liverpool an education suited to their wants, upon most moderate terms, and at same time to maintain indissolubly connexion between sound religion and useful learning (Rules). Designed to supply at a moderate expense to three classes of society a sound education based upon principles of Church of England. Three schools entirely distinct one not being intended to be preparatory for the other.

The upper school is designed to afford a liberal education, and consists of a classical and a modern division.

The middle school furnishes a complete commercial education.

The lower school provides a practical education for the trading classes. . . .

Principal must be in priest's orders and M.A. of Oxford, Cambridge, or Dublin; may not take private pupils or engage in permanent clerical duties unconnected with institution (Rules).

I. UPPER SCHOOL

Exhibitions. – Five of from 54*l*. to 40*l*. per annum, and one of 25*l*., tenable for three years and a half at Oxford, Cambridge, or Dublin.

Two open scholarships, annually, of 15*l*. each, tenable at school for two years; and three of 7*l*. 14*s*. each, tenable at school for one term.

Subjects of Instruction prescribed. – Include classics, Hebrew, English literature, and composition, geography, civil and ecclesiastical history, modern languages, mathematics, natural history and philosophy, chemistry, drawing, and such other useful learning as committee determine (Rules). In classical division education similar to that in great public schools given to those destined for universities and learned professions; in modern, (or exceptional) pupils prepared for general and mercantile pursuits, as well as those connected with engineering, architecture, &c. (Prospectus, A.D. 1868).

State of School in Third Term of 1868

General Character. – Classical. In age of scholars, first grade.

Masters. – Six classical, one mathematical (all graduates of Oxford or Cambridge), one French, one German, one natural philosophy, &c., one drawing, one arithmetic, &c., one drilling (Prospectus, A.D. 1868). In A.D. 1867 principal's emoluments were 968*l*. 2*s*. 6*d*.

Day Scholars. – 114; just half between 10 and 14 years of age; majority from within two miles, some from 12 to 15 by railway; pay for general work, under 10, 17*l*. 17*s*.; above, 23*l*. 2*s*. Exhibitioners nothing. Stationery and drilling 12*s*. each. Do not attend on Sunday. . . .

Instruction, Discipline &c. – Boys on admission must be able to read in junior department, and give evidence according to their age of having learnt something, either Latin or French, arithmetic, &c.
Classification in senior department by classics and mathematics; in exceptional division by English subjects, modern languages, and mathematics; in junior department by Latin, English, and arithmetic. In contemplation to make such modifications of school course to suit special cases as are not inconsistent with uniformity of work necessary for class teaching. Scripture reading for a quarter of an hour daily; one hour's divinity in each class; periodical examinations and lectures by principal. Eighteen boys exempted from learning Church Catechism. Prayers from Liturgy morning and evening.
Promotions by terms work and examination.
First class examined once a year by University examiners appointed by principal; other classes continually by principal, and twice a year by

a committee of masters helping him. Books and medals given publicly once a year.

Punishments: impositions, deprivation of half or whole holiday, and caning on hand; last commonly before class. All punishments must be reported to head master weekly. Expulsion by head master only.

Playground adjoining college about an acre, cricket field of about seven acres in the suburbs. Drilling taught as part of system.

On average of last five years, four or five boys have within one year of leaving school gone to Oxford or Cambridge.

School open about 40 weeks in the year. Boys in school 29 hours in the week; majority of lessons prepared out of school.

II. MIDDLE SCHOOL

Subjects of Instruction prescribed. – Comprise Latin classics, English composition, history, geography, mathematics, especially in their practical application, arithmetic, principles of mensuration, French, German, drawing, vocal music, book-keeping, and writing, with natural philosophy and chemistry for senior pupils (Prospectus, A.D. 1868). . . .

III. LOWER SCHOOL

Subjects of Instruction prescribed. – Comprise English grammar, composition, and history, geography, arithmetic, book-keeping, Latin, French, drawing, vocal music, writing, chemistry, and elementary mathematics (Prospectus, A.D. 1865).

[25] A Plea for Better Educational Opportunities for the Middle Classes

J. L. Brereton, *County Education. A Letter, Addressed to the Right Hon. Earl Fortescue* (1861) pp. 5–7. The Rev. Joseph Lloyd Brereton, spendthrift and educational enthusiast, was prominent in the County School movement.

But the resources of the parish, however unitedly put forth, will not, except under a forced and artificial system, do more than procure the first elements of instruction, – reading, writing, and arithmetic, – and probably from ten to twelve years of age will be the limits where these advantages will cease. At that age the resources of different classes will naturally cause a variety of plan. The children of the labourer will be at once absorbed in industrial employment; the children of the gentry and clergy will be already launched in the great stream which, through the various channels of public schools and private tuition, and by the outlets of university distinction and professional attainment, is rushing on to the free and rich expanse of Educated Life.

The degrees given by the universities have raised some three or four schools through the country into the proud position of the English public schools. These, with supplementary private tuition, provide efficiently for the education of the wealthier classes, and if any English gentleman goes into life practically uneducated, unfit for his station, he is the exception, not the rule; the fault has been in his own circumstances or conduct, not in the means which society has furnished for the youth of his class.

Meanwhile the education of the middle ranks remains to be provided. They are above the necessity of limiting their learning-years to the earliest childhood. They have already a stake in the welfare, and a share (though too small) in the honourable duties and privileges of the nation; and have therefore a claim for liberal as well as professional education; while perhaps they neither can afford the expense nor would desire the associations implied in the present public school and college career. To them the universities are only valuable as improving the atmosphere above them; and, on the other hand, the efforts made for the education of the labourer are only interesting as they affect the happiness and usefulness of those upon whom their own position is based. Meanwhile their own special wants are not provided for, and while they look to the advantages of the higher class unattainable to themselves, and to the assistance rendered not only by the free hand of Charity, but by the strong arm of Power, to the class below them, what wonder, if a sense of injustice and isolation widens the gap which does economically, but ought not socially to exist between the employer and the labourer, the capitalist and the landowner?

To this deficiency in the means of education provided for the middle ranks of society, even more than to the claims of religious freedom, must be ascribed the pressure to which the universities themselves have been subjected, and the loud call, to which they are reluctantly responding, to open their gates, and extend the area of their foundation. But common sense knows that it is easy to spoil an old institution like an old building, by extending it beyond its capacity, and altering the characteristics of its excellence. And who can doubt that the necessary reforms and improvements of these honourable and successful seminaries will be more wisely and permanently conducted if somewhat of the pressure from without can be relieved? Fresh streams admitted through graduated inlets are beneficial, but a flood is destruction. If this view be correct it will be for the security of the higher ranks, and the preservation of those existing educational privileges to which not only they, but, through their improvement, the whole commonwealth is largely indebted, that some plan should be devised to secure adequate educational advantages for the great body engaged in commerce and agriculture, who, from property and importance, have a just claim to the assistance, not of government grants, but of public institutions and privileges.

Their present resources are to be found in such old grammar schools as have not kept pace with the public schools above alluded to*, and numerous commercial schools, conducted by private teachers, with no fixed system, and without a definite object; mere competition tending, as in other instances, rather to cheapness than to excellence. The improvement of these existing schools must depend upon the amount of publicity and honour that can be brought to certify and reward their success; and to this point I will presently advert; I only allude to them here that it may not be supposed that in suggesting additional schools I contemplate the supplanting of those now in operation. On the contrary, it appears that the increase and improvement of public schools favours the enterprise of private undertakings. But supposing the calculation to be correct, that at twelve years of age the advantages offered by parish schools must generally cease, and that with those schools the opportunities of the labouring class will also end, it remains that from the age of twelve to fifteen there will be a numerous class of children whose parents can make some sacrifice to secure for them a farther share of instruction, but whose means will be too limited to bear the whole expense of a boarding school. Those in towns or very large villages could perhaps support a day school, or share as day-scholars in the tuitional advantages of boarding schools. But a very great number of the rural population, the small farmers and tradesmen, would remain, as now, sufferers from the lack of means, and places of education. They could pay for the instruction, but not, at the same time, for the maintenance of the children away from their own homes.

To meet this want might not certain divisional schools be established on the principle that the parents should pay the amount of fees necessary for the salary of the masters; but that the maintenance of the establishment should be dependent on the industry of the scholars?

Note

* Not only have they suffered by being thrown out of competition for the open University degrees and honours; but the progress of the present principles of University reform is operating to their injury by the destruction of many close and local foundations, which had the effect of connecting counties and neighbourhoods with the influence of the great centres of education.

[26] Educational Élitism

H. Staunton, *The Great Schools of England* (1865) pp. xviii–xxi. Howard Staunton, the illegitimate son of a peer, received little formal education; he was a noted chess player and editor of Shakespeare.

England cherishes the exceptional and anomalous, and nothing can well be more exceptional and more anomalous than her great Endowed Schools. Though most of them arose when the Middle Ages were drawing to an end, they are yet in the main supremely mediæval in character, and it is difficult to see how the mediæval element can be removed without changing their nature. Utilitarianism, left to itself, would probably sweep them away altogether, and substitute an equivalent in the shape of the German *Gymnasia* or *Realschulen*. But Utilitarianism is not the highest wisdom, and these Schools have to be regarded less in themselves, perhaps, than in relation to a particular fashion of society. No English institution can be fairly measured by an ideal standard; for if so estimated nearly every English institution would be forthwith condemned. The simple question must be whether a particular institution harmonizes with other institutions, and with a certain rude, vague, yet quite intelligible something, which may be called the English Scheme of Life. The Great Endowed Schools are less to be considered as educational agencies, in the intellectual sense, than as social agencies.

In many respects they are undoubtedly defective. They neither furnish the best moral training nor the best mental discipline, nor the most salutary and substantial mental enrichment; they do not form the most accomplished scholars or the most heroic, exalted, and disinterested men, but they are the theatres of athletic manners, and the training places of a gallant, generous spirit for the English gentleman. This is the highest merit claimed for them by the warmest and most discerning of their admirers. England will, doubtless, in due time succeed in creating institutions aiming mainly at stimulating and storing the mind; but by no process of transfigurement are the great Endowed Schools likely to be rendered institutions of this stamp. To be convinced of this, let any one read the valuable evidence given before, and the elaborate Report published by, the late Schools' Commission. The Members of the Commission were notable alike for integrity and intelligence. Their prejudices – if prejudices they had – were all of a conservative kind. Eton and the other Schools were dear to them as the homes and sanctuaries of their boyhood. We are not, therefore, to deem their opinions, conclusions, and suggestions those of innovators, but the results of sound sense, and of enlightened experience, tempered by patriotic feeling. Now it is plain the Commissioners wish the Institutions not so much to be remodelled as to be amended. The Schools are still to be more aristocratical than cloistral, more classical than national. It is here that we encounter the pith and pinch of the case. How far the Schools carry out the intentions of the founders should be treated as a subordinate point, though by no means to be lost sight of. It is of vastly more importance to decide to what extent they achieve a national purpose. The aristocratical element has immense force in England. The English aristocracy is the only aristocracy in Europe which is still powerful, and even the progress of democracy adds seemingly to its strength. The aspiration of the English aristocracy is to be, not the best educated, but for practical purposes the most cultivated. This class, however, does not exist for its own sake; does not exist merely to monopolize certain privileges; it exists that it may be the national ornament and bulwark; it exists that it may crown that social hierarchy which should symbolize the hierarchy of nature.

Now it is in reference to the interests of the social hierarchy that the English aristocracy should be always contemplated, otherwise its doom may be the same as that which befell the aristocracies of Venice and of Poland. If English society as a whole is intensely aristocratic, the English Universities, the great English Endowed Schools, the English Church, the English Army, the English Navy should be aristocratic also, though still in entire subserviency to the most glorious of the national destinies. Theorising on the subject will profit little, and the English are wisely impatient of theories. But it is evident that conservative realists as the English may be, prone though they are to let the aristocratic element have its due empire, they must yet allot the foremost place to the National idea. It is not then timid conservatives, neither is it innovators, theorists, utilitarians, common-place mechanical reformers, that should deal with the Great Endowed Schools; but what we may fairly term the heart, and conscience, and reverence of the nation. If the noblest instincts of the people were consulted, they would assuredly oppose organic change in these venerable institutions, but they might demand that their cloistered aspect should be diminished, their aristocratic associations elevated, their classical power expanded and fertilized, and their national leaven and lineaments increased. The best friends of these Schools confess that they contain much that is pedantic, much that is puerile, much that is antiquated, much that is obsolete, much that is obstructive, and not a little that is barbarous, and that, like other English institutions, they are apt to confound stolidity with solidity. Let then abuses be removed; let absolute obscurantism cease, and let such improvements be adopted as commend themselves, not to superficial progress, but to the most exalted wisdom.

[27] Commercial Education, 1850

Master W. Hudson, 'On Barter' (1850). Mr Potter's Academy, Spofforth near Wetherby (Castle Museum, York).

— *Barter* —

Is the exchanging of one commodity for another, and informs the traders so to proportion their goods that neither may sustain loss.

Find the value of that commodity whose quantity is given; then find what quantity of the other at the rate proposed, you may have for the same money.

When one has goods at a certain price ready money but in bartering, advances it to something more, find what the other ought to rate his goods at in proportion to that advance, and then pro-ceed as before. ————

How much tea at 9s per ℔ can I have in barter for 4 cwt 2 qrs of chocolate, at 4s per ℔? ——

$$As\ 1\ \overset{\text{℔}}{} :\ 4\ \overset{s}{} :: \ 4\ \overset{cwt}{} \ 2\ \overset{qrs}{}$$

$$\frac{4}{18}$$

$$\frac{28}{144}$$

$$\frac{36}{504}$$

$$\frac{4}{}$$

$$20\ \overline{2016}$$

$$\overline{100\ 2}\ \text{£ 16s value of the chocolate}$$

Barter is the exchanging of one commodity for another and informs the traders so to proportion their goods that neither may sustain loss.

Find the value of that commodity whose quantity is given; then find what quantity of the other at the rate proposed, you may have for the same money.

When one has goods at a certain price ready money but in bartering advances it to some thing more find what the other ought to rate his goods at, in proportion to that advance, and then proceed as before.

How much tea at 9s. per lb. can I have in barter for 4 cwt 2 qrs of chocolate at 4s. per lb.

```
       lb   s    cwt   qrs
  As    1 :  4 ::  4     2
                   4
                  ___
                   18
                   28
                  ___
                  144
                   36
                  ___
                  504
                    4
                  ___
                 2016
            100£  16s, value of the chocolate
```

[28] Commercial Education, 1856

Master A Houseman's penmanship exercise book (letter dated 26
November 1856). Mr Potter's Academy, Spofforth, near Wetherby
(Castle Museum, York).

London 26th Nov. 1856.

Mess.rs James Duncan & Co.
Aberdeen.

Gentlemen,

*In reply to your letter of the 18th Instant
containing your kind order, we beg to return you our best thanks
and have much pleasure in informing you that the execution of it is proceeding, and in a few days we shall be able
to advise you of the shipment.*

*The improvement noticed last week as having
taken place in the Colonial Markets, has not been supported
to a greater extent than the wants of the dealers required. A
decline therefore has taken place in some articles, the
chief of which are Sugar, Tea, and Rum. The Corn
Market was, during last week, well supplied, particularly
with Wheat, and to effect sales, a decline of 2/ per Quarter
was submitted to.*

*Waiting your further commands, we remain
with the greatest respect,*

Gentlemen

Your most obedient Servants.

A. T. Houseman & Co.

Messrs James Duncan and Co   *London 26th Novr 1856*
Aberdeen

Gentlemen,

In reply to your letter of the 18th Instant containing your kind order, we beg to return you our best thanks and have much pleasure in informing you that the execution of it is proceeding, and in a few days we shall be able to advise you of the shipment.

The improvement noticed last week as having taken place in the Colonial Markets has not been supported to a greater extent than the wants of the dealers required. A decline therefore has taken place on some articles the chief of which are Sugar, Tea and Rum. The Corn Market was during last week well supplied particularly with wheat and to effect sales a decline of 2/- per Quarter was submitted to.

Waiting your further commands we remain with the greatest respect,
    Gentlemen,
            Your most obedient Servants,
                A. T. Houseman and Co.

[29] The Classical Curriculum at Rugby School in 1861 and 1895

Public Schools' Commission, vol. II, *P.P.* (1864), XX, p. 482; *Secondary Education Commission*, vol. IX, *P.P.* (1895), XLIX, pp. 404–5.

I

FIFTH FORM, SECOND DIVISION, 35 BOYS. MR. ANSTEY

Lessons and Compositions during the Year ending at Midsummer 1861

		Lessons	*Compositions*
Sunday	10¼ to 11¼.	Old Testament, history, or Greek Testament, occasional recapitulation lessons.	
	7¼ to 8¼.	Greek Testament with parallel passages.	
Monday	4 to 5.	Greek play, Homer, Herod or Demosthenes, 38 lines.	
	10 to 12.	Mathematics, with Greek Grammar repeated.	
	4½ to 6.	Latin or Greek sentences, *viva voce*, repeated at a subsequent lesson.	
Tuesday	7¼ to 8¼.	35 or 40 lines of Greek play, Homer, Herod or Demosthenes, with Greek Grammar repeated.	
	10 to 12.	Modern languages. Half Holiday.	
	12 to 1½.	Latin verse, elegiacs or hexameters 16 lines (looked over by tutors, and marked when shown up by master of form).	
Wednesday	7¼ to 8¼.	Virgil, Horace, 40 lines, Ovid's Fasti 40 lines, with Latin Grammar repeated.	
	10¼ to 11¼.	Demosthenes, or Greek play 35 lines, with Greek Grammar repeated.	
	4 to 5.	Cicero's Orat. or Livy, 40 lines with Latin Grammar.	
	5¼ to 6¼.	Latin sentences viva voce, afterwards repeated.	
Thursday	7¼ to 8¼.	Ovid's Fasti or Virgil 40 lines, with Latin Grammar repeated.	Prose copy set, and done out of school (looked over by tutors, and looked over and marked by master of form.)
	10 to 12.	Modern languages. Half Holiday.	
Friday	7¼ to 8¼.	History and Geography lesson, 12 to 15 pages.	
	10 to 12.	Mathematics.	
	3¾ to 5.	Cicero's Orations or Livy, with Latin Grammar repeated.	
	5¼ to 6.	Greek iambic copy.	
Saturday	7¼ to 8¼.	Cicero's Orations or Livy.	Prose copy on Thursday, produced and sent to tutors, afterwards (on the following Wednesday) brought to and marked by master of form.
	10¼ to 11¼.	Demosthenes, Theocritus, or Greek play, with Greek Grammar repeated. Half Holiday.	

Summary of lessons

	Hrs
Greek	6
Latin	7
Mathematics	2¾
Modern languages or Natural Philosophy	2
Divinity	2
History	1
Total	20¾

MIDDLE SCHOOL, UPPER MIDDLE FORM, FIRST DIVISION, 38 BOYS. MR. L. F.
BURROWS

Lessons and Compositions during Year ended Summer Holidays 1861

Summary of lessons	Hrs.
Divinity	2
Latin or Greek construing, with	
grammar and lines	10
History	1
Modern languages	2
Geography	1
Composition	3 or 4
Mathematics	$3\frac{1}{2}$
TOTAL	$22\frac{1}{2}$ or $23\frac{1}{2}$

MIDDLE SCHOOL, UPPER MIDDLE FORM, FIRST DIVISION, 37 BOYS. MR. T. W. JEX
BLAKE

Lessons and Compositions during the Half-year ending June 1861

Summary of lessons	Hrs
Divinity	2
Greek	4
Latin	4
History and Geography	2
Compositions	5
Mathematics	$3\frac{1}{2}$
Modern languages	2
TOTAL	$22\frac{1}{2}$

UPPER MIDDLE FORM, SECOND DIVISION, 34 BOYS. MR. A. G. BUTLER

Lessons and Compositions during the Half-year ending Christmas, 1860

Summary of lessons	Hrs
Divinity	2
Greek	4
Latin	5
History	1
Composition	5
Modern languages	2
Mathematics	$3\frac{1}{2}$
TOTAL	$22\frac{1}{2}$

II

Grade	School	Name	Form	Religious instruction (hrs)	English (hrs)	History (hrs)	Geography (hrs)	Arithmetic (hrs)	Greek (hrs)	Latin (hrs)	French (hrs)	German (hrs)	Mathematics (hrs)	Physical science (hrs)	Drawing (hrs)	Manual instruction (hrs)	Music and singing (hrs)	Book-keeping (hrs)	Shorthand (hrs)	Physical exercises (hrs)	Other subjects (hrs)	Total no. of hours per week (hrs)	Remarks
1st Grade Endowed	RUGBY SCHOOL		*Classical Side* Forms I & II	1	1	—	—	—	8	6	2 or 0	0 or 2	4	4 or 0	—	—	—	—	—	—	—	24	In Form IV the 4 hours French may be given to extra classes.
			III	1	1	1	1	—	5	6	4	4	4	2	1	—	—	—	—	—	—	24	
			IV & VI	1	2	1	1	—	6	7	2	—	4	1	1	—	—	—	—	—	—	24	
			Modern Side Forms I*-II	1	3	1	1	—	—	3	4	4	4	4	1	—	—	—	—	—	—	24	
			III	1	2	1	1	—	—	4	4	4	4	2	1	—	—	—	—	—	—	24	
			IV	1	3	1	1	—	—	4	5	4	4	2	1	—	—	—	—	—	—	24	
			V–VI	1	3	2	1	—	—	5	5	—	4	2	1	—	—	—	—	—	—	24	
			Army Class	1	1	3 or 0	1	—	—	—	3	4	9 or 6	0 or 3/4	1	—	—	—	—	—	—	24	
			Specialists	1	1	1	—	—	2	2	2 or 0	2 or 0	4	0 or 4	—	—	—	—	—	—	9*	24	* Special work in science & mathematics.

[30] Science a Poor Relation in the Public School Curriculum

Royal Commission on Scientific Instruction and the Advancement of Science,
P.P. (1875) XXVIII, pp. 59–60.

First of all, I think, really comes the very grave obstacle, that if Science
is intended to be introduced into a school at the present day, a crowded
curriculum is to be met. The curriculum in most schools is already so
large that it is taken for granted that it cannot be extended. It therefore
becomes a question of eliminating something before Science can be
properly introduced. The next question is, what should be eliminated?
And this question is one extremely difficult to be answered, or at all
events it is answered with difficulty; although if a school were merely
considered as a place of training, and not a place where useful
knowledge is imparted, the difficulty would really be seen to be a lighter
one than it is supposed to be.

It is stated at Marlborough that the boys' time is already absorbed by
studies which have of late years been largely multiplied, and which in
most cases they know to be essential to their future prospects in life,
seeing that most of them will have to be examined in all those
subjects. . . .

But the want of time, after all, is only one of the difficulties. In the old
schools the tone of the school is distinctly against Science, not so much
on the part of the Masters as on the part of the parents, and, to a great
extent, on the part of the boys themselves; and I believe it is from this
point of view (and I express my opinion with much diffidence) that the
introduction of Science into the modern sides merely of schools, whether
of this class or of any other class, will eventually be a matter extremely
unfavourable to Science. Not only will Science be looked upon as on
sufferance, but its training power will be entirely disregarded. . . .

There is ample evidence to show that where Science has been best
taught its effect upon the boys is most acknowledged. Thus at Eton, as
already seen, it is acknowledged that the subject has done good work for
the boys. At Wellington it is acknowledged that the past feeling of
inferiority to other subjects is perhaps hardly just, and I am sure that the
Head Master of Clifton College is quite willing to acknowledge the
importance of a Scientific training, although he states that a prejudice
against Science, as a new study, to some extent lingers in the minds of
both men and boys.

Another real obstacle is connected with the Science Masters. It is
stated in evidence that in the great schools the Science Masters, as a

rule, are not sufficient in number, and are not sufficiently trained. When Science has been introduced into a school, it has been introduced very much as any other subject would be – any other subject, I mean, of quite an inferior kind, and one, like most of the old studies, in which the book is all sufficient. The Science Master has faced his work, lectured to his classes, prepared his experiments, revised his note-books, prepared his examination papers, and has then either broken down, or has appealed for more help, which he has not been able to obtain.

I have referred in another section to the evidence concerning the training of the Masters, which goes to show that although the present staff of Science Masters is altogether inadequate, more might be done by the existing staff, if, as a rule, they were more conversant with the methods of teaching and experimentation. . . .

Another obstacle which is urged, and which I believe to be more unreal than is generally imagined, is the cost of introducing the new study. No doubt a Laboratory is needed; no doubt a special class room is desirable, but in many schools these requirements have been met without any additional expenditure; but when once the *locale* is found I believe that Science can be introduced at one tenth of the cost which is usually supposed to be that which is absolutely essential.

But to come back to the real obstacles, we find what I have had to refer to in other sections of my report, viz., the utter absence of an assured career for any student of Science. At Eton it is stated that the rewards for success in Classics are so great, that a boy must hesitate about endangering his progress in them, and it is difficult to reward him adequately for success in Science. Another Eton Master also refers to the belief amongst parents and Masters, that Science does not pay.

At Marlborough it is acknowledged that the demand for Science teaching amongst parents is very small. The general opinion seems to be that an ordinary knowledge of Science does not open the way for any career in the future, and that a boy is more likely to win for himself a future position by following the studies which form the main curriculum of teaching.

At Wellington the feeling that Science does not pay as well as other subjects do is also distinctly referred to.

Again let us take the case of Christ's Hospital. Most of the boys leave that school before 16, and at present there are hardly 30 boys in the school over that age. These are all aiming at University Scholarships; and it is stated by the Head Master that to these hitherto Classics and Mathematics have been found the only, or at least, the readiest, avenue.

The Head Master at Rossall not only points to the greater inducements held out by the Universities for the study of Classics and Mathematics, but he refers to the unsettled state of opinion as to what is the real aim of scientific study; and the instinctive feeling of the boys that, as at present taught, Science is not equal to Latin and Greek, or Mathematics, for educational purposes.

[31] An Elementary School's Curriculum – Clifton Road, Norwood, SE25

First Report of the Royal Commission to Inquire into the Working of the Elementary Education Acts, P.P. (1886) xxv, pp. 542–3.

INFANTS

Time given to each Subject

Subject	Classes						
	1st (h. m.)	2nd (h. m.)	3rd (h. m.)	4th (h. m.)	5th (h. m.)	6th (h. m.)	Babies (h. m.)
Prayers	1 40	1 40	1 40	1 40	1 40	1 40	1 40
Holy Scripture	3 20	3 20	3 20	3 20	3 20	3 20	3 20
Registers	50	50	50	50	50	50	50
Reading	3 30	3 30	3 30	3 30	3 30	3 30	3 30
Writing	1 0	1 0	1 0	2 0	2 30	2 30	2 30
Arithmetic (Paper or Slates)	2 30	2 30	2 30	2 30	2 30	2 30	Nil
Mental Arithmetic	1 15	1 15	1 15	1 15	1 15	1 15	1 15
Dictation	3 30	3 30	3 30	2 30	30	30	Nil
Natural History, Objects, or Geography	1 0	1 0	1 0	1 0	1 0	1 0	1 0
Kindergarten Occupations	1 30	1 30	1 30	1 30	1 30	1 30	3 20
Needlework	3 0	3 0	3 0	3 0	3 0	Nil	Nil
Needle threading	Nil	Nil	Nil	Nil	Nil	Nil	1 30
Tables or Number	30	30	30	30	30	30	2 20
Drill, Singing, Recitation	1 25	1 25	1 25	1 25	1 40	1 40	2 30
Recreation	1 15	1 15	1 15	1 15	2 30	2 30	2 30

TIME TABLE SUMMARY – BOYS

Subjects, &c.	1st class Time h.	m.	2nd class Time h.	m.	3rd class Time h.	m.	4th class Time h.	m.	5th class Time h.	m.	6th class Time h.	m.
Prayers		20		20		20		20		20		20
Registers	1	0	1	0	1	0	1	0	1	0	1	0
Scripture	2	30	2	30	2	30	2	30	2	30	2	30
Reading	3	20	3	20	3	20	4	5	4	40	4	40
Arithmetic	3	45	3	45	4	25	5	5	5	5	5	5
Spelling and Dictation	3	45	3	45	3	45	4	30	4	30	4	30
Geography and Mapping	2	10	2	10	2	10	1	20	1	30		45
Grammar and Poetry	1	30	1	30	1	30	1	30	1	30	1	30
Music		45		45		45		45		45		45
Writing or Composition	1	30	1	30	1	30	1	30	1	30	2	15
Drawing	2	10	2	10	2	10	2	10	1	25	1	25
Drill		45		45		45		45		45		45
Specific subjects (1)	1	20	1	20	1	20		—		—		—
" (2)		40		40		—		—		—		—
Play or tables		50		50		50		50		50		50
Mental Arithmetic	1	10	1	10	1	10	1	10	1	10	1	10
TOTALS	27	30	27	30	27	30	27	30	27	30	27	30

[32] Scientific Instruction at a Higher Grade School and an Organised Science School

Secondary Education Commission, vol. IX, *P.P.* (1895), XLIX, pp. 414–15. *Second Report of the Royal Commission Appointed to Inquire into the Working of the Elementary Education Acts, P.P.* (1887) XXIX, p. 1017.

School			English subjects					Languages				Sciences			Art subjects			Commercial subjects					
Grade	*Name*	*Form*	*Religious instruction*	*English*	*History*	*Geography*	*Arithmetic*	*Greek*	*Latin*	*French*	*German*	*Mathematics*	*Physical science*		*Drawing*	*Manual instruction*	*Music and singing*	*Book-keeping*	*Shorthand*	*Physical exercises*	*Other subjects*	*Total no. of hours per week*	*Remarks*
			hrs	hrs	hrs	hrs	hrs	hrs	hrs	hrs	hrs	hrs	hrs	hrs	hrs	hrs	hrs	hrs	hrs	hrs	hrs	hrs	
													C	P									
3rd Grade	Leeds Central Higher Grade Board School (Boys' Department).	4th year's course	–	1½	1	½	–	–	4¾	3	–	7	3½	2	2	–	–	–	½	½	–	26¼	The school includes an organised science school. Boys in Form I., 2nd year's course, give 2 hours, and boys in Form II., 1 hour a week to German in addition to the regular 26¼ hours. Boys taking the 3rd year's course give 1¾ hours to manual instruction on Saturday.
		3rd year's course	¾	¾	¾	–	–	–	1½	2	2	5	6	3½	2	1½	–	–	–	½	–	28¼	
		2nd year's course:																					
		Form I	¾	½	½	–	–	–	1½	2		5	5	2	2	2	–	–	½	½	2*	28¼	
													M	2									
													C	P									
		II	¾	1	½	½	–	–	1½	2	1	5	4	4	2	2	–	–	½	½	1	27¼	
													M	1									
		1st year's course:											C	P									* Geometry
		I	¾	1¾	¾	½	–	–	⅔	1¼	–	5	5	3	1½	2	–	½	½	½	2*	26¼	M = Mechanics
		II	¾	2	¾	½	–	–	⅔	2	–	4½	4¾	3	1½	2	–	½	½	½	2	26¼	C = Chemistry
		III	¾	1½	¾	½	–	–	⅔	2¼	–	5	4¾	3	1½	2	–	½	½	½	2	26¼	P = Physics

CENTRAL BOARD SCHOOL, MANCHESTER

Science School – Time Table from 1st September 1886 to 30th April 1887

Class A

Monday

9 to 9.50	10 to 10.30	10.30 to 12	2 to 3.30	3.30 to 4.45
Scripture	French	Mathematics	Magnetism	Book-keeping

Tuesday

9 to 9.50	10 to 11	11 to 12	2 to 3.15	3.15 to 4	4 to 4.45
Scripture	Freehand draw	Geom. draw	Acoustics	Mathematics	Exercise

Wednesday

9-15 to 10.45	10.45 to 12	2 to 3.15	3.15 to 4.45
Practical chemistry	Theo. chemistry	Machine construction	Geometry

Thursday

9 to 9.50	10 to 11	11 to 12	2 to 3.15	3.15 to 4	4 to 4.45
Scripture	Mathematics	Theo. mechanics	Chemistry (elem.)	French	Exercise

Friday

9-15 to 10.45	11 to 12	2 to 3.15	3.15 to 4	4 to 4.30
Pract. organic chem	Theo. org. chemistry	Physiology	French	Exercise

[33] Industrial Training in Elementary Schools

Letter of Lord Brabazon to *The Times* (11 October 1886), reprinted in his *Some National and Board School Reforms* (1887). An energetic philanthropist, the Earl of Meath was especially active in support of public parks, Early Closing, and physical education; he originated the idea of 'Empire Day'.

SIR, –A paper containing the following questions has been sent by the Royal Commission on Education to the managers of schools.

1. Is the course of teaching prescribed by the Code suited to the children of your school?

2. What changes, if any, would you desire in the (Education) Acts? in the Code? in the administration?

3. Would you recommend the introduction into your school of practical instruction – A. In any of the industries of the district? or in the use of tools for working in wood or iron?

4. B. (for girls) in the domestic duties of home?

I hope the answers to these questions will be that the course of teaching prescribed by the Code is not calculated to effect the object of education, namely, to enable boys and girls to earn their own living when they grow up, and to perform efficiently the duties to which they will be called when they reach the estate of manhood and womanhood.

I trust that the managers will point out that all boys (no matter what is their station in life) should be taught to use their hands, and that girls should be educated so as to become good housewives. . . .

The depression of trade, the misery to be found in our large towns, the drunken habits of some of our people, are in a measure owing to the want of proper training in youth in industrial handicrafts and technical arts on the part of the boys, and in household work on the part of the girls, so that able-bodied men are unable to find work, and women when they marry have no idea how to make a home neat or happy, or to make the most of limited resources. . . .

The children of our Board Schools are being taught many subjects, such as French and even Italian, which they cannot possibly retain, looking at the early age at which they leave school and the necessity which drives most of them to earn their living immediately on leaving school. A clever child who had learnt some trade well enough to earn good wages, instead of a miserable pittance, or none at all, could always learn these extra subjects, with a much better chance of retaining them, a little later in life at one of the numerous institutions where evening classes are held. In our very laudable desire to obtain for the nation a high standard of general culture and in omitting to teach them the use of the tools by which the mass of them will hereafter have to earn their living, we are unintentionally leading them to believe that the bread which has been gained by the sweat of the brow is less honourably earned than that which is the result of mechanical quill-driving. Now I am sure this was not the intention of the late Mr. Forster or of the promoters of the Bill of 1870. They did not wish to cast a slur upon labour or to make a difference in the honour attaching to different kinds of work. 'All work is honourable,' says Carlyle.

The practical result of this one-sided training is that every boy or girl on leaving school is desirous of engaging in work which is neither manual nor what is mis-termed menial. As the demand for clerks is limited, the only result of this overstocking of the supply of writers or copyists is that those who obtain employment are obliged to be content with wages which the artisan would reject with scorn, and the remainder, who are not fortunate enough to obtain the miserable pittance – well, they go to swell the ranks of the unemployed. They are useless at home, useless as emigrants, and, with bitterness and despair in their hearts, they are ready to blame everyone – Providence, society, capitalists – for the miserable condition of their existence, the real culprit all the time being, in my opinion, in a great measure the national system of education. What I have said of the boys is, with a slight alteration, true of the girls. These mainly desire to become governesses – a class notoriously overstocked and underpaid. Of the four subjects a knowledge of which is most essential to women of all classes – hygiene (including an acquaintance with the rudiments of the art of healing), cookery, household work, and needlework – only the latter is compulsorily taught at school, and that imperfectly. . . .

It appears to me self-evident that, unless we are prepared to be left behind in the competition of nations, we must follow the example of America, Germany, France, Belgium, Austria, Holland, Sweden, and Switzerland, and make technical and industrial training a prominent and compulsory portion of our educational system. . . .

In view of the present distress and depression in trade and agriculture, when all classes must exercise the greatest economy and thrift, it is imperative that our boys should be taught to labour, and our girls to become good housewives.

I am your obedient servant,

BRABAZON

[34] Clara Salter's Penmanship Book, example on Labour, June 1887 (Castle Museum, York).

Labour.

This world has work for us : we must refuse
No honest task, nor uncongenial toil.
Fear not your foot to tire, nor robe to soil ;
Nor let your hands grow white for want of use.

Clara Salter

Fulneck. June 1887

LABOUR

This world has work for us: we must refuse
    No honest task, nor uncongenial toil.
Fear not your foot to tire, nor robe to soil;
    Nor let your hands grow white for want of use.

Fulneck, June 1887.   CLARA SALTER

III. TEACHERS AND THE CLASSROOM

To the outsider all classrooms at all times look very much the same, and the concerns in the Victorian age of the public-school master and the elementary school teacher appear superficially very similar; thus [40] displays, like the documents on the elementary school, a respect for order and discipline in Harrow School as necessary means for the improvement of pupils. Yet as [51] trenchantly reveals, the teachers' tasks in the two sorts of school were performed within quite different assumptions and constraints. In the public school, master and pupils had the same view of the purpose and value of the schoolroom. In the elementary school parents and pupils often failed to share the teacher's attitude towards education, and the regular attendance thought necessary to ensure it [41, 49].

Conflict with recalcitrant pupils and parents added an extra dimension of difficulty to the elementary head-teacher's life. Teachers themselves often lacked formal education and a self-confident culture; they were young and inexperienced, and sometimes scarcely older than their pupils [46]. As a result one perennial concern of the educationist and the principal was the need for system, organisation and an almost military precision in the classroom [35, 36].

The immaturity and working-class origins of most entrants to elementary teaching encouraged authority to provide a training which in every detail registered deference, subordination and paternalist control [42, 43]. At the same time their ignorance, as much as the endless problems of their job, fostered a concentration on teaching them all the knowledge deemed necessary for their pupils eventually to learn, and on the practicalities needed to impart it successfully [43, 45, 46]. For teachers brought up so closely in leading strings it was natural to provide books of ready-made lesson plans. Our example [37] reveals the assiduous categorisation and pedantry of so much Victorian instruction. It could have been the framework for an interesting lesson, but only if it were given by a teacher knowledgeable enough to do without the book. As used by many, it provokes the justified criticisms of [38], and Edward Thring's moving rejection of ratiocination in favour of intuition and empathy [44] – though Thring does not really propose a feasible and convincing way to train people so that they might achieve them.

If their arid formal education sufficed to confer competence in very similar ways of instructing children, it leaves mysterious the excitement some teachers managed to create in their classroom, and the passionate love for their task which survived the slow millstones of routine. For many, it seems clear, the inner self was nourished by private reading, to whose existential significance several witnesses testify [46, 49]. By turns inspired by noble vocation and downcast by mundane grind, the teacher's self-image was ambiguous and changeable [47]. Doubts were aggravated by uncertainties of social status, for which complaints over pay, though themselves real enough, were often a mask [50]. This blurring of self-definition reflected in part society's confused attitudes. A quasi-sacramental view of the teacher's role was common. But only rarely was it held to entail true partnership with the clergy. Most often, teachers were seen as filling a lowly place in a firm hierarchy, as artisans of moral instruction and the copybook [48, 51]. Meanwhile, even kind and intelligent inspectors could be blindly ignorant of the difficulties of the teacher's life – the refractoriness of children's minds and the slow pace of possible progress [39]. By the world outside, the classroom was little understood.

[35] Work and Discipline in the Monitorial School, 1810

Epitome of Joseph Lancaster's Inventions and Improvements in Education (1810) pp. 40–5.

OF ORDER AND COMMANDS

It is unavoidable, on a large scale of education, to do without giving many commands, and some of a very trivial nature. On my plan, many of the commands, which would be given by the master, are given by the monitors. As it is not proper that commands, without number, and perhaps of a nature opposite to each other, should be given at random by the monitors, it becomes needful to limit the number that are to be given, as much as may be. It is an important object to secure implicit obedience to those commands on the part of the scholars: and, for the monitors to acquire as prompt a manner in giving them, as will secure the attention of the classes, and lead them to a ready compliance. The first of these objects is easily attained. It is only to write down on paper the commands most necessary to be given by the monitor to his whole class; and, it is essentially needful, that he should not vary from the rule once laid down. The general commands common to all schools are detailed in the Appendix.

The practice of giving short commands aloud, and seeing them instantly obeyed by the whole class, will effectually train the monitor in the habit of giving them with propriety. Thus, for instance, 'Front,' 'Right, or Left;' '*Show Slates*, or clean *Slates*,' are all things that must be occasionally done in school. Having a series of commands applicable to the duties of classes and of a school, is only defining what already exists in the nature of things, and which would be done in a vague manner unless so defined and commanded.

The classes should learn to measure their steps when going round the school in close order to prevent what else would often occur from their numbers, treading on each other's heels, or pushing each other down. In this case, measuring their steps commands their attention to one object, and prevents their being unruly or disorderly. It is not required that the measure should be exact, or be a *regular step*; but, that each scholar shall attempt to walk at a regular distance from the one who precedes him. When a new scholar is first admitted, he is pleased with the uniformity, novelty, and simplicity of the motions made by the class he is in. Under the influence of this pleasure he readily obeys, the same as the other boys do. None of these commands are in themselves, an hardship; and they are well supported by the force of habits easily acquired, from the circumstance of being congenial to the activity of the youthful mind. The power of example greatly facilitates the establishment of order. Children are mostly imitative creatures: they enter a new school; they see all in order around them; they see promptness and alacrity in obeying every command that is given; they do as they see others do, by the influence of their example. Before the effect of novelty is worn off, new habits are formed; and the happy children who are trained under the mild and generous influence of the British system of education, learn obedience with pleasure, and practice it with delight, without the influence of the rod or cane to bring them to order. . . .

Paper of Commands on Coming Out to Shew Writing

Out. Front. Look – (to the Right or Left, by a motion made with the hand by the commanding monitor.) – Take up Slates. *Show Slates.* – (Here the monitor inspects.) – Left hand Slates. Right and Slates. Single. – (In a line.) – *Double.* Step forward. Step Backward. Go. Show Slates, to the Master, or Inspecting Monitor.

On Returning to the Class

Look.   Go.   Show Slates.   Lay down Slates.   In.

On Going Home

Out.   Unsling Hats.   Put on Hats.   Go. . . .

Rules for Appointing Monitors of Tuition

First, the monitors appointed must understand, and be quite perfect in the lessons they are to teach, as to good reading and spelling.

Secondly, they must understand the mode of teaching.

Thirdly, in the first five classes, monitors may be appointed from the next superior class, to teach the one immediately below it. Thus the second, or two-letter class, will furnish monitors who may teach the first, or alphabet class; the third will supply monitors for the second; the fourth for the third; and the fifth for the fourth; the sixth class will supply a choice of monitors for the fifth, for itself, and for the order of the *school*. *Under* the seventh class, each class will supply boys to teach the class below it; this will ground the monitors in the lessons they have themselves last learned, by the act of teaching them. From the sixth class upwards, the classes will supply boys to act as monitors, and teach themselves; the teachers of the sixth, seventh and eighth classes, may be chosen out of the said classes, as any boy who can read can teach; the art of tuition, in those classes, depending only on the knowledge of reading and writing. The system of inspection of progress in learning, as it respects the scholar, is *only* on *his* part mental; neither inspection nor the mode of instruction require any other qualification, on the part of the teacher, than the mere art of reading and writing, united with orderly behaviour.

Of Monitor's Tickets, Superintendant's List, and the Office of Monitor-General

Every monitor should wear in school a printed or leather ticket, gilt, and lettered thus: – Monitor of the first class – Reading Monitor of the second class – Monitor of the third class, with variations for Arithmetic, Reading, Spelling, &c.

Each of these tickets to be numbered. A row of nails, with numbers on the wall, marking the place of each ticket, to be placed in every school-room; the nail numbered 1, being the place for the ticket No. 1. When school begins, the monitors are to be called to take their tickets; every ticket left on a nail, will shew a regular monitor *absent*, when an occasional monitor must of course be chosen. . . .

All the monitors should have a written or printed paper of their 'Duties,' which they should particularly study, and repeat once a week. Those duties, which are the same in all schools, and which apply generally to the mode of teaching, may be had *printed, as see the APPENDIX, containing a list of things wanting in the outfit of a new school.* These duties each monitor should paste in the books belonging to his class. The larger series of papers on the duties of monitors, should be read for a class lesson by all boys selected as regular, or auxiliary monitors, in order to prepare them, by a knowledge of their duty, for the proper discharge of it.

[36] Organising an Elementary School

National Society Monthly Paper (June 1851).

May I ask if any schoolmaster has yet found such important depart-ments as reading, arithmetic, and writing, make satisfactory progress when left entirely to the care of pupil-teachers? It seems to me to be of

the last importance, and to be the basis of all progress, that the reading
should be under the immediate superintendence of the master. Reading
cannot be called a purely mechanical, but rather a highly mental
exercise. But I must ask, again, how is a master thus circumstanced to
guide and develope the teaching powers of his apprentices? When and
how are they to acquire skill in oral teaching? A rather varied
experience in teaching brings me to the conclusion that, under ordinary
circumstances, any system which confines the entire time and energies
of the master to one place and one class of instruction for the whole
school morning is defective, and unless his teachers be advanced,
radically so. . . .

I must first say we have three rooms: one (now having a gallery added
to it) used for oral teaching, but not exclusively; one used generally as a
reading room; a third for writing. There are 100 children, mixed; and
the younger ones are drafted off as an infant class. The school is divided
into three classes; each class having daily an oral lesson, as set forth in
the enclosed time-table: two of them in the morning, one in the
afternoon. The first hour in the morning is devoted to reading by the
upper classes, superintended by the master, aided by one pupil-teacher
and one child monitor; the lower classes are at other work under the
mistress and the assistant. During the second hour the master gives his
gallery lesson to the second class, while the first class are at the desks.
The third hour is occupied in oral lesson to the first class, while the
second are at the desks. The lower classes have their gallery lesson
during the first hour in the afternoon, after which the master is at liberty
to superintend the work at the desks, and the reading of the lower classes
in turn. It will be seen, then, that our school is divided into three
divisions (besides infants); we have three rooms, each appropriated
generally to its particular branch of instruction, one of them being oral
teaching. The whole school comes in turn under this teaching, which is
always given by the clergyman or master. Here ends our obligation to
the Tripartite system. Our modification of it differs, then, in the
following respects from that at West Ashton. The master regularly
superintends the reading of the upper classes, and occasionally that of
the lower. There are only two oral lessons, of about fifty minutes each, in
the morning, and one in the afternoon. No children monitors are
employed, excepting one for reading, the school being divided into five
sections for this exercise. Our staff of teachers are four, viz. master,
mistress, and two pupil-teachers. For some lessons, such as tables, &c.,
the lower classes are united under the care of the mistress and one pupil-

teacher; the two pupil-teachers taking turn, to enable one to be engaged with the master in the superintendence of the first and second classes. I must add, the work is so arranged that one of the pupil-teachers is invariably present at one oral lesson daily; a plan I consider absolutely necessary to their proper instruction. It is not presumed that this arrangement is perfect, or approaching to perfection; but so far as it goes, it has answered well. I shall be thankful for any suggested improvements.

In conclusion, I feel constrained to say we can hardly hope for any *national* plan of teaching till we are supplied with a suitable and uniform series of books. Valuable as no doubt Mr. Moseley's suggestions are as to teaching, infinitely more valuable are the propositions he has put forth respecting the preparation of a series of school books. Let us hope his suggestions will take a form, and result in the production of such a series of works as may render our teaching more uniform and more effective. – I am, &c.

THE MASTER, *St. Buryan National Schools.*

NOTE.– At the suggestion of her Majesty's Inspector, Mr. Tinling, I sometimes unite the first two classes for the oral lessons. I am not sure that it answers: it is right, however, to add, the number in those classes is much larger than at the time of his visit.

The following table will shew what the children are doing each portion of their school-hours; and, of course, children kept at home during any part of school-time will lose the lessons given in that time.

GENERAL TIME-TABLE

FIRST CLASS

Morning				Afternoon			
Hour		Lesson	Length lesson	Hour		Lesson	Length lesson
9 0 to 9 20		Prayers	20	2 10 to 3 20		Copying, &c.	70
9 20	10 0	Read	40	3 20	3 50	Tables	30
10 0	10 50	Write	50	3 50	4 0	Playground	10
10 50	11 0	Lessons	10	4 0	4 10	Spell	10
11 0	11 10	Playground	10	4 10	4 55	Cipher	45
11 10	11 55	Oral Lesson	45	4 55	5 0	Dismiss	5
11 55	12 0	Dismiss	5				

	Morning					Afternoon		
Hour		Lesson	*Length lesson*		Hour		Lesson	*Length lesson*
9 0 to 9 20		Prayers	20	2	10 to 3	0	Lessons	50
9 20 10 0		Read	40	3	0 3	20	Tables	20
10 0 10 50		Oral Lesson	50	3	20 3	50	Read	30
10 50 11 0		Playground	10	3	50 4	0	Playground	10
11 0 11 55		Cipher	55	4	0 4	55	Write	55
11 55 12 0		Dismiss	5	4	55 5	0	Dismiss	5

	Morning					Afternoon		
Hour		Lesson	*Length lesson*		Hour		Lesson	*Length lesson*
9 0 to 9 20		Prayers	20	2	10 to 3	0	Oral Lesson	50
9 20 10 0		Spelling	40	3	0 3	20	Repeat Lessons	20
10 0 10 50		Write on Slates	50	3	20 3	50	Tables	30
10 50 11 0		Playground	10	3	50 4	0	Playground	10
11 0 11 55		Read	55	4	0 4	55	Read	55
11 55 12 0		Dismiss	5	4	55 5	0	Dismiss	5

	Morning					Afternoon		
Hour		Lesson	*Length lesson*		Hour		Lesson	*Length lesson*
9 0 to 9 20		Prayers	20	2	10 to 3	0	Scripture	50
9 20 10 0		Write, Slates	40	3	0 3	20	Repeat Lessons	20
10 0 10 50		Read	50	3	20 3	50	Tables	30
10 50 11 0		Playground	10	3	50 4	0	Playground	10
11 0 11 55		Hymns	55	4	0 4	55	Read	55
11 55 12 0		Dismiss	5	4	55 5	0	Dismiss	5

The Oral Lessons are on various subjects, including Scripture, Liturgy, Geography, Grammar, History, and Vocal Music.

[37] Notes for an Elementary-School Lesson on Elephants

Handy Book of Object Lessons (1875). The lesson seems to have been designed for ten-year-olds.

THE ELEPHANT

Matter	*Method*
I Locality Elephants are found in Asia, Africa, Hindostan, and parts of Further India, or India beyond the Ganges;[1] but they are most frequently met with, in a wild state, in Africa.	There is a very large animal which is generally to be seen in a wild beast show: What is its name? The Elephant. [1] Show these countries on the map.
II Description of the Elephant (*a*) *Size.* The Elephant is the largest animal we have. It varies in height from 7 to 10 feet.[2]	[2] Compare with objects in or near the school to give the children an idea of the size of an elephant.
(*b*) *Body.* Very bulky – weighs several tons and is covered with short bristles.	
(*c*) *Head.* Very heavy – sometimes weighs 300 lbs.[3]	[3] Considerably above two cwts. (The upper classes might work the sum on the Bk. Bd.)
(*d*) *Neck.* Very thick and short.[4]	[4] Why? Shew the result if the elephant had a *long* neck.
(*e*) *Trunk.* Serves both as a nose and also as hands. It consists of a number of elastic rings, and is so made that it combines great strength with the utmost delicacy of touch. By means of it the elephant is enabled to tear off large branches of trees, pick up a pin, untie a knot, or open a door. The trunk is also its chief means of defence.	
(*f*) *Ears.* Pendent[5] and very large.	[5] What does this word mean? Elicit other animals having pendent ears.
(*g*) *Tusks.* Common to both sexes. They are generally from 4 to 6 feet long, and are composed of solid ivory.	[6] Why? To support the body.
(*h*) *Legs.* Very thick and straight, like pillars.[6]	

III Habits
When wild, elephants wander in vast herds. They are very fond of bathing, and are there-

fore often found in or near the water, where
they frequently wallow in the mud[7] and afterwards repose beneath the shade of some forest
tree. Their food consists of vegetables, shrubs,
and the branches of trees.

When tame, they are fed on hay, roots, &c.,
but will eat cakes, fruits, nuts, &c., and are
often taught to perform a variety of tricks, such
as ringing a bell, untying a knot, &c.

Elephants are docile, but they are also very
revengeful of injuries (illus.: the tailor of Surat.)

IV How Captured
A herd is surrounded by hunters, who drive the
elephants into an enclosure. Here they are
bound to trees, beaten often by tame elephants,
called 'decoys,'[8] kept without food for a week or
a fortnight, after which they generally become
docile.

V Uses
(1) As beasts of burden[9] or draught, especially in time of war, when they are made to
pull heavy cannon along the rough roads of
their native country.

(2) To assist in launching vessels. (Give the
story of one which was reproached by its master
as a 'lazy beast.')

(3) The ivory of their tusks is made into a
variety of useful and ornamental articles.

[7] Why? It cools them: the
countries in which they are
found being very hot.
(Comp.: boys bathing in
summer.)

[8] Why? Because they 'de-
coy' or entrap the wild ones.

[9] What are beasts of burden? Elicit names of such animals in this country.

[38] HMIs' Comments on Object Lessons
The Teachers' Aid (22 December 1894)

INSPECTORS ON OBJECT LESSONS

The introduction of a new compulsory subject into the Code is looked
upon with considerable misgiving by a large number of teachers. The
Inspectors' views and methods bulk so largely in the success or failure of
any school, that it is a wise proceeding, when breaking new ground, to

know what these officials have to say on the subject. Their wide and varied experience should make them valuable guides into the unknown.

It is with the intent to place before teachers what to do and what to avoid that the following notes on object lessons have been extracted from recent Blue Books.

Of the ignorance of the teachers – chiefly, we presume, of the pupil teachers, whose lessons the Inspectors are supposed to hear – we have many complaints.

Mr. Mostyn Price notes a lack of knowledge in the two subjects –(a) Simple phenomena of nature, (b) Lessons on familiar scenes.

Mr. Fowler deplores 'the strong tendency with unskilful teachers to *rote* work.' 'Certain facts,' he says, 'in a set form of words, are learnt by heart by frequent repetition, and this has a deadening effect on the intelligence of the little ones.'

Mr. Williams says: 'The object lessons are apt to be mechanical and wanting in interest and information, and the reason is that the teachers who give them do not know enough about the subjects to make their lessons instructive and interesting.'

Mr. Kinnersley, in a very lively paragraph, inveighs strongly against the emptiness and puerility of many of the lessons to which he is condemned to listen. He says: 'The absolute inanity of the ordinary instruction in these subjects fills the Inspector with despair.'

'The cow which coils its long tongue round the blades of grass and tears them off; the reindeer which lives on snow; the camel which lives in the sandy desert; the ostrich which lives on iron nails; . . . These are the denizens of the infants' mistress' Noah's Ark, and their amazing habits are handed down by tradition, or recorded in a textbook of object lessons, to which, as to an inspired work, she refers the sceptical examiner.'

Formality is a Deadly Sin – and most of the Inspectors have something to say on this point; but they also recognise the fact that 'the object lesson is a severe test of teaching.' The object lesson is not a *lecture*, but a lesson.

Methods – Scattered up and down the pages of the Blue Books are many hints of what the Inspectors look for in these object lessons.

Mr. Brodie, in summing up the opinions of his colleagues on this subject, pleads for the proper

(1) *Grading, grouping* and *adapting* of the lessons. He says: 'What is more objectless than an object lesson given at random, and one day on cotton; another on the elephant, still too much supposed to be always

picking up pins with his trunk; and again on rain, on the railroad, on the Post-office. All needs *grading, grouping* and *adapting* to the different ages.'

(2) *Tracking out the How and the Why.* Mr. Parez, speaking on Elementary Science Lessons, urges that the experiments should be given for definite ends, and laments that 'no real attempt has been made to cultivate in the scholars the habit of tracking out the *how* and the *why* of everything that comes under their observation.'

(3) Lessons should be *observational, experimental* and *conversational*. Mr. Turnbull says: 'In order to teach the scholars to observe, the teachers themselves should receive some training of their observing faculties.'

Mr. Barry finds 'that in some schools the object lessons are still lectures in which the children are not called upon to take part. . . . Sometimes they are given without any objects or pictures, so that the scholars have no opportunity of exercising any observation for themselves.'

Mr. Brewer hopes that care will be taken that the Elementary Science Lessons are 'not verbal, or at best pictorial, but observational and experimental.'

Mr. Holt White strikes the note of the newer teaching when he bids us remember that 'children are naturally most inquisitive little creatures if their imaginative faculties have their play, and it should be the object of teachers to stimulate this natural and laudable curiosity by giving suitable conversational lessons, combined with plenty of questioning upon such objects as they are able properly to illustrate, rather than dull formal lectures which may be easy to give, but which do not in the least interest the little children or engage their attention.'

(4) The lessons must be illustrated by *pictures* – the *objects* themselves by *models* of the *objects* and by *blackboard sketches*. Almost every Inspector who writes on the subject notes a lack of illustrations. Mr. Airy, however, has a few cheering words of praise for the teachers in his district.

'The power of illustration by rough chalk drawings is being actively and successfully cultivated. Object lessons are now not very often mechanical and unheeded lectures to listless, if credulous, sufferers, but brightly illustrated conversations "to children who watch the teacher's chalk with open eyes."'

(5) *Language Lessons*. Mr. Turnbull hopes that 'the object lessons will be used for the development of *power* to *use language*.' And he warns teachers not to suppose that when this power to express clearly and correctly the result of the lesson is wanting, the power to *think* is present.

He would have one 'daily conversational object lesson or other lesson in speaking.'

[39] A Headmistress Gives Her Views on a Diocesan Inspection
Cambridge, Park Street School Log Book, 17 April 1889 (Governors of the Old Schools, Cambridge).

Scripture Examination to-day.
Exam conducted by Rev. A. Stokes & Rev. – Clarke.

The classes examined by the Rev. A. Stokes were worried very much by his incessant worrying if *every* hand was not out. 'Two or three hands not out'. 'Back row not answering' (perhaps only 1 out of the 12 had her hand down) 'I want every hand out'. These were the constant remarks from the Inspector, tiring out the patience of the girls who could answer *every* question, and worrying those who were not so fortunate.

A great deal of time was thus wasted – not one subject being thoroughly examined except the Catechism, upon the repetition of which in the Upper Standards I consider too much time to be wasted.

Mr Clarke got through a great deal of work, as he did not seem to expect *every girl to answer every question.*

Both Inspectors were exceedingly kind and courteous. The questions mostly were fair. A few that would be much better omitted will be copied in this book.

3rd Std. Children from 8 upwards – 'What did the Israelites help to build?' *Pyramids* was answer required, but which I need not say was not obtained.

This same Std. was also asked how many years after Joseph did Moses live?

The 1st Std. – children of 6 and 7 in giving answers about our Lord's Temptation, were required to answer in the exact words of the Bible. This requiring far too much of children who had only been out of Infant room 5 months.

The Infants were asked 'How are we to be saved from our sins?' The children gave 'By Jesus' blood', but the only answer Mr Stokes would take was 'By *faith.* This was a similar question to one given to infants last year. What do you mean by the '*Trinity*'?

[40] Discipline and Character-Building in Harrow School, 1879

Edward D. Rendall and Gerald H. Rendall, *Recollections and Impressions of the Rev. John Smith M.A.* (1914) pp. 43–8. Smith took the First Fourth (the third form from the bottom of the school) at Harrow. What follows are instructions to a master taking his form for a time.

THE FIRST FOURTH

1879.

The first day of term. – On Friday at first school after having collected the Form into your room make them sit down in Bill Order: tell them what lesson to prepare for 11 A.M. (Greek would be best). Let the old boys go; keep all the others who are new to the Form, and give them a few words of advice; never to be late for 1st school; always to speak the truth; to be frank and straightforward; always to have clean hands, neat hair, and well-brushed clothes; and to avoid all ornaments except the simplest *little* pin for their necktie. Read out the List of Books to them that they may get the necessary orders from their Tutors.

At 11, keep at the end all who are new to the Form. Have a number of slips of paper in readiness to save time; give each boy one. Tell him to write down in full his surname, all his Christian names; his birthday and age this year (1879); what he is or what he will be in the coming months; his House and Tutor; his direction at home. When they have finished call up each in Bill Order; read over what he has written to be sure there is no mistake, let him go. When alone copy all these papers carefully into your mark book.

For evening exercise. – The New Boys to write an autobiography. Where they were born, brought up; what they have done and *suffered*: it is very important to know Boys' illnesses or accidents as soon as possible.

[Look this over at leisure, so as to keep each case as individual as possible.]

The Old Boys to write an account of their holidays. Tell the New Boys that they must have all their books stamped at the beginning of the second week. Take no excuse.

Repetitions have generally been written out; but this is not a good plan; feeble health compelled me to adopt it, but I shall rejoice in knowing this temptation to unfairness does not exist. Let them be said *viva voce* as you think best. Turned repetitions are the most wearisome and hateful part of our work. I have always devoted Monday 12–1 and Wednesday 12–1 to the purpose of hearing them. A turned repetition can always be heard a verse at a time or two lines at a time. Only they must be heard somehow; or the whole tone of the Form is lowered.

The *Greek Reader* is worth 200 marks. Take off 2 for every mistake, Gk. or Eng., 2 for every accent or iota subscript left out; subtract 5 for each erasure, 5 for each word not honestly looked out. It is a great trouble to me to find some Boys putting fictitious meanings again and again to avoid trouble. Do not punish them, for they are young, but impress upon them the solemn duty of truthfulness and accuracy in looking out their words.

Punishments. – For talking or eating in Form send a Boy to the bottom; for repeated bad exercises send him to Extra School. Do *not* set lines, if you please; they injure the writing and do no good. Prayer, patience, forbearing threatening; [above all, the Son of Man came not to be ministered unto but to *minister*;] these will help you wonderfully. Then always see a boy's Tutor before you punish; and often a troublesome Boy becomes a Friend by a quiet chat about home over a cup of tea in your rooms. Hospitality is a great source of good discipline.

In the course of the 1st Fortnight ask those who cannot swim to stand up: make a mark against their names; and from time to time inquire what progress they are making: when the whole Form was reported able to swim I used to go down to the Bathing Place at the end of July; see each Boy *jump* in at 5th Form end, and swim across. If I were satisfied I gave them a first school in honour of it. [I rely upon you to *make* every non-swimmer learn.]

Officers. – As soon as possible appoint the officers for the Term, letting Boys choose in Bill order, except the head boy who *ex officio* always supplies you with Books; opening them at the proper place, and showing you where the lesson begins. You must also ask some very good writer to provide you with a card of the Form every Sunday at 3 P.M. for registering answers, repetitions, etc., and some other good writer to give you a list of the Form on plain paper every Monday at second school.

Two Boys to supply bands for exercises. [They buy them themselves because it is for the public service.]

Two Boys to supply pencils. [When you want a new one for looking over exercises.] [These must be H.B. costing 1*d*.]

Two Boys to be special messengers: most necessary office: praise them warmly when they are prompt, and never let them return *re infecta*.

Two Boys to be Watchmen or Timekeepers. To remind you when to stop for prayers or marking.

Two Boys to act as Memory; to remind you about setting exercises, or

giving them out: or asking certain questions of public interest. [If Y–
does not get his remove, ask him with my love to be first memory again;
he did it admirably last term.]

Two Boys to collect exercises on Sunday mornings and Chapel
mornings or whole Holidays; fellows who are sure to be in time; and
able to say NO to any petitioners with late exercises.

Two Home-boarders to pick up papers etc., on alternate days at the
end of each school, so that the rooms may be perfectly free from litter.

Two Sanitory Inspectors to attend to windows and doors; get rid of
unpleasant odours, etc.

If ever any officer wishes to resign through pique, because he has
failed and been scolded, *never* accept his resignation. Tell him he is a
public servant with no right to resign; and comfort or scold him as you
think he requires.

Watchwords of IV.1, to be read out at the beginning of Term, and when
any New Boy joins. Also to be applied constantly as occasion requires.

1. It is as easy to be a minute too soon, as a minute too late. [N.B. –
You must never be late yourself.]

2. Cleanliness is next to Godliness. [Look at the hands at first school
before beginning actual work, and send away any with dirty nails; in
the summer there is no excuse; they go to the bottom when they come
in.]

3. A difficulty is a thing to be overcome. [Never let them say, 'I
can't.']

4. Duty before pleasure any day.

5. The richest man is he who has the fewest wants. [Drive this into
them for future years.]

6. He who returns the blow is really he who begins the quarrel.
Latterly was added:–

7. Never put off till to-morrow, what ought to be done to-day.

Some time during the first month ask each Boy for his Motto: make
him explain it to the Form. If not, explain it yourself when possible. The
half-hour so spent is very interesting, and sometimes very valuable to
stimulate.*

Ministry etc. – Ask the Form from time to time the names and offices of
the different ministers: and any important events. Expect them to know
the chief picture in *Punch*; and any portraits in *Illustrated* or *Graphic*.
Read to them when you like about gallant deeds such as those of Chard,
Bromhead, Melvill, Coghill; tell them to pray for a man under a cloud,
like Lord C. See that they know who Sir Wm. Harcourt is, John Bright

and other vigorous speakers. Take them through the names of Shakespeare's Plays: Milton's Poems; Scott's Novels; Dickens, if you like; Thackeray, Lord Lytton; great musicians; great painters; great engineers; anything to stimulate their minds, and call out dormant interests.

N.B. – In looking over exercises, *never* have any arrears. If possible look over each set on the day on which you receive them. *Marking exercises*. An abstract of Scripture or History is worth 80, *if finished*. Take off five for every proper name misspelt – the same name not counting more than three times: five for every erasure: five for absence of date, or absence of stops. If the exercise is not honest, only a little bit of each chapter given, or only a part instead of the whole lesson set, give no marks, and speak very earnestly to the defaulters about the danger of scamping their work: its ruinous consequences in after-life; if well written, well done, and no *erasures*, add ten or fifteen or even twenty if first-rate.

J. S.

Note

* 'I well remember one school which he gave to family mottoes. To my own, *Suivez Raison*, he gave the vigorous translation 'Follow the Right,' and preached an eloquent sermon on it, but his words were still more burning when the next boy gave him *Nil Desperandum*.'

[41] An Elementary schoolmistress at Odds with Pupil and Parent, 1884.

Log Book of Harlton School, Cambridgeshire (June 1884).

June 20th James Mace has not been this week.

24th This morning James Mace refused to hold out his hand for the cane so I caned him on the shoulders. I had not hit him before he turned round and tried to kick me, in fact he did kick, though he did not hurt. I did not send him home but punished him for it. The Revd. O. Fisher being ill I did not send for him. At noon the boy being kept in, his mother came in a frightful passion fetched her boy and abused me in a frightful manner.

24th I sent a monitor for a policeman when she departed with her boy.

25th This afternoon James Mace made his appearance at school. I kept him out of his class, but he did his class's work and was well behaved. He did not know his geography lesson, so was kept in partly for that & partly to make up for being taken away the day before. His mother came again and fetched him away, being very impertinent in the use of her language. The reason of this outbreak is this. She will not send the boy to school but keeps him at home to nurse. I have sent his name to the Attendance Inspector; therefore the woman vents the displeasure she feels at being obliged to send him on me. The boy is $10\frac{1}{2}$ & has not passed third standard yet. . . .

The people here are so enraged at having to send their children to school that they put them up to rebel so that they should be turned out and be able to go to work.

[42] Discipline and Instruction in a Teachers' Training College, 1852

Homerton College, Cambridge, archives. Until 1895 the college was situated in east London.

HOMERTON COLLEGE RULES [1852]

The following Rules have been prepared with a view to promote the comfort and future welfare of the Students of Homerton College. It is confidently expected that every Student will maintain a spirit and deportment worthy of his profession as a Christian; and, under the influence of the highest motives, conform to the prescribed regulations, promote order and harmonious feeling, and that universal propriety of conduct, which is so intimately connected with the success of every Student, and the reputation of an Institution whose position in public estimation should be constantly regarded by all its inmates.

In all cases not provided for in these Rules, it is understood that the permissions specified are only to be obtained from the Principal, or the Mistress, and, in their absence, from such parties as they may have appointed.

General Arrangements

The Students in the male department will, except on Sundays, use the Eastern side gate between the hours of 8.30 A.M. and 5 P.M.; and, at other times, the principal front door of the College.

The Students in the female department will use the western front door of the College, but will have access to the Practising Schools from the garden.

The Students in the female department returning after 8.30 P.M., and the Students in the male department after 9 P.M., are required to enter by the principal front entrance, and to insert their names in a book kept for this purpose. All the Students are expected to be within at the time specified, unless permission to return at a later hour has been obtained.

No Student is at liberty to go out after 9 o'clock, P.M., without permission; and it is expected that the evenings be conscientiously devoted to study. . . .

Dormitories

The Students are expected to rise at 6 o'clock, A.M., and to retire to rest at 10 o'clock, P.M.

The Students in the male department are not to go, *under any pretence*, to their Dormitories between the hours of 9 and 12 o'clock, A.M.; *and not to use them, at any time, for the purposes of study.*

No Student is at liberty to have a candle in the Dormitories or Class Rooms, or to light the Gas after it has been put out by the Censor.

Duties of Censor and Monitor

Every Student in rotation is to act as Censor for one week. The Censor is to ring the bell, and knock at the doors of the bed rooms at the time for rising; to put out the lights in the Class Rooms at 10 o'clock, P.M., and the lights in the Dormitories at 10.30 P.M.; to endeavour always to preserve order and general propriety of behaviour; and to report any violation of the Laws of the College.

A Monitor in each class will be appointed to see that all the Students in the class are present at the times fixed for their meeting; to lower the Gas when the Students leave the Class Room, to prepare the Lecture Room for the duties of the class, to maintain diligence and order, and to keep the Class Room neat.

Meals

The Students are to take their meals in the Dining Hall at the appointed times, viz. – Breakfast after family worship, – Dinner at 1 P.M. – Tea at 5.40 P.M. – and Supper at 8.45. On the first Sunday in the month, the dinner-hour will be 1.30 P.M., and on Saturdays at 2 P.M. No student will be allowed to have any meal except at the stated times, without express permission.

No Student is allowed to introduce any friend to the Class Rooms, or to any meal.

The Servitor is to ring the bell ten minutes before, and at the time of each meal. It is expected that the Students will make suitable preparation for their appearance in the Dining Hall, take their appointed places promptly and orderly, and avoid all conversation during meals. . . .

Family Worship

The Students are required to be present at family worship, 8 o'clock, A.M., and 9 o'clock, P.M., and to provide themselves with Bibles, and hymn and tune books.

Sunday Arrangements

Every Student in communion with a Christian Church is expected to bring a letter from his or her pastor, which will secure occasional communion with some Church in the immediate neighbourhood, and to continue in fellowship with that Church while resident in the College.

No Student is allowed to remain at home on Sunday during the time of Morning or Evening Service, without permission. No visitors are allowed on Sundays.

HOMERTON COLLEGE TIME-TABLE–FEMALE STUDENTS

A.M.

		7–8	Teacher	9–10	Teacher	10–11	Teacher	11–12	Teacher
Monday	1.	Spelling & Dictation	J. G.	History	L.	Arithmetic	J. G.	Geography	S. G.
	2.	Ditto	„	Grammar	S. G.	Com-position	P.	School Manage-ment	L. S.
Tuesday	1.	Botany	P.	Grammar	S. G.	Com-position	S. G.	School Manage-ment	L. S.
	2.	Physio-graphy	S. G.	Arithmetic	J. G.	Domestic Economy	J. G.	History	L.

P.M.

		12—1	Teacher	2—3	Teacher	3—4	Teacher	4—5	Teacher	6—7	Teacher	7—8.30	Teacher
				2-3.30		3.30—5				6-6.45		7—8.30	
Monday	1.	Domestic Economy	J. G.	Private Study		Recreation				Private Study			
	2.	Geography	S. G.	Ditto		Ditto				Ditto			
Tuesday	1.	Repetition & Reading	S. G.	Recreation		Singing		V. M. Private Study		French	L. S.	Private Study	
	2.	French	F.	Ditto		Private Study		Singing	V. M.	Private Study			

PART TWO: DOCUMENTS173

[43] Learning and Living in a London Teachers' College, 1875

Report of the Board of Education for the year 1912–13, P.P. (1914) XXV,
pp. 51–5.

. . . during the seventies, the students, about 130 in number, had no
place for recreation worthy of the name, no library and reading-room;
no pictures appeared on the walls of the dingy class-rooms, and there
were no facilities for sitting out of doors or meeting in the open air.

The paved yard of irregular shape, surrounded by forbidding walls,
was all too small even for the ordinary drill exercises taken once a week,
in two sections; whilst the small and badly-equipped gymnasium could
only be used by a few men at a time – the enthusiasts in boxing and
Indian club exercises. In short, it may be said that the College
authorities made practically no satisfactory provision for physical
exercises and games.

Recreation took the form mainly of walking through the neighbour-
ing streets for an hour before dinner and half-an-hour before tea.

The ordinary class-rooms were used for recreative reading after class
hours, and few men could find a comfortable place in which to sit, and
in winter the fires could be approached by only a small section of those
who needed warmth and brightness. Magazines and newspapers were
purchased by the students from funds subscribed by them and handed
to a committee of some of their fellow students, duly elected to perform
the necessary duties.

Similarly, concerts and debates were organised by the men, and these
(all of them interesting, some ennobling) took place at regular intervals
after the classes were closed for the day. The resident superintendent
took a personal interest in these meetings, and the men were
encouraged by his presence and commendation. The principal classroom – 'The Theatre' – was used on such occasions.

The men slept in cubicles, separated by wooden partitions some 6 feet
high, arranged in long rows down the corridor 'landings.' The rooms
were plainly furnished, but scrupulously clean. No real privacy was
possible; and during the winter the bedrooms were subjected to
draughts and were bitterly cold.

On Saturday afternoons and evenings no restrictions were placed on
the men. Some spent their time with acquaintances or relatives residing
in London, many visited the parks or other places of interest, the
majority walked about rather aimlessly, a few participated in the sports
described above. At 9.30 p.m. each man had to return in time for

prayers and roll-call, except, at his parents' request, he had obtained a half-hour's or an hour's extension of time for visiting friends at a distance and locomotion was difficult.

Sunday, too, left all the men free, providing they attended some place of public worship. Each student had to fill in a solemn declaration on the following Tuesday, as to where he had spent the morning, afternoon, and evening of Sunday. There is no reason to believe that the confidence of the College authorities was seriously misplaced in the case of the men generally, for most of them had come up from homes where the religious observance of the Sabbath was a part of the very lives of the parents.

This freedom gave opportunities to thoughtful students to hear the more celebrated preachers of the day and to discuss them afterwards. It is an interesting fact that the majority went to Church.

During these years no serious breach of the regulations is remembered. Amongst so many men drawn from towns and villages, N., S., E., and W., there may have been a few undesirables, but their influence scarcely affected the majority of self-respecting and thoughtful students.

Slight breaches of the rules were only natural, such as sitting up to talk (or even sing) after the lights were out, or smoking within bounds in the dark corners of the ill-favoured yard – this was a cardinal sin, but one that perhaps was discreetly overlooked. The men, it must be remembered, were at lessons all day, they had no real chance to take reasonable recreation, or cultivate friendships by social intercourse. These law-breakers – the smokers – were amongst the best of the men and the conditions might almost be held to condone their offence. Ailing men were expected to see the doctor when he called. Students suffering from colds, &c., could obtain from the housekeeper a ticket which enabled them to receive each a basin of porridge (or gruel) from the kitchen, and permission was granted them to retire to bed before the regular time. Strong men, well-muffled up round the throat, secured what they wanted; more timid fellows were told to drink cold water.

Some brief notes as to the instruction may be added.

The Principal of the College taught Scripture, History, English Grammar and Literature, and Chemistry and Latin and French, assisted by the Vice-Principal. In each subject the method was soulless. For 'Scripture,' pages of useless 'notes' were dictated at high speed, and of the few men who transcribed them, still fewer ever read them afterwards. The annual College Examination included questions upon the Scriptures, and most of these questions were well within the grasp of men who had read their Bibles from childhood and so were well calculated to satisfy the College Committee as to the effectiveness (?) of the scriptural instruction; but few references to the dry notes upon which much valuable time had been wasted, were known to appear. . . .

The instruction in Music, Geography and Physiology was left in the able hands of a devoted tutor who will always be gratefully remembered by those who were fortunate enough to sit under him. His memory was phenomenal and his logical marshalling of facts, his graphic presentation of all things are still matters for wonder. His patience with men who seemed hopeless in musical matters and the encouragement he gave to them, raised many to hope that they might in time overcome their natural defects, and often the hope was not in vain. The lectures in Geography and Physiology were as realistic and informative as the limited resources of the College allowed. Above all, the tutor's high sense of duty reflected on and animated the men, and he has been to many of them an exemplar and a friend in the years that have since passed.

The training in practical teaching consisted of –
    (1) Weekly lectures in 'Method.'
    (2) Preparation of 'Notes of lessons.'
    (3) Practical work in the Schools.
and   (4) Criticism lessons before the officers of the College, and some of the students of his year.

The Master of Method was, in his day, regarded as at the head of his class. His personality counted for much – every student respected him, and perhaps feared him a little, though his efforts were conspicuous in the sincere desire to uplift the children through the teacher – the teacher, high-minded, well-equipped and expert.

His lectures were welcomed by the classes and dealt mainly with the practical work in the everyday Elementary School, methods of teaching each subject, plans for organisation, hints on discipline, and the like.

Although Psychology was not dealt with *as a subject*, the master was full of suggestion as to mental processes and their development in the Elementary School, from his own reading and more so from his own intelligent observation and his more than usually fruitful experience.

The directly practical portions of these lectures were afterwards published in book form, so that the influence of this master served a wider purpose outside the College walls at a time when such instruction was most required by the rapidly growing world of elementary teachers who had to help themselves. The book has served its purpose well.

Each student spent a fortnight (?) in the Practising School and was in actual charge of a class. The lessons of the school syllabus were taught by him, after due preparation during 'private study' time in College. The 'notes of lessons' were carefully written out; indeed, an undue amount of time was spent in elaboration, in designing and illustrating the subject page of the 'notes.' – (This system, at least made men careful and methodical.)

Whilst in school the students were under the constant supervision of one of the assistants who reported to his chief the success or failure of each student's efforts.

The 'Criticism' lessons given before the officers and fellow students proved to be a greater ordeal than the daily work in school, especially where men had not been accustomed so to teach during the years of their apprenticeship as pupil-teachers. The lesson was drawn by lot a week beforehand and the class to be taught was brought into the 'Theatre' of the College from the schools.

Students made notes on the lesson given; (Language used, illustrations, sequence, &c., &c.) and some were asked to read their criticisms. The officers followed with their own comments; marks were given by each officer and added to the student's College record in due course.

[44] Edward Thring's Views on Teacher-Training

From a letter to the Vice-Chancellor of the University of Cambridge, 22 February 1878 (Cambridge, University Department of Education archives). The headmaster of Uppingham School was replying to an enquiry about the desirability of training secondary-school teachers in the university.

I would however dismiss at once all thought of making learners study the history of education and its rival systems as part of the process; and all thought of examinations in the bookwork of the subject.

This kind of headwork appears to me to be utter treason to the truth. The first thing to discard from a teacher's mind is the idolatry of knowledge, and to get him to understand that mind-treatment is his subject, and that the power of adapting himself to a stupid mind is alone teaching power.

The worse the material the greater the skill required in the teacher, should be his motto, and St Augustine's axiom 'that a golden key which does not fit the lock is useless, and a wooden key which does is everything' should be engraved over every schoolroom in England. There is much bungling of golden keys, and much destruction of locks. Let book-knowledge then and examinations be set aside.

There remains the fact that both Universities possess gentlemen of practical experience as teachers of schools, and always will do so. If those gentlemen gave the result of their experience in lectures, and explained the kind of minds they found had to be dealt with, and by what various methods and devices they reached them, much good might be done. If they showed how to interest, to reward, to punish, to get pupils in a state to listen at all, and drew constant attention to the high artistic excellence of teaching as teaching, the minds of men would at least be open to the great truth that how to get at thoughts and feelings is the problem of a teacher, not how to put a subject in a clearcut form. There might then possibly be a glimpse of the truth that the most perfect and flawless statement of a subject may be the worst teaching, and proceed from a mind incapable of ever becoming a teacher's mind; inasmuch as severe and accurate outline of statement is oftentimes the exact opposite to that gentle, searching forbearance, that tender regard for weakness, which humbles itself to the pupil's level, and is not satisfied with turning the blaze of a knowledge lantern on the outside of the shut door of the mind.

[45] The Pupil-Teacher's Life: Rote-Learning about Gibraltar

Moffatt's Pupil Teacher's Course. Second Year (1888) pp. 112–13, 178–9. Typical pages from a book for fourteen-year-old trainees.

GIBRALTAR

Situation   Gibraltar is situated at the entrance to the Mediterranean Sea, on a rocky promontory connected with the Spanish peninsula by a narrow sandy isthmus. The rock is strongly fortified, and commands the entrance to the Mediterranean. It is about 1,150 miles from Southampton.

Extent and Population   Length, 3 miles; *breadth,* ¾mile; *area,* 1¾ square mile. Population, about 25,000, including the English garrison. The population varies considerably, according to the number of British soldiers present at any one time.

Physical Features   The rock rises to a height of about 1,450 feet, and is inaccessible on the north and east. On the west it slopes gradually down to the Bay of Gibraltar. This being the vulnerable side, it is defended by fortifications of enormous strength. The rock itself is excavated into galleries containing guns of great strength. The southern extremity is called Europa Point.

Occupations of the People   Agriculture is carried on to some extent. The climate being warm, southern fruits are cultivated. The commerce is considerable, mostly with England. The *imports* are upwards of £1,100,000; the *exports*, £100,000. Much smuggling is carried on in the port of Gibraltar, to the great annoyance of the Spanish authorities.

Productions   Not very important. Southern fruits, as oranges, figs, etc., are grown. There are some wild animals, as rabbits, partridges, apes.

History   This rock was known to the ancients under the name of Calpe, one of the Pillars of Hercules. It belonged successively to the Romans, Saracens, Spaniards, and English. The latter came into possession of it in 1704, when it was captured by Sir George Rooke. The Spaniards have made several efforts to recover it, but unsuccessfully. From 1779 to 1782 it sustained a memorable siege by the combined French and Spanish fleets and armies; but was gallantly and successfully defended by General Elliott. In 1842 it was constituted a see of the English Church.

Town   The town of Gibraltar lies at the foot of the rock, on the north-west. The harbour is not good, being exposed to the winds and the sea. The trade is chiefly in manufactured goods imported from England. The nearest Spanish town is Algesiras, lying on the other side of the Bay of Gibraltar, at a distance of 5½ miles.

Miscellaneous   Gibraltar is connected with England by means of steamships and the electric telegraph. It is one of the packet stations on the route to India through the Suez Canal.

Questions for Examination

The following questions are selected from previous Government Examination Papers:–

1. Show, as you would to children, what articles in ordinary use for breakfast are imported from British Colonies . . .

14. I have friends coming home from China, South Africa, Queensland, Malta, and Jamaica. What presents is each of them likely to bring home as specimens of the productions or workmanship of the country?

15. Draw out full notes of a lesson to a Fourth Standard on Gibraltar, its position, physical features, history, and importance. Illustrate your notes by a map of the coast line from Cape St. Vincent to Cape Palos.

16. Name the British possessions in Asia, describe the position of each, and say how it is valuable to this country.

[46] The Pupil-Teacher's Life: Teaching Standard III in Swindon, 1890

F. H. Spencer, *An Inspector's Testament* (1938) pp. 74–86. Spencer became an HMI and then Chief Inspector for the London County Council.

My father was one of the type of skilled artisan not by any means uncommon, men of intelligence with intellectual interests which they are only partly able to exercise. 'Going to college' appealed to him, and he hardly discriminated between Balliol or Trinity and a Training College for Teachers then in the back streets of South London. Moreover, I should not have to tumble out of bed at 5.15 in the morning in winter to be 'at my work' by 6; and there would be more than a week's holiday in the year. So a pupil teacher I became. It was for me a natural avenue of employment. I had no overweening desire to be a fitter and turner, nor even a pattern-maker. An engine-driver, willingly. But the would-be engine-driver must begin as an unskilled 'cleaner' on a lower social plane than the skilled mechanic, so that career was barred by unquestioned social convention. . . .

So far as the academic side was concerned, my pupilage was largely a fraud. The Code laid down that a pupil teacher was to have at least one hour's instruction a day from the head master, who apparently could delegate this duty, or part of it, to certificated assistants. In our school these 'lessons' purported to take place every day from Monday to Friday inclusive from seven to eight in the morning. 'Shonnie' himself was down for Wednesday mornings. One or other of the assistants attended on the other four days. In fact, 'Shonnie', who took English, chiefly grammar and the reading of a play of Shakespeare, could be relied upon never to arrive before 7.30. On the other mornings things varied according to the conscientiousness of the various masters, of whom the more intelligent were, as a rule, the less conscientious. . . .

For two of the assistants – those who successively took mathematics and could really teach me something – I usually arrived by 7.30. The first of these was a really clever man of two- or three-and-twenty, who had a fine academic mind. Had he got to one of the old universities, I am sure he would have been a distinguished scholar. I admired him also because he was one of the best and most capable handlers of boys I have ever known. Unfortunately he remained during only half of my apprenticeship, securing a better post in one of the growing suburbs of outer London. A hundred pounds a year in a London suburb was a very great improvement in livelihood and life on £70 a year in Swindon. We lost our more capable men to London and the large towns. . . .

On no other side did I get any real education. There was no one to teach me any language but my own, though I picked up some French in an evening class, and one of 'Shonnie's' assistants started a rather futile class, after school hours, in Latin. This was abandoned in a month or two because four out of the five of us could or would make no progress, and our teacher himself had but a fragmentary and fallible knowledge of the language. In history we just learned facts out of a date-book. And I got some background out of Scott's novels. Geography was a thing of names, meaningless, wearisome names, and our instructor was dull, stupid and conscientious beyond words. We learned topographical fact by teaching: so I usually cut the instructional geography morning. I can still recite all the rivers of Asia from the Obi and Yenesei round to the Euphrates, for didn't I drill the list into Standard VI in the year 1890? . . .

Pupil teachers, however, were regarded not as pupils or students, but primarily as teachers; and I was plunged into the pedagogic business at once and at the top of the school. The 'science class' of a year or so earlier had enlarged itself into a class of thirty, who had stayed on, though eligible to leave school. The class was just one of the old grant-earning Science Classes held under the South Kensington Department, long before its amalgamation into the Board of Education. Anyhow, it was taught by a respectable and hard-working assistant, who had several 'first-class advanced' South Kensington certificates, and whose business it was to get as many elementary 'passes' as possible out of his present pupils. For each pass was worth 30s., and thirty passes in two subjects would mean £90. In the achievement of this high aim I was to assist. The class did elementary algebra and geometry, and, as a separate subject, 'Practical Plane and Solid Geometry', science subject 1 in the nomenclature of South Kensington, if I rightly remember. They also took physiography, as I had done, a subject (and not a bad one) invented, I believe, by T. H. Huxley to cover a general study of the external physical world. I could easily coach part of the class in the 'science' which I had 'done' a year or so earlier. And, you will notice that 'Agriculture' had been dropped as too blatantly unsuitable for those whose certain future was an engineering workshop. So we plodded on. I helped those boys, a year younger than myself, to solve simultaneous equations, and I supervised their practical plane geometry, and I did odd jobs, such as giving out papers, correcting exercises, and multiplying test papers on a jelly-graph. Occasionally the class was left to me; and little disciplinary trouble arose: for the master, a serious and efficient person, if not present, was in the offing, I was not unpopular, for I was still sergeant-major of the school battalion, was 'Shylock' in the Trial Scene, a good cricketer, and an effective if clumsy footballer. Moreover, I was by this time a big, boney lad, and the tendency to manslaughter exhibited in the playground a year before was not unremembered.

This, however, lasted only a few months, and was my last experience as a helper rather than as the responsible teacher of a class. In each succeeding year I had a class of my own; and I remember very clearly that in three successive years they were Standards 111, v and v1. Our 'standards' (years or forms we should call them now) were large, usually numbering, until the top of the school was reached, some 120 boys.* This number was divided, unequally, into three classes, taken respectively by a certificated assistant, an 'ex-P. T.' and a pupil teacher. Practice varied somewhat. But a typical arrangement was that the P. T. took about thirty of the best boys, who would in any case be likely to pass the annual examination, the ex-P. T. would have about fifty of the mediocre pupils most of whom would probably pass, and the remainder, the forty worst, who needed real hard work, would be taken by the certificated master. To the least-experienced and least-qualified teacher the best boys. The best-qualified man usually devoted himself to the hard but necessary task of getting 'the duffers' through the examination. That was how things worked out in a large school under an annual examination and payment by results. . . .

So I went on for nearly five years, in the matter of knowledge owing

almost nothing to the farce which was called instruction, getting some
fragmentary knowledge of mathematics and science by working with
assistant masters anxious to get more 'sciences' to their credit,
devouring literature, chiefly classical novelists, Scott, Dickens,
Thackeray, George Eliot, not forgetting W. H. G. Kingston and
Talbot Baines Reed, because I found these entrancing, picking up odd
knowledge from the *Boy's Own Paper*, and from *Whitaker's Almanack*,
learning a little French at an evening class (one night a week attended
intermittently), failing to learn to play the piano, but becoming
passionately interested in such music as was available at that date in
that town; withal teaching hard five-and-a-quarter hours every day,
and subconsciously absorbing the craftsmanship of the trade, I was
without proper intellectual discipline or any scholarly criteria, or any
standard of comparison except with two fellow-pupil-teachers of the
same vintage as myself, who were decent, companionable lads: but I
somehow realised by occasional intercourse with others outside my
elementary school world that there were lamentable deficiencies about
my kind and me.

Note

* The effect of the law of school attendance at the time was this. In Standard v
there would be 120 boys, in vi about eighty to ninety, in vii and Ex. vii together
about thirty.

[47] A Working-Class Intellectual and his Private School, 1830

Life of Thomas Cooper, written by Himself (1872) pp. 72–6. Cooper
(1805–92) was a self-educated shoemaker, later prominent in the
Chartist movement.

A good constitution and the skill of my kind physician, under the
blessing of the Almighty, enabled me at length to leave the sick bed. But
I was very weak for some time; and when I attempted a little manual
labour, it brought on a peculiar nervous tremor that almost frightened
me, and which compelled me to desist, time after time. My friend
Hough, and my acquaintance – who afterwards became a dear friend –
Charles Kelvey, took counsel together, and proposed to me that I
should try the profession of a schoolmaster. I agreed, for I felt I could
not work again on the stall; and they sought out a large club-room
which was already furnished with forms and boards, that would serve

for desks, and made themselves responsible for the rent for the first half-year. I issued handbills; and on the tenth of March, 1828, just ten days before I became three-and-twenty, I opened school.

My school was eagerly patronised by the poor; and I had a few of the children of the middle-class. People in the little town had been talking for years about the remarkable youth that was never seen in the streets, and was known to wander miles in the fields and woods, reading. He was believed by some to be a prodigy of learning; and they would send their children to be taught by him. In the course of twelve months I had a hundred scholars on my list, had an average attendance of eighty, and had to think of engaging an assistant.

If it could ever have entered into my nature to set about making money, now was my first 'good chance.' But it could not, and never will. I have had several 'good chances,' since that passed away; and I could never make use of them, or suffer such a purpose to enter my mind. We cannot all 'make money,' although it is necessary that somebody should. I have said, and said it solemnly, that I cannot 'make money,' and I do not believe that anything which could possibly happen to me in the world could turn my nature into the path of money-getting. But there is something besides that I cannot do. I cannot avoid throwing my whole nature into an undertaking, when I once enter upon it, either from a sense of duty or for self-gratification.

My school was a perfect passion with me for a time. I was in the school-room often at five in the morning until nine at night, taking my meals in a hasty, imperfect way, while the boys were gone home to take theirs. I had quill pens to make in great number, the first work in the morning; and for a time I had early classes each morning. Then again, in the evenings, although other day-schools broke up at five, I drew the elder scholars around the globe, and described the countries upon it, until a late hour, or talked to them on some part of history, or described the structures of animals, or, to keep up their attention, even related a story from the 'Arabian Nights.'

I spent at least fifty pounds on the walls of the large club-room, by covering them with pictures of every imaginable kind, and filling the corners with large plaster figures and busts. The sill within every window of the school-room was fitted up with small divisions, so that the boys might have a miniature museum of pebbles, coins, etc. I was intent on making their school-room their delight. The pictures fastened themselves on the eyes and brain of one poor boy, John Spicer, the child of a lowly shoemaker. That child did some wondrous things, as beginnings, in art. He was a born genius, and would have gained distinction had he lived.

Four children of an officer of excise were entrusted to my care by their father; and the two elder boys were an important trust. They were highly intelligent, were ripe in arithmetic, and in the school where they had been learning Latin had been put into Horace. But I found the advancement was false. They really did not know what they were about. I did not understand the custom of helping lads out with one half of their translation, and yet never showing them how to translate. I had learned no old teachers' tricks.

So I placed Cæsar's Commentaries before them, and taught them how to select the nominative in each sentence, then the verb, and then the noun governed by the verb, and so on, until they became happy labourers at the book, because they understood it, and felt they were achieving something worth talking about. They also commenced the study of Euclid, daily; and so I had a stimulus for keeping up my knowledge of Geometry and Latin, in those two pupils.

There was no desire on the part of the parents of any other pupils in my school, that they should learn Latin. But I wished to teach it to all. Soon, I had copies of declensions and conjugations written out on sheets of paper, with lists of the prepositions, and so on; and gave them to a good number of the boys to commit to memory. And to the very last day of my life that I sustained the office of daily schoolmaster, I had the declensions, or conjugations, repeated by the boys, as they stood in class, every morning. The Latin Accidence, I may say, is so firmly fixed in my memory, from hearing these daily repetitions, for about nine years of my life, that I think I could as soon forget my own name as forget any part of it.

A few of the boys to whom I thus taught Latin gratuitously made such promising progress as to enable me to form them into a separate class for the translation of Cornelius Nepos. But the great body of them were never able to construe a Latin sentence. They had no taste for it themselves; and they had no stimulus at home. The stupid listlessness of the parents of my pupils was, indeed, my hindrance from the first; and, in time, it produced disgust.

'I want our Jack to larn to write a good hand. What's the use of his larning Latin? It will nivver be no use to him.'

Such were the kind of thanks I had from the poor, when I tried to benefit their children, without any cost to themselves! After the few boys had passed away who had been my first scholars, and I had to begin anew with dull intellects, amid harsh discouragements from their parents, I lost the passion for my profession as a schoolmaster; and I began to feel it, what I fear thousands beside myself have felt it to be – unwelcome drudgery.

[48] An HMI's View of the Teacher's Task

Minutes of the Committee of Council (1846), John Allen's report, *P.P.* (1847) XLV, p. 76.

Unless our teachers be living in the fear of God, and be struggling to do their work as that which has been allotted to them by Him, and in the faithful discharge of which they may confidently look for spiritual help, all the pains that may be bestowed on our educational establishments are comparatively useless. It is acknowledged that right moral training is the first object to be aimed at: but what means are so effectual to this end as the example of the teacher? Children are acute observers, and it is notorious that they learn more by the eye than by the ear; a gesture or a glance will set their imaginations at work; they expect also a sort of perfection in those who are set over them as their guides: most careful, therefore, should we be to do all in our power to avoid that shock to their moral sense which must result from the observation of gross faults in those whom it is their duty to respect. *Maxima debetur pueris reverentia.* It is remarkable also how much skill in the production of merely intellectual results is attained by those whose qualifications may have been originally scanty, but who love their work, and persevere with zeal therein. After visiting a school of humble pretensions in a village in Hertfordshire, where the teaching seemed to me to accomplish, in an admirable manner, the highest purposes aimed at by such an in-stitution, I was very much struck by the observation of a lady who was daily at work therein, rendering cheerfully her unbought services, who said to me, 'We endeavour to train these children aright for what will be required of them hereafter, assured that if we succeed in this, they will not be found deficient in the discharge of those duties that may be required of them here.'

My desire that teachers should realize the responsibility of their position has led me to regard with extreme jealousy any proposal that might seem to limit the services of a schoolmaster for the poor to the communication of secular instruction; unless the teacher feels that he is intrusted with the training of the noblest part of the child's nature, I do not believe that, in ordinary cases, the most serious men will give themselves to the work of school-keeping. Certainly the teacher who regards mainly the intellectual development of his pupils, loses that which is a great solace to such as, on the highest grounds, follow this calling. It may be considered wearisome to be day after day before an irregular class of half-reclaimed urchins teaching them that twice two are four; and, under the most favourable circumstances, the school-master's calling is necessarily a harassing one, involving, when honestly persevered in, a great expenditure of spirit and energy; but if the teacher, standing at his class, feels that the little ones around him are his flock, whom he by his care and industry may be the means, under the Chief Shepherd, of feeding and guiding to their future and enduring, as well as their present and transitory wellbeing, surely he will have hope and encouragement in his work: as he is intrusted with a talent of the highest value, he will feel that if he be faithful in the use thereof he will receive at the last the highest reward. Such an one may be expected to crave more of that support which is given to all that rightly ask for it, and without which nothing that is truly good can ever be accomplished by man. Such an one, moreover, as it seems to me, ought not to be fettered in the exercise of his discretion as to the occasion, manner, and extent of such appeals as he may deem needful to be made to those motives which must be most effective with his pupils, their fear and love of God, and their regard to His written will. The schoolmaster of the poor ought (in my judgment) to be trusted with the most important teaching of the poor – a fellow-labourer with the minister of religion. If the schoolmaster be not so trusted, many favourable opportunities for dropping here and there seed which may prove fruitful in infinite good, will, as I think, be lost. Commonly, those observations that seem to rise spontaneously, and that take children by surprise, produce impressions more lively than direct teaching; they are remembered by us, and acted upon during all our subsequent lives.

[49] Training and Teaching in Wales, c. 1850

J. H. Davies (ed.), *The Life and Opinions of Robert Roberts, a Wandering Scholar, as told by Himself* (Cardiff, 1923) pp. 256–60, 283–5. Roberts was born in 1832.

As Bob Evans said, we were a very miscellaneous lot. Two or three were tolerably well educated, could write grammatical English, and knew some Latin and Greek; but the greater number were much less advanced, although the previous examination prevented the entrance of any so deplorably ignorant as some of my old fellow students at Bala. There was but one teacher, the Principal, and in consequence we were taught in one class for most subjects. It is true that the Master of the Model School, Mr. Foster, used to give lessons in the evenings, but he was too ignorant for his lessons to be of any use. We had also a Music Master, whose weekly lessons were equally void of beneficial result. Our principal was an active hard-working man, somewhat given to follow the newest crotchet out of the papers for the schoolmaster, or some such authority, and a little desultory in his teaching; but he had plenty of energy, and was a good man at bringing up the ruck to a fair state of proficiency. The chief fault I found with the system was that I had not enough work; it was so easy to get up the ordinary lessons, and I had no encouragement to work systematically for myself. However, I did work, to some extent, and made considerable progress, especially in mathematics, for which, the Principal, being a Dublin man, had a liking.

One week out of six was spent at the 'Model School' for the purpose of obtaining a practical knowledge of the art of teaching. As a rule, this we greatly objected to as a waste of time. The Model Master was looked upon by most of us as something of a humbug; we knew that he was very ignorant in book-learning, and had no faith in his capacity for imparting knowledge; we thought the he had picked up a few dodges, and by unblushing cheek imposed upon the public, who thought him a wonder. And the Caernarvon boys were so thoroughly savage in their manners, and behaved so rudely to the 'Trainers' as they called us, that our attempts at teaching them were on the whole a grievous failure, and the week at the school was a weariness of spirit. If we attempted to chastize any of these promising pupils, we were sure to have a crowd about us on our way home; enraged women volleying Billingsgate, and their precious offspring volleying stones after us. Appeal to the Head Master was useless, for he would say that this unpopularity only indicated our want of efficiency as teachers. When I went to Caernarvon first, this street war was almost an everyday occurrence; one or two timid students were frightened away. As we saw that it was becoming intolerable, we signified to the Headmaster that we must henceforth take canes in our own hands, and fight them into good behaviour, cost what it may. We had a tremendous conflict for about a week, but our determination carried the day; and we had something like peace.

We were, of course, Church schoolmasters, but there was not one of us who had any previous Church teaching. Indeed, I do not think that there was one of us who had been brought up in the Church of England from infancy. We were all a sort of converts, mostly from Methodism, and if we had any religious teaching it was a Dissenting sort. Now here was a fine field for instilling Church principles. We had thrown away old beliefs and associations, and wanted some new definite teaching to replace the old. But there was not the slightest attempt at any dogmatic teaching. Our churchmanship was of the evangelical sort, low, and slow; the teaching of the Prayer Book was eschewed as dangerous, and savouring of Puseyism, which was worse than Dissent and next door to Popery. Anything more meagre than our Liturgical lessons cannot be conceived, and it would be hard to find anything more cold and lifeless than the service in the genteel English Church which we were forced to attend. . . .

I had been at Caernarvon four months when the Principal received notice that an examination would be held at that town in a month's time for Certificates of Honour. Several schoolmasters had already sent in their names as candidates, but there was some difficulty about student candidates, for the college had not long been established, and there were very few of us likely to pass. The Privy Council made a certain grant for each student that passed: hence the Secretary to the College Committee (I believe the funds were low that year) was very anxious that some of us might obtain the desired honour. Still it would not do to have too many candidates plucked, so there was a preliminary examination of the more advanced students for the purpose of selecting candidates. The result was that only three were declared eligible, Bob Evans, myself, and another. I was at first reluctant to go in, thinking my youth a barrier. I was only sixteen, but the Principal over-ruled my objections, and I consented. I was sorry that I had not received longer notice, as I might then have worked harder, and prepared for it, but as there was no help for it, I did my best to make use of the month that remained. Bob and I worked early and late, Sundays included, but the range of subjects was too wide for us to do much with all of them in that space of time. I tried the most approved "crams" and worked at them vigorously for a few days, but fortunately I abandoned that system as useless, and confined myself to those subjects in which I felt myself most deficient, trusting to my general knowledge for the rest. . . .

On my return from Caernarvon, my schoolroom was finished, and a few days afterwards, it was opened. It was a large building, capable of holding about three hundred children, and there was a good house adjoining. The population was so great that though there were three other large schools within a mile, we entered 300 names the first day, and it soon appeared that a still larger building would be required. A large number were very young, and had never attended school; very few could read or write, and there was a roughness of manner among them which was rather repelling. But I was fortunate enough to obtain the services of some elder boys and girls, who were of great assistance to me in teaching, and the youngest children being placed under the care of a mistress, my work was much lightened. Still, it was a heavy undertaking for a youth of seventeen: the strain upon the physical powers was great, and the responsibility of such a charge was greater than I could well realise, but I had sufficient confidence in myself and entered upon the work without fear or hesitation. I worked very hard, and succeeded in getting my assistants to work hard, too: the visible progress was small and slow, and I was at times a good deal disheartened at the apparent disproportion between the improvement and the labour bestowed, but it came at last: in about a year's time the school was brought into a fair state of efficiency. I found a considerable amount of unreasonableness among the parents, unreasonable expectations of rapid progress, silly complaints about trifling matters of discipline, and other little disagreements of that sort: but that annoyance wore away as the parents acquired confidence in me. I also found that the more I was known to the parents, the less difficulty I had with the children; this encouraged me to cultivate their acquaintance. They were rough, and what is called unmannerly, in their conduct and conversation; but the roughness was all of the outside: at heart they were a friendly social people. The men were generally intelligent, fond of reading, much given to polemics and politics: for labouring men who had received but little early education, they were the best informed people I ever saw. The women were greatly inferior to the men. They married young, were very ignorant, coarse, given to incongruous finery, and spoiled their children sadly. I was amused to see the mothers bring up their children for enrolment on the opening day, with their mouths full of toffee, India rock, or other sweetmeat, and thought it a pity they could not be sent to school as well as their offspring. My female assistant, a married woman, lived in my house, and cooked for me. . . .

I was in receipt of an income much more than sufficient for my wants, and absolute necessaries were cheap at Bethesda, consequently there was a larger sum at my command than I had before possessed. The few debts I had contracted were paid. I was enabled to assist my parents with their rent, and to give my brothers and sisters a helping hand. I had no inclination to spend money on clothing and finery, but I was tempted to be extravagant in books. I bought a large number during my two years' stay at Bethesda: good, bad, and indifferent, for there was not much care taken in the selection. Neither were the books on the whole, what may be called 'useful books': they were odds and ends, very miscellaneous. There was an old edition of the *Encyclopaedia Britannica*, a number of volumes of *Blackwood*, bought for waste paper, a Barnes commentary on the Bible, a few classical authors, and a good number of historical works. There is no knowing how far this recklessness in book-buying might have led me if it had been long indulged in, but I had a horror of debt, and when to my horror I found myself with a balance on the wrong side at the end of the first half-year I 'pulled up' and bought no more for a long time. There was a circulating library at Caernarvon which supplied me with abundance of reading matter at a cheaper rate than buying the books, and I usually found one of my neighbours who would accompany me in a walk to Caernarvon on a Friday evening.

[50] The Schoolmaster's Position in Society

National Society Monthly Paper (April 1851).

SCHOOLMASTERS' SALARIES

March 4th, 1851

SIR, – Upon perusing your Paper for March, I find a letter bearing the signature of the Rev. W. Ewart, the purport of which, I presume, is to bring before the readers of your truly valuable paper, and particularly the managers of schools, the inadequate remuneration which school-masters receive for their labour. So kind an introduction of a subject at once so necessary and so important to all schoolmasters, coming from an influential source, deserves our grateful notice. I am enabled from practical experience (as doubtless are hundreds of others) to confirm the statement made by the Rev. W. Ewart, that schoolmasters are the worst remunerated class of persons in society. To make the subject appear more clear, I will venture to trespass upon your space for a little matter of fact. I have, with a sister, been conducting a school for 40*l.* per annum, with house and coals. Now if I ask the agricultural labourer what he would do with such an income as I have enjoyed, he would doubtless, upon a sensible knowledge of a certain number of mouths at home, exclaim with a sigh, 'I wish I could get it.' But if I ask my fellow-schoolmasters what they would do with it, those who, unfortunately, have had courage to test their constitutions upon it will assert, 'We cannot do with it; it is not sufficient for food, raiment, and many other additional expenses entailed upon us by our office.' The obvious and well-known distinction between the position of a schoolmaster and a labourer will supply ample reasons why one can, and the other cannot, live on such an income. But why is the schoolmaster not better paid? Because, it will be argued in certain localities, they have no funds. In others (and there are very many still existing of this sort), only so much has been given for so many years; what so and so lived upon others can live upon. But what does this shew? I certainly think it looks very like careless indifference to the office, or to the person who fills it. That till within these few years, any poor, lame, deaf, decrepit, or broken-fortuned man who was likely to require a share of the poor-rates, was considered fit for the office of schoolmaster, is a well-known fact. Necessity being the parent of invention, the most beautiful little salaries were invented that can be imagined, and these in many cases, out of love for old customs, have been continued. But the day is past when the office of schoolmaster was looked upon as a lightener of rates and a species of parochial patronage; the day was when the village schoolmaster was considered as a kind of toy, only safe in his office while he pleased all. But, thanks to the rapid strides of education, the dignity of the office is daily increasing. The schoolmaster is now better educated and instructed in the duties of his calling than heretofore; and I am quite sure, in the same degree as he is supported and upheld, so will his office increase in usefulness and importance, and become, what I firmly believe it is fast approaching to, the most onerous and responsible position next to that of a clergyman in a country parish. – I am, &c.

PRO BONO PUBLICO

SIR, – In glancing over the advertisements of your monthly publication, every well-wisher must regret to see the very low salary offered to schoolmasters. This induces me to offer a humble suggestion. At the present day, in almost every parish, a collector of parish taxes is employed; this office ought to be given to the ill-paid schoolmaster, and the work done on a Saturday. It is folly to suppose young men will be induced to apply their talents to the numerous requirements laid down by the Government, unless something more is done to enhance their pay. They can easily get into the drapery, or other respectable employment, at a salary of 30*l*., 40*l*., or 50*l*. per annum *with board*; while to the poor schoolmaster, with his arduous duties, is only offered 20*l*. or 30*l*. per year *without board.* – Permit me, sir, & c.

A VILLAGE SCHOOLMASTER

[51] A Clergyman's Views on Teachers and Schooling the Poor

Report from the Select Committee on Education, P.P. (1865) VI, 386–8. The witness is the Rev. Charles Lloyd, Rector of Chalfont, Bucks, and diocesan inspector of schools.

6794. The importance of a certificate has been much urged as the only means of guaranteeing the moral and intellectual qualifications of the teachers; is that your opinion, or do you think that the condition of the school itself is a sufficient guarantee for the moral and intellectual character of the teacher? – I think that a certificated master has this advantage, that he has a greater knowledge of the machinery of education than those who have not passed through that process of education; but it by no means follows that he is more competent to deal with the wants of a rural parish. There are a great variety of things which go to make a good schoolmaster; for instance, a knowledge of the habits of life of the people amongst whom he lives and whose children he is training; and they often come from a training college wholly and entirely ignorant of those points which are very valuable in the after-life of the children.

6795. Do you consider that masters and mistresses who have been brought up in training colleges are the best suited to the wants of your own neighbourhood? – If I had my choice, I should like to have a man begin as an untrained master, feel the wants of his school, and then be led on to go to a training college (and I have seen myself most admirable results through that course), in order that he may gain the additional knowledge which he sees he requires to enable him to deal with the children. . . .

6802. Have you had to do with teachers who were extremely well qualified to instruct children, but who were nevertheless most incapable of passing an examination for a certificate? – Yes; I have had to do with four such teachers, persons whom I have selected from the parish as having evidently the gift of teaching, which they proved to me by their extremely judicious management of classes in the Sunday school. One man I took literally from the plough-tail, and he became a very first-rate schoolmaster. His was a very melancholy end. I believe at the present moment he is a beggar in the streets of London. He came up three times to pass his examination for his certificate and (I must say, to my great astonishment, until I had tried him myself to put down his ideas on paper) he utterly failed, and that so disheartened the man that he took to evil habits, and is an utterly ruined character. He was a first-rate teacher. I think I never saw in my life a man with the power of interesting children in the way that he had; and it is a sore grief to me at the present moment, to think that that man is cast away. I believe that if he had got a certificate he would have been now of the greatest possible utility as a teacher in schools.

6803. Was he a self-taught man? – He was a self-taught man. I took a great deal of trouble with him myself, and then we sent him up for a short time to the Westminster Training School, but it was for a very short time.

6804. How many children had he under his charge? – He had a school of 80 boys.

6805. How far did he conduct their education? – Wholly.

6806. Were they ever under inspection? – Yes; they were under Government inspection.

6807. What report was made? – A fair report: not of a very high character.

6808. Was it such a report as would have entitled the school to a capitation grant, had he been certificated? – I think so.

6809. Was the man discharged in consequence of his failure to obtain a certificate? – No, he fancied he could keep a school himself, and went away; unfortunately a gentleman in the neighbourhood took him in hand, and set him up to keep a boarding school.

6810. When you say that you never saw a man with such a natural power of teaching, and nevertheless the report of the result was only a fair one, how do you reconcile the difference between those statements? – He wanted the methodical teaching that the inspector required of him.

6811. How was it that, being so good a teacher, he failed to bring his children up to the proper standard? – The system which he usually followed was to make the children question each other very much, he suggesting the questions previously, or giving a general outline of the subject. When the Government inspector came the whole of his usual system was put a stop to, and a very rigid, and silent and cold inspection was substituted, which entirely chilled the whole school, and I never saw it conduct itself so badly; I was very much disappointed myself.

6812. You think that the inspector's examination was not one calculated to draw out fairly the intelligence and information possessed by the children? – Precisely so. . . .

6818. What were the two or three other cases that you mentioned? – I found a woman, a labourer's wife, whom I put into the school; she is a very first-rate lace-maker; her children have passed a very fair diocesan examination, not a Government examination; and the last time I was in her school, which was about two months ago, she had, I think, one of the nicest schools I ever saw, containing over 80 children. Her powers of conveying information are very great, but as for passing an examination it would be absurd to offer her. Though she is but a poor writer herself, she teaches the children to write; and I inspected their copybooks and found them extremely good; and the cleanliness, order, and discipline of the school were very remarkable. The same was the case with another person who was once a servant in my own house. Finding that she had great teaching powers I placed her in the same position, and with very great success. I have an infant-school mistress at this present moment with an infant school of 70 children, who was selected by my wife out of my own nursery; she is very fond of children, and I do not think there is a single inhabitant in the parish who would not say she was quite a boon to the parish by the way she manages the school as an infant-school mistress. . . .

6822. You do all you can to encourage them to obtain as much education as they can get? – I do not know whether you understand by education what I mean by education, which is to fit them for their place in life; I do not like a child to stay very long in the school in that state of life, because I think it unfits him for his after duties. If a boy never leaves school till he is 14, he does not know how to manage a horse, or to collect a body of sheep, or anything of that kind; and therefore I think the great object is for them to come and go. . . .

6843. It is not the custom, is it, to send the tutors of our public schools and universities to training colleges, in order to learn how to teach, as distinguished from acquiring information themselves? – No, certainly not.

6844. Is not the gift of teaching partly a natural gift belonging more or less to different persons, and in some more developed than others, but depending very much upon a man's own experience and observation? – Yes, I think very much so. The only difference seems to me, that in the case of our tutors they are conveying information to persons in their own rank of life, or thereabouts, and therefore they are only conveying to them a representation, as you may say, of their own character, whereas a master has to teach people who are of a different character.

IV. EDUCATION AND GIRLS

Throughout the nineteenth century the educational needs of girls were considered to be different from those of boys, although the nature of these differences varied according to the girls' social class.

For the upper- and middle-class girls the acquisition of some accomplishments was regarded as desirable: a 'blue-stocking' argued that they were pleasant if inessential adornments [52] while at an expensive establishment for young ladies they dominated the curriculum [53]. A cheaper way to acquire these social graces was through a governess whose sole qualification for her post was frequently her gentility [54]. Whether acquired in the home or at school a shallow veneer of culture was all that was required to reveal the traditional qualities of womanhood according to more conservative mid-Victorians [55]. A defensive tone in [55] suggests a changing climate of opinion on the role of women in society. A less passive ideal was indicated by an early plea for physical activities in girls', as well as the boys', school [56]. The Taunton Commission urged the necessity of recognising the fundamentally equal capacity of girls' and boys' intellects in recommending that girls' schooling should be made more like that of boys [57]. But that there remained a substantial gap between these liberal objectives and much conservative practice was indicated by [58].

In the newly established proprietary and endowed schools for girls the headmistress's belief in the essential equality of the male and female intellect led to a conscious imitation of boys' public schools both in an academically orientated curriculum and in the provision of games [59, 60]. However, there was a more even apportionment of the school day between the humanities, ancient and modern languages, mathematics and science so that classics did not dominate the curriculum to the same extent [61]. It is interesting to notice that traditional accomplishments still formed a part of a girl's education whether as extras [60] or as compulsory subjects [61]. The ethos of these new schools was also strikingly different from that of the boys' public schools in their 'plain living and high thinking' [62].

With the expansion of schools for middle- and upper-class girls in the second half of the nineteenth century the success of a new academic model for female education seemed to be assured, but wider academic opportunities continued to be challenged, and polemical debates had to be won, if a favourable public opinion was to be maintained. Although the Taunton Commission had considered girls to be physically capable of regular schooling [57] medical arguments which cast doubt on their fitness to do so were imported from the United States shortly afterwards. Dr E. Garrett Anderson rebutted them authoritatively and suggested that both sexes had their adolescent problems [63]. In the 1880s concern over the danger of schoolchildren's overwork breathed new life into the issue of sex differentiation in education, but the alleged size of the problem for schoolgirls was deflated in a woman teacher's commonsense reply [64]. Miss Beale's magisterial analysis of the nature of girls' education refuted the allegation that it was manufacturing female pedants [65]. The meticulous concern that was taken over both pastoral and academic matters – which was implicit in [64] and [65] – is revealed in [66] as the conscious implementation of their chosen vocation by women teachers.

Girls in elementary schools were encouraged to perceive the sexes as playing sharply different roles [67]. There was a growing emphasis on domestic subjects for the working-class girl, although there was ambivalence as to whether this was a solution to the 'servant problem' of the middle classes, or an attempt to improve the comfort of working-class households [68]. The permeation of other subjects by a concern for domestic economy [69] was indicative of a hidden curriculum which differentiated the teaching of boys and girls to a far greater extent than the formal timetable of the elementary school would have indicated [70]. The rigid timetable of the elementary school might conceal the exotic, as well as foster the formal, exercise, as in the delightful examples of ten-year-old Minnie Bulmer's work [71].

The education of working-class boys and girls within a common building meant that there was less differentiation between the sexes than existed in the separate facilities provided for middle- and upper-class boys and girls. Those who had taught poor boys and girls together recognised that there were differences in intellectual aptitude between them, but argued that such diversity brought educational advantages [70, 72]. By the end of the nineteenth century, a progressive educationist, who had begun a coeducational experiment in a boarding school for middle- and upper-class pupils, concluded [73] that it had been beneficial for both sexes. And [74] suggests the extent to which by the end of our period there had been an erosion of received ideas on the need to provide a sexually differentiated education.

[52] Accomplishments are Only Part of a Girl's Education

M. Wollstonecraft, *Thoughts on the Education of Daughters* (1788)
pp. 15–18.

EXTERIOR ACCOMPLISHMENTS

Under this head may be ranked all those accomplishments which
merely render the person attractive; and those half-learnt ones which do
not improve the mind. 'A little learning of any kind is a dangerous
thing;' and so far from making a person pleasing, it has the contrary
effect. . . .

Girls learn something of music, drawing, and geography: but they do
not know enough to engage their attention, and render it an
employment of the mind. If they can play over a few tunes to their
acquaintance, and have a drawing or two (half done by the master) to
hang up in their rooms, they imagine themselves artists for the rest of
their lives. It is not the being able to execute a trifling landscape, or any
thing of the kind, that is of consequence – These are at best but trifles,
and the foolish, indiscriminate praises which are bestowed on them only
produce vanity. But what is really of no importance, when considered in
this light, becomes of the utmost, when a girl has a fondness for the art,
and a desire of excellence. Whatever tends to make a person in some
measure independent of the senses, is a prop to virtue. Amusing
employments must first occupy the mind; and as an attention to moral
duties leads to piety, so whoever weighs one subject will turn to others,
and new ideas will rush into the mind. The faculties will be exercised,
and not suffered to sleep, which will give a variety to the character.

Dancing and elegance of manners are very pleasing, if too great a
stress is not laid on them. These acquirements catch the senses, and open
the way to the heart; but unsupported by solid good qualities, their
reign is short.

The lively thoughtlessness of youth makes every young creature
agreeable for the time; but when those years are flown, and sense is not
substituted in the stead of vivacity, the follies of youth are acted over,
and they never consider, that the things which please in their proper
season, disgust out of it. It is very absurd to see a woman, whose brow
time has marked with wrinkles, aping the manners of a girl in her
teens. . . .

Exterior accomplishments are not to be despised, if the acquiring of them does not satisfy the possessors, and prevent their cultivating the more important ones.

[53] A School for Young Ladies, 1836

Life of Frances Power Cobbe as told by Herself (1904 edn) pp. 60–4. Frances Cobbe was a noted philanthropist and crusader for women's rights.

When it came to my turn to receive education, it was not in London but in Brighton that the ladies' schools most in estimation were to be found. There were even then (about 1836) not less than a hundred such establishments in the town, but that at No. 32, Brunswick Terrace, of which Miss Runciman and Miss Roberts were mistresses, and which had been founded some time before by a celebrated Miss Poggi, was supposed to be *nec pluribus impar*. It was, at all events, the most outrageously expensive, the nominal tariff of £120 or £130 per annum representing scarcely a fourth of the charges for 'extras' which actually appeared in the bills of many of the pupils. My own, I know, amounted to £1,000 for two years' schooling.

I shall write of this school quite frankly, since the two poor ladies, well-meaning but very unwise, to whom it belonged have been dead for nearly thirty years, and it can hurt nobody to record my conviction that a better system than theirs could scarcely have been devised had it been designed to attain the maximum of cost and labour and the minimum of solid results. It was the typical Higher Education of the period, carried out to the extreme of expenditure and high pressure.

Profane persons were apt to describe our school as a Convent, and to refer to the back door of our garden, whence we issued on our dismal diurnal walks, as the 'postern.' If we in any degree resembled nuns, however, it was assuredly not those of either a Contemplative or Silent Order. The din of our large double schoolrooms was something frightful. Sitting in either of them, four pianos might be heard going at once in rooms above and around us, while at numerous tables scattered about the rooms there were girls reading aloud to the governesses and reciting lessons in English, French, German, and Italian. This hideous clatter continued the entire day till we went to bed at night, there being no time whatever allowed for recreation, unless the dreary hour of walking with our teachers (when we recited our verbs), could so be

described by a fantastic imagination. In the midst of the uproar we were
obliged to write our exercises, to compose our themes, and to commit to
memory whole pages of prose. On Saturday afternoons, instead of play,
there was a terrible ordeal generally known as the 'Judgment Day.' The
two school-mistresses sat side by side, solemn and stern, at the head of
the long table. Behind them sat all the governesses as Assessors. On the
table were the books wherein our evil deeds of the week were recorded;
and round the room against the wall, seated on stools of penitential
discomfort, we sat, five-and-twenty 'damosels,' anything but 'Blessed,'
expecting our sentences according to our ill-deserts. It must be
explained that the fiendish ingenuity of some teacher had invented for
our torment a system of imaginary 'cards,' which we were supposed to
'lose' (though we never gained any) whenever we had not finished all
our various lessons and practisings every night before bed-time, or
whenever we had been given the mark for 'stooping,' or had been
impertinent, or had been 'turned' in our lessons, or had been marked 'P'
by the music master, or had been convicted of 'disorder' (*e.g.*, having
our long shoe-strings untied), or, lastly, had told lies! Any one crime in
this heterogeneous list entailed the same penalty, namely, the sentence,
'You have lost your card, Miss So-and-so, for such and such a thing;'
and when Saturday came round, if three cards had been lost in the
week, the law wreaked its justice on the unhappy sinner's head! Her
confession having been wrung from her at the awful judgment-seat
above described, and the books having been consulted, she was
solemnly scolded and told to sit in the corner for the rest of the
evening! . . .

   That a pupil in that school should ever become an artist, or authoress,
would have been looked upon by both Miss Runciman and Miss
Roberts as a deplorable dereliction. Not that which was good in itself or
useful to the community, or even that which would be delightful to
ourselves, but that which would make us admired in society, was the
raison d'être of each acquirement. Everything was taught us in the inverse
ratio of its true importance. At the bottom of the scale were Morals and
Religion, and at the top were Music and Dancing; miserably poor
music, too, of the Italian school then in vogue, and generally performed
in a showy and tasteless manner on harp or piano.

[54] The Plight of the Governess

Eliza Cook's Journal (25 May 1850). Eliza Cook was a poet and journalist.

The private teacher is, in many instances, a 'lady', born amid polished society, belonging to an 'eminently genteel family,' educated well, possessing varied and rich acquirements, accustomed to the elegancies of life, and nursed in all the refined ideas and tastes belonging to her station. Her father is not rich, but derives competence through his profession, whatever it may be. She is one of many daughters, and finds herself single at a time when the accidents of fortune render it imperative that she should embrace some means of support for which her abilities and acquirements may fit her.

What has she to do? The common resource is private tuition. She engages herself either to educate children in a family, or 'gives lessons' in the languages, 'affords instruction' in the arts, or 'imparts the accomplishments,' which ladies study.

In a private family her position is often the most unenviable. She is below the head of the house, and above the servants. Oftentimes superior in every respect, to those whose patronage supports her, she is frequently subjected to insulting slights from the family, and consequent impertinence from the menials. Her position is below the drawing-room and above the kitchen – in a kind of cold, and comfortless middle sphere. She is sometimes admitted into 'a mixed party,' but never into 'a select circle,' and her treatment is always marked with patronizing condescension. Those who employ her act towards her with cold, and often, equivocal civility; her pupils – ready in the education of pride and supercilious haughtiness – endeavour to make her feel her position, and the servants show her an obviously unwilling and incomplete respect. Accustomed to independent action, nursed in ideas of dignity and self-respect, the fetters of dependence gall her, and the treatment she experiences from society serves in no way to allay the irritation.

Such, in all instances, is not the case; but, if it be, the teacher has no help for it. The personal qualities of particular individuals sometimes – we would fain hope often – render the teacher's position less painful; but the other picture, unfortunately, too truly, in many instances, represents the condition of a woman, who earns support by the tuition of children in a private family.

Thousands who, in early youth, have been led to hope for better things, earn a precarious and painful support by irregular teaching in different houses, and they taste, in its fullness, the bitterness of the position, which has driven them from a home of comfort and independence to struggle with the turbulent waves of the world.

There is another, which is considered a superior class of teachers, who rent handsome apartments in somewhat fashionable quarters, where they give instruction in music, drawing, and other accomplishments. Their rates of remuneration are often high, and they also pay visits for the purpose of teaching in the houses of the rich. The carriage is frequently sent for them. They are treated with courtesy, and not unfrequently realize an income which enables them to live in elegance and comfort.

But they are known only in 'society' as teachers, whether of painting, drawing, music, or singing. Their 'connection' only recognise them in their professional capacity; they are seldom introduced in the houses where they attend, and, if they are, seem rather to be treated after a condescending fashion, than admitted as a guest. One or two professionals give a tone to a musical party, and they are, consequently, occasionally invited.

'Who is that lady?' 'Oh, only a person who teaches the pianoforte?' is the frequently-heard fragment of a conversation between host and guest. 'She plays very finely, and I thought you might like to hear her, so asked her.'

To be employed in the task of education, therefore, of whatever kind it may be, is *spoken of* as honourable, but secretly regarded as derogatory, below the level of 'gentility.'

[55] Superficiality not Solidity is Desirable in a Girl's Education

Saturday Review (8 October 1859). The *Saturday Review* was a notoriously anti-feminist journal.

THE INTELLECT OF WOMEN

There is a set of persons who are always troubling themselves about the intellect of women, and who wish to persuade the world that women are labouring under some great wrong, which would be instantly remedied if men would but dispassionately consider the facts of the case. . . .

The great argument against the existence of this equality of intellect in women is, that it does not exist. . . .

So long as the solidity of education is limited by the consideration that the girls, when they have become women, must exercise their special gifts, there can be no objection to it. The education of women in England has greatly improved within the last twenty years, and nothing has contributed to the improvement so much as the employment of men to aid in their education. It is now a very common practice with girls' schools to have male lecturers in history, astronomy, geography, and so forth. The classes instituted by distinguished foreigners in London for instruction in Continental languages and literature have been very successful, and parents, by adopting a system so strange to English domestic habits, have shown how deeply they have the education of their daughters at heart. Then, the heads of the best schools show the keenest avidity to bring within the range of their instruction every new department of human knowledge. Directly any sets of facts, or supposed facts, have been brought into any sort of scheme, young ladies learn them. Men are half dazzled and half amused at finding how quickly female patience and female trustfulness are brought to bear on new fields of learning. It is wonderful, for example, to find what some young ladies know about Egyptian history. They can tell off hand when Thoth the Second succeeded Rameses the Fourth, and seem to have formed or imbibed a shrewd opinion as to the respective merits of those two princes. In geography, again, their acquirements are prodigious. When a man comes across the name of one of the great standing difficulties of geography, such as the name of a South-American Republic, or a Scotch county, he is at sea. He has a sense, closely resembling a vague sense of smell, that the places are somewhere in South America and somewhere in Scotland. But a woman is quite at home, and when she reads of a shocking accident in Bolivia or Cromarty, she knows perfectly, not only where those territories are, but what are their chief towns, and what their chief towns are most famous for producing. We really cannot see that English girls need any greater solidity of education than they already possess. If a change is required in any direction, it is probably in the direction of learning the English language and literature more thoroughly. French girls are made to devote a great portion of their educational time to learning French; and although the excess to which this is carried springs mainly from the Catholic notion of teaching girls only what is safe, and cannot therefore be a precedent for Protestants, yet the example might be advantageously followed to some extent, and Englishwomen might be forced to bestow more attention than they do now on standard English authors, and on the construction, compass, and niceties of the English language.

Perhaps it may be thought that the acquirements of women are rather too superficial and extensive. It is certainly necessary that they should learn some things thoroughly well, in order to gain a conception of what thorough knowledge is; but a certain superficiality of knowledge is by no means unsuited to them. Philosophers say that women have the deductive intellect, and not the inductive. By this is practically meant that they have great quickness in suggestion, in the detection of possible consequences, and in hazarding skilful remarks. In order to do themselves justice, they must therefore have a kind of notion of what the subject is that falls under discussion, and a general conception of the elementary facts on which it rests, and the technical expressions it carries with it. Directly they have got so much, their deductive intellect can begin to work. They do not proceed by arriving at argumentative conclusions from clearly-defined premisses, but they throw out observations which they cannot tell how they came by, but which give the discussion a new turn, and open up new lines of thought. However equal, therefore, their intellect may be, yet, as it works in a different way from that of men, their education must be accommodated to this difference. . . .

If they are to do the same lessons, they must want, it may be thought, the same recreations; and both sexes ought to balance the composition of Latin Elegiacs by cricket and football. We do not feel attracted by the programme. Young ladies surely can attain and preserve health without anything like public games; and if it is only meant that brothers and sisters should play together at home, they do that already, and very wisely, without any philosopher being required to instruct them.

[56] Physical Exercise Need not Lead to Freckles for Young Ladies

A. Maclaren, 'Girls' Schools', *Macmillan's Magazine*, x (1864) 413–15. Archibald Maclaren pioneered the development of gymnastics in England during the 1860s.

But it is when we begin to examine the subject of the exercise which girls at school receive that the great error of all comes to light – the error which increases tenfold the evil results of every other. There is not a want that has been enumerated as affecting boys, there is not an ailment through which they must pass, but must be experienced also by girls.

They grow as rapidly; the laws of their development are the same; there is no single reason why they should be denied their share in this all-important agent of health; yet the idea of making any provision for its employment – nay, the idea of employing it at all – seems never to have been contemplated. The two-and-two walk is the sole and single form of exercise that appears ever to have presented itself as being necessary or even desirable. Can we wonder, then, that the hollow chest and twisted spine are so sadly frequent, or that the habit of long-continued sitting should act so fatally upon the healthful and symmetrical development of the whole body? Is it strange that so few grow to womanhood either healthy or graceful? Is it not rather a matter of wonder that any should do so at all? . . .

But I am asked, What would you have girls do? . . .

Neither cricket nor foot-ball would be a good exercise for girls; and there are excellent reasons against leap-frog. But there are very many other valuable, health-promoting games with hand-ball, racket or battledore, grass-hoops, &c. essentially fit for girls; and there can be no doubt that a retired nook in a private meadow, field, or park, might be obtained for the practice of these and similar exercises, where their growing feet might press the soft, springy greensward, where the sweet fresh air might fan their fair young faces, and their eyes might look upon the varied colours of earth and sky. And all this might be accomplished without fear or risk of freckle or tan; for the straw hat and silk gloves would preserve the most delicate complexion, while to it would be added the beautiful bloom of health. These exercises would be for half-holidays, and then only when the weather was unequivocably fine; but the hours for recreative exercises between studies should be spent in the playground. 'Playground! What can a girls'-school want with a playground? What can girls want with a playground? What can girls want with a place for out-door sports?' They want it, because it is more important to health, comfort, and happiness, present and prospective, than any other place or thing in the establishment; they want it because the possession of every other desirable object – large dormitory, large school-room, baths, liberally-supplied and varied table – is trifling in comparison with a view to health, growth, and development. Give them this and you give them the talisman which turns everything it touches into gold! Continue to deprive them of this, and in vain will you try materially to improve their condition, because on exercise the extent and limitation of all the other agents of health depend. Let the same provision be made for girls' as for boys' schools – a provision for every kind of playtime and leisure, for all seasons and states of weather; a place in the country for half-holiday recreative exercises, and, attached to the school, a double playground, open-air and covered-in. Do this, and the mental and physical energies of your daughters will be increased a hundredfold; do this, and fifty per cent will be deducted from the annual register of deaths from consumption.

[57] Girls Have the Same Intellectual Capacity as Boys

Schools' Inquiry Commission, vol. I, *P.P.* (1867–8) XXVIII, part I, pp. 546–54.

We have had much evidence showing the general indifference of parents to girls' education, both in itself and as compared to that of boys. It leads to a less immediate and tangible pecuniary result; there is a long-established and inveterate prejudice, though it may not often be distinctly expressed, that girls are less capable of mental cultivation, and less in need of it, than boys; that accomplishments, and what is showy and superficially attractive, are what is really essential for them; and in particular, that as regards their relations to the other sex and the probabilities of marriage, more solid attainments are actually disadvantageous rather than the reverse. . . .

It cannot be denied that the picture brought before us of the state of Middle-Class Female Education is, on the whole, unfavourable.

The general deficiency in girls' education is stated with the utmost confidence, and with entire agreement, with whatever difference of words, by many witnesses of authority. Want of thoroughness and foundation; want of system; slovenliness and showy superficiality; inattention to rudiments; undue time given to accomplishments, and these not taught intelligently or in any scientific manner; want of organization, – these may sufficiently indicate the character of the complaints we have received, in their most general aspect. It is needless to observe that the same complaints apply to a great extent to boys' education. But on the whole the evidence is clear that, not as they might be but as they are, the Girls' Schools are inferior in this view to the Boys' Schools. . . .

That much of this, as we have before intimated, may be said, still more might have been said some time ago, of boys' education, is plain. The corresponding question arises, whether similar methods of improvement with similar objects in view, should be adopted in the one case as in the other?

208 EDUCATION AND GIRLS

The question is two-fold. First, have girls similar (it need not be equal) capacity for intellectual attainments with boys? Secondly, if they have, does it follow that their training should be the same? The state of society, the need of some peculiar culture in their case, may necessitate modifications; and there may be important differences in degree, if there are not in kind.

On the first question there is weighty evidence to the effect that the essential capacity for learning is the same, or nearly the same, in the two sexes. This is the universal and undoubting belief, – and the un-questioned practice corresponds to it, – throughout the United States; and it is affirmed, both generally and in respect to several of the most crucial subjects, by many of our best authorities. It is impossible to read the account of a really efficient Girls' School, such, for instance, as the Ladies' College at Cheltenham, under Miss Beale, without acknowl-edging the truth of this to a great extent. Mr. Hammond reports that in mixed schools taught by masters he found no noticeable difference of attainments in the two sexes.

But if we go on to consider, with regard at least to the average and the greater number of girls, how far we should apply this view in practice, we may probably come to a conclusion somewhat of the following kind: that there *is* a practical difference to be observed in degree and in time – that the foundation, the main and leading elements of instruction, should be the same in the two cases, and further, that ample facilities and encouragement, and far more than now exist, should be given to women who may be able and willing to prosecute these studies to a higher point; but that the complete assimilation of the education of the sexes, such as prevails in America, should not be attempted.

It must be remembered, in dealing practically with the question, that it is only on the whole, and balancing one quality against another, that we can speak of the equal intellectual capacity of the sexes. Many differences, such as the tendency to abstract principles in boys contrasted with the greater readiness to lay hold of facts in girls – the greater quickness to acquire in the latter with the greater retentiveness in the former – the greater eagerness of girls to learn – their acuter susceptibility to praise and blame – their lesser inductive faculty – and others, are dwelt on by our witnesses.

The view we have above taken is supported by such statements and opinions as these: that up to the age of 12 girls hold their own in the ordinary subjects of instruction with boys; that their education should be the same up to the point when the professional instruction of boys begins, or up to the age of 16; that it should be similar, but not carried so high.

[58] A Woman's Aspirations

Miss Fanny Triffitt's penmanship book – 'A Woman's Aspirations' (1872), Holgate Classical and Commercial Seminary, York (Castle Museum, York).

Man may for wealth and glory roam,

But woman must be blest at home.

To this should all her studies tend,

This her great object and her end

Man may for wealth and glory roam,

But woman must be blest at home,

To this should all her studies tend,

This her great object and her end

Fanny Triffitt, 1872.

Man may for wealth and glory roam,
But woman must be blest at home,
To this should all her studies tend,
This her great object and her end

Man may for wealth and glory roam,
But woman must be blest at home,
To this should all her studies tend,
This her great object and her end

[59] North London Collegiate School in the 1880s: A Feeble
Imitation of a Boys' School?

M. Vivian Hughes, *A London Girl of the Eighties* (2nd edn, 1978) pp.
35–7.

Coming into the school at the age of sixteen I saw its glaring faults and
àbsurdities. The whole seemed to me an elaborate machine for doing
the minimum of useful things with the maximum of fuss. I didn't see
then, as I saw later, that Miss Buss was faced by a herculean task. The
endless anxieties she caused her pupils were as nothing to her own big
anxiety. She was a pioneer, and almost single-handed, in getting some
kind of systematic education for girls. She had no school to copy, no
precedent of any kind. Her private school had been so successful that
she found herself before long with five hundred girls – all to be taught
something and to be trained along Victorian lines of good behaviour.

To be taught something – but what? Negatively the problem was
easy. All the hitherto satisfactory ideals of accomplishments and
'finishing' must be wiped out, but what was to take their place? While
the education of boys had been gradually shaped from ancient times,
engaging the attention of philosophers, that of girls had as a rule no
other aim beyond making them pleasing to men. This idea was to Miss
Buss anathema, and she failed to see all its great possibilities when really
well done. To be deeply pleasing to a husband, and widely pleasing to
other men, seems to me as good an ideal as a woman can have. But
instead of facing squarely the real needs of future wives and mothers, as
the vast majority of girls were to be, Miss Buss seized the tempting
instrument at her hand – the stimulus to mental ambition afforded by
outside examinations. By this means the curriculum was ready-made.
And thus, for better or worse, the education of girls became a feeble

imitation of what the boys were doing, for the public examinations made no distinction of sex, and no woman's voice was heard at the examination boards.

A more serious problem than the curriculum was the discipline. The girls came day by day from a great variety of homes, and never before had there been so many at work together. Here the example of the boys' Public schools was no help. Three essentials of their system were entirely lacking: games, effective punishment, and respectable learning.

I don't think it ever occurred to Miss Buss that games are far more than games, that they provide a vent for high spirits, develop natural obedience, and prevent mental overstrain. True, we had only a tiny yard of open space, nothing to call a playground, but there was a big gymnasium where games could have been freely played. All we did in it was Swedish exercises – bouncing balls or balancing poles – and marching round to music. Were they afraid that if we played free games we might start a riot? Even our short breathing-space of a quarter of an hour in the middle of a long morning's work gave us no freedom except to talk. We filed down into a basement room, bought a bun or a biscuit at a table as we passed, and then stood in *rows* till the time was up. I used to recall with a pang the jolly games of rounders in the grassy garden of my private school, whence we returned to work all hot and recreated.

Punishment as the boys knew it was impossible. Caning was out of the question, and detention was almost equally so. The bulk of the girls came from considerable distances, and the double journey for an afternoon school had to be ruled out. Consequently the lessons had to be over by half-past one, to allow time for getting home for dinner. But parents had complained that the girls had not enough to do during the afternoon and evening. Therefore, since hobbies were considered frivolous, the curse of homework was started. A detention would involve stopping at school for dinner, and an imposition would add to the already over-burdened homework, so neither of these was widely practicable.

Reproof, therefore, was the only form of punishment available, and it is hardly to be wondered at that Miss Buss had brought it to a fine art. It ranged from the mild disgrace of 'signing' to the third degree in the private room. Very rarely, I believe, expulsion was used. The knowledge that there was always a waiting list of pupils gave Miss Buss absolute power, and this must always be dangerous for a woman. Now by nature she was generous and kind-hearted, and did most sincerely long for the loyal co-operation of her pupils in making the school a success. To this end she delivered every week a moral lecture, and would frequently enlist our cheerful compliance with the innumerable rules. 'Multiply the results' was her great slogan for deciding whether a rule was necessary or not. She would point out that one girl running downstairs might not be dangerous, but what if five hundred did? One shoe-bag untidily hung doesn't matter, but five hundred look bad. One girl talking makes no disturbance, but five hundred do. The fallacy of this argument never struck her. Or did it? and that's why she repeated it so often? I think that her sleep must often have been broken by the nightmare of five hundred girls all running amok at once.

Underlying all this iron discipline must have been the subconscious fear that the assistant teachers could not carry on if there were much freedom for questioning and discussion in class. Hard as it is to realize to-day, a well-educated and cultured woman-teacher was extremely rare. It was in this direction that Miss Buss made her greatest mistake. Instead of searching far and wide for the best, she almost invariably chose women who had been through the school and could be relied on to follow her methods; no doubt from a subconscious fear that those methods might be called in question by some lively and original member of the staff. After all, fresh ideas are always upsetting.

Not quite so easy to understand was the objection to the teachers having any interests outside their work. Now it is obvious that no teacher, and no parent, can inspire children if he thinks too much about them; he must have some wider outside interest about which they must be left guessing. But for Miss Buss the school, the scheme, the orderly plan – this was the one absorbing thought.

[60] Prospectus for Wycombe Abbey, 1896

E. Bowerman, *Stands There a School* (1966) pp. 88–9.

Head Mistress

Miss DOVE, Certificated Student of Girton College, Cambridge, 1874; for fourteen years Head Mistress of St. Leonards School, St. Andrews, Fife.

Assistant Mistress

Miss A. R. BURNE, Certificated Student in Honours of Girton College, Cambridge, 1884. Other Mistresses will shortly be appointed.

PROSPECTUS

HIGH WYCOMBE is a pleasant town among the Chalk Downs and Beech Woods of Buckinghamshire, thirty miles from London on the Maidenhead and Oxford Branch of the Great Western Railway. Wycombe Abbey is on the outskirts of the town; it is a large and commodious building situated within its own beautiful grounds of thirty acres, and has been most favourably reported on, both as to position and arrangements, by Dr. W. H. Corfield, Professor of Hygiene in University College, London. The Abbey is large enough to accommodate the Head Mistress, and some of her Assistants, and about a hundred girls. For this purpose it will be divided into four Houses. Each House will be under a House mistress and will have its own sitting rooms and dormitories and tables in the Dining Hall, but all will be under the immediate superintendence of the Head Mistress.

A Gymnasium and Workshop will be among the first necessaries to be provided, and the buildings already include a Hall 120 feet long with a floor properly laid for dancing.

The grounds include a lake, an avenue of limes, other fine trees, an extensive tennis lawn and abundant space for cricket pitches, hockey grounds, and a golf course.

The School is intended to provide for girls an education which, while moderate in cost and especially adapted to their requirements, shall be as complete on all its sides as that given to boys at the great Public Schools.

The number of girls in the School is intended to be two hundred.

The subjects of instruction will be Scripture Knowledge, Arithmetic, Literature, History, Latin or German, French, Physiography or Harmony, Gymnastics, and Part Singing. The different branches of Mathematics and Natural Science, Greek or German, and Italian will be gradually added.

The hours of study will be strictly limited, and a good deal of valuable training will be given through the medium of handwork.

The girls will attend the Parish Church of High Wycombe, and religious instruction will be given by the Head Mistress.

The School will open on 23rd September. Applications for admission must be made to the Head Mistress, who will supply all information and the requisite forms. Preference will be given to those who wish to enter at the beginning of the School year in September.

Girls desiring to enter are expected to show by means of an

examination, which may be conducted in their own homes, that they
have an adequate knowledge of:

ENGLISH – Grammar and Elementary Analysis

LATIN – All the Declensions and the Active Voice of the Regular
Verbs

FRENCH – Elementary Grammar, including Regular Verbs.

ARITHMETIC – The Simple and Compound Rules, Factors and
Vulgar Fractions.

Also Political Geography and General Information. They must write a
neat, clear hand, and be able to read distinctly and with expression, and
to spell correctly. Special excellence in other subjects may under certain
circumstances exempt from Latin.

The above Examination should easily be passed by girls of thirteen or
fourteen, and will, to begin with, be used chiefly for the purposes of
classification.

Girls are admitted on the Nomination of a Shareholder, with the
sanction of the Council. A girl whose parent is unable to obtain a
Shareholder's Nomination may be nominated by the Council, and pay
an Entrance Fee of £10.

The School year is divided into three Terms of twelve weeks each,
beginning about the last week in September, the middle of January,
and the first week in May.

The Holidays consist of sixteen weeks in the year – usually four weeks
at Christmas, three weeks in April, and about two months in Summer.

The School will be examined every July by the Oxford and
Cambridge Schools Examination Board.

Fees per Term (payable in advance)

For Girls who enter under 15 years of age   £32
For Girls who enter over 15 years of age   £38
A small sum is charged for Concerts and School Entertainments.

Extra Subjects   Fees per term

Piano	£2 2 0 to £4 4 0
Singing	£3 3 0
Violin	£3 3 0
Drawing	£2 2 0
Dancing by a Pupil of Mrs. Henry Wordsworth	£1 10 0

THE GIRLS' EDUCATION COMPANY (Limited) *May* 1896

[61] Truth, Beauty and Service at a Girls' School in the 1890s

B. Dunning (ed.), *Francis Holland Church of England School for Girls. Graham Street Memories* (1931) pp. 41–2, 45–6.

Forty years ago, or forty years on, whichever way you think of it, two small girls were received by Whybrow, most faithful of porters, at the red sandstone doorway of the C. E. H. S., Graham Street, when they came for the entrance examination. Forty years at this distance of time seems but little removed from fifty, and 1890, not so long after the foundation of the School. And yet even then there was already the tradition of an heroic past under Miss Westmacott, and of a school in Eaton Terrace; stories too of the four beautiful Ashleys in long black pinafores and of the elder sisters of girls still in the school – Villiers, Todds, Furses, Haigs.

A good deal of that heroic past with its Victorian ideal of plain living and high thinking endured into the nineties. There was no drop of hot water to thaw frozen fingers struggling with knotted boot-laces after a frosty walk to school, or to wash grubby hands before a music lesson; no seats in the Hall for Prayers except at end of term break-up, when each Form-mistress was presented with dazzling flowers in baskets with great loop-shaped handles. On other days all the Forms stood or knelt in regular ranks; now and then someone fainted on those hot summer mornings, but fainting was despised as a feeble thing. There was no stained-glass in the windows to hide the curling smoke from the laundry outside; and there was nowhere to spend a free hour for members of the Sixth, one of whom will always connect the books of Samuel with revision carried out seated on the stone stairs leading to the dressing-room, the chill somewhat mitigated by using the scarlet Scripture notebook alternately with the green star-spangled exercise book as a cushion.

But we would not have had it otherwise; we were rather proud of enduring some hardness, and it certainly did us no harm, although modern theories of health would scarcely have approved of bringing streaming colds to school and disposing of them thoughout the Form. No doubt too some of the methods of pedagogy would not altogether satisfy 'Modern Ideals in Education'; but one Old Girl at any rate will never cease to be grateful for the fine teaching and the insistence on the true religion and sound learning, which the founders of the school aimed at for themselves and us. Canon Holland came every Friday to

school and took Scripture in several forms; and successive Canons of
Westminster also came.

It was a never-failing source of interest to note the terms in which we
were addressed: Canon Furse increased our self-respect by his vigorous
'young women'; Canon Foakes Jackson, swaying from side to side on his
high chair, his hands entwined around the blackboard pointer upright
on his knee, addressed his lessons in Church history to 'gurrls.' We
learned much from both; but from Canon Holland we learned
something of the quality of true saintliness. With utter simplicity he
taught the Gospel of St. John to his 'dear children,' and it might have
been St. John himself in his old age who was speaking.

It is harder to write of those who are here sharing in the Jubilee; of
Miss Holmes who in 1890 had not, I think, long succeeded to the
headship, and Miss Wolseley-Lewis who followed her in the summer
term of 1894. They were very different, and yet they had much in
common. They ruled the School with wisdom and justice, and with the
sympathy born of understanding and humour. Their presence was
everywhere felt; and, if in the lower and middle school they inspired a
wholesome awe and respect, it was a respect tempered by an affection
which became more and more predominant in the closer contact in the
Fifth and Sixth Forms. In their Scripture lessons they made us think: it
was a hard discipline to spend Sunday evening in deciding the question:
'Is joy a duty?' with no extraneous aid beyond Bible, Prayer Book and
Concordance. They made duty a real thing, and they made us sensitive
to truth and beauty and service. These ideals ran tacitly through the
School, although there was but little preaching, and these lessons were
learnt through the sound teaching of ordinary school subjects and the
rigid standard of work exacted. . . .

Ascension Days spent at Canterbury are vivid in the clear May
sunlight, for the sun always shone for the Guild of C. C. C., and it was
something like genius that drew up the programme which never varied
from year to year. The afternoon train from Charing Cross carried some
eighteen or twenty of us, and as many more from Baker Street to
Canterbury. The Guild Office and the admission of new members in St.
Anselm's Chapel came first after our arrival, followed by high tea with
pies and buns in a great tent in Canon Holland's garden. Then came
games on the lawn until we could see no longer, and then Compline in
St. Anselm's Chapel, where a light burned to guide us in the darkness as
we stumbled and groped our way up the mysterious aisle; next, ginger-
beer and more buns in the tent, and then, best of joys, the procession

round the Precincts as Canon Holland, lantern in hand, deposited us and our bags by twos and threes at the houses of hospitable dignitaries.

In the morning there was the adventure of discovering the front door, seen only in the dark, and the way to the Cathedral for the special Celebration of Holy Communion. After breakfast there was the walk or drive to Harbledown Woods and sheaves of wild hyacinths; and after lunch the visit to the Cathedral, when Canon Holland on the very spot made 'live history' of the Martyrdom under one Henry, and the destruction of the Martyr's Shrine under another. The conclusion of the whole matter still rings in the ear: Henry VIII ordered 'the bones to be brent.' Then the bells rang for Evensong and all too soon Ascension Day was over, though the joy was prolonged to the last by continuous singing in the train all the way to London. Friday saw us back in School, as we are back in School to-day in memory. It is a memory of a discipline of body and mind which secured part of the natural order of things; a memory of a keen interest in all sorts of learning; and a memory of much happiness in companionship. It was a full life, and for all *gratias agimus*.

[62] An Academic Curriculum: (i) Sheffield High School for Girls (ii) Aston, King Edward's Grammar School for Girls

Secondary Education Commission, vol. IX, *P.P.* (1895) XLIX, pp. 418–21.

School			*English subjects*					*Languages*				*Sciences*	*Art subjects*			*Commercial subjects*					
Grade	*Name*	*Form*	*Religious instruction*	*English*	*History*	*Geography*	*Arithmetic*	*Greek*	*Latin*	*French*	*German*	*Mathematics*	*Physical science*	*Drawing*	*Manual instruction*	*Music and singing*	*Book-keeping*	*Shorthand*	*Physical exercises*	*Other subjects*	*Total no. of hours per week*	*Remarks*
			hrs	hrs	hrs	hrs	hrs	hrs	hrs	hrs	hrs	hrs	hrs	hrs	hrs	hrs	hrs	hrs	hrs	hrs	hrs	C = Chemistry P = Physics B = Botany O = Object lesson N = Needlework
1st Grade, Proprietary	Sheffield High School for Girls	*Upper School*																				
		Form IA	1½	¾	–	–	–	–	4	1¾	–	3½	C 1¾ P 4¾	–	–	–	–	–	1	–	19	
		B	1½	1	¾	–	1½	–	3¼	2¼	2½	3	P 1½	–	–	¾	–	–	1	–	19	
		IIA	1½	1	¾	–	1½	–	3¼	2¼	2½	3	1½	–	–	¾	–	–	1	–	19	B = Botany H = Harmony N = Needlework
		B	1½	2½	1	–	1½	–	3¼	2	2½	3	1½	–	–	¾	–	–	1	–	19	
		Middle School																				
		Form IIIA	1½	1½	¾	¾	2½	–	–	3	2½	2½	B ¾	1½	–	¾	–	–		–	19	
		B	1½	1½	1½	¾	2½	–	–	2¾	2½	¾	2	1½	–	¾	–	–	1	–	19	
		IVA	1½	1½	1½	1	2½	–	–	2½	2¾	¾	1¾	1½	–	¾	–	–	1	–	19	
		B	1½	2¼	1½	¾	3¾	–	–	2½	3¼	–	¾	1	–	¾	–	–	1	–	19	
		Lower School																				
		Form VA	1½	3¼	1½	1½	3½	–	–	2¼	–	–	O 1½	1½	N ¾	¾	–	–	1	–	19	
		B	1½	2¾	2	1½	3½	–	–	3	–	–	¾	1½	¾	¾	–	–	1	–	19	
		VIA	1½	5	½	¾	3¾	–	–	2¼	–	–	2	¾	–	¾	–	–	1¾	–	19	
		B	1½	4¼	–	¾	2¼	–	–	2¼	–	–	1½	2	1¼	¾	–	–	2½	–	19	
2nd Grade, Endowed	Aston, King Edward's Grammar School for Girls	Form I	¾	¾	¾	¾	2¼	–	3	3	3	3	B 1½	1½	N ¾	¾	–	–	¾	H ¾	23¾	
		II	¾	1½	¾	¾	2¼	–	3	3	2¼	3	1½	1½	¾	¾	–	–	¾	¾	23¾	
		III	¾	1½	1½	¾	2¼	–	2¼	2¼	2¼	2¼	1½	2¼	¾	¾	–	–	¾	¾	22½	
		IV	¾	2¼	¾	1½	3	–	–	3	3	1½	1½	2¼	¾	¾	–	–	¾	–	22½	
		V	¾	3	¾	1½	3	–	–	3	3	–	1½	3	¾	¾	–	–	¾	–	22½	
		VI	¾	3¾	1½	1½	3¼	–	–	2¼	–	–	1½	3	¾	¾	–	–	¾	–	21	

[63] Sex in Mind as Well as Body?

E. Garrett Anderson, 'Sex in Mind and Education: A Reply', *Fortnightly Review*, xv (1874) 582–8. Elizabeth Garrett Anderson was the first woman to qualify in England as a doctor.

The April number of the *Fortnightly Review* contains an article under the heading of Sex in Mind and in Education, by Dr. Maudsley. . . .

Dr. Maudsley's paper consists mainly of a protest against the assimilation of the higher education of men and women, and against the admission of women to new careers; and this protest is founded upon a consideration of the physiological peculiarities of women. It derives much of its importance from the assumption that what is now being tried in England has already been tried in America, and that it has there produced the results which Dr. Maudsley thinks are inevitable. When, however, we turn to Dr. Clarke's book (from which the American evidence quoted by Dr. Maudsley is taken) we find that the American system is, in many important features, and especially in those most strongly condemned by Dr. Clarke and the other witnesses, widely different from that now being advocated in England. . . .

The position Dr. Maudsley has undertaken to defend is this . . . that the physiological functions started in girls between the ages of fourteen and sixteen are likely to be interfered with or interrupted by pursuing the same course of study as boys, and by being subjected to the same examinations; and, 2nd, that even when these functions are in good working order and the woman has arrived at maturity, the facts of her organization interfere periodically to such an extent with steady and serious labour of mind or body that she can never hope to compete successfully with men in any career requiring sustained energy. Both with girls and women, however, it is the assimilation of their education and the equality of their aim with those of boys and men which, in Dr. Maudsley's eyes, call for special condemnation. And in each case he grounds his objection on the fact that physiologically important differences are found in the two sexes. . . .

The educational methods followed by boys being admitted to be better than those hitherto applied to girls, it is necessary to show that these better methods would in some way interfere with the special functions of girls. This Dr. Maudsley has not done. He has not attempted to show how the adoption of a common standard of examination for boys and girls, allowing to each a considerable range in the choice of subjects, is likely to interfere more with a girl's health than passing an inferior examination for girls only. Either would hurt her if unwisely pressed, if the standard of competition were unduly keen, or if in the desire for mental development the requirements of her physical nature were overlooked.

What we want to know is what exactly these requirements are, and especially how much consideration girls and women ought to show to the fact of the periodic and varying functions of their organization. . . .

It is, we are convinced, a great exaggeration to imply that women of average health are periodically incapacitated from serious work by the facts of their organization. Among poor women, where all the available strength is spent upon manual labour, the daily work goes on without intermission, and, as a rule, without ill effects. For example, do domestic servants, either as young girls or in mature life, show by experience that a marked change in the amount of work expected from them must be made at these times unless their health is to be injured? It is well known that they do not.

With regard to mental work it is within the experience of many women that that which Dr. Maudsley speaks of as an occasion of weakness, if not of temporary prostration, is either not felt to be such or is even recognized as an aid, the nervous and mental power being in many cases greater at those times than at any other. . . .

As to the exact amount of care needed at the time when this function is active and regular, individual women no doubt vary very much, but experience justifies a confident opinion that the cases in which it seriously interferes with active work of mind or body are exceedingly rare; and that in the case of most women of good health, the natural recurrence of this function is not recognised as causing anything more than very temporary *malaise*, and frequently not even that.

The case is, we admit, very different during early womanhood, when rapid growth and the development of new functions have taxed the nutritive powers more than they are destined to be taxed in mature life. At this age a temporary sense of weakness is doubtless much more common than it is later in life, and where it exists wise guardians and teachers are in the habit of making allowance for it, and of encouraging a certain amount of idleness. This is, we believe, as much the rule in the best English schools as it is in private schoolrooms and homes. . . .

The time given to education is being prolonged, and the pressure in the early years of womanhood, when continuous work is less likely to be well borne, is being lightened; girls are no longer kept standing an hour or more at a time, or sitting without support for their backs; school hours and school terms are shortened; and, above all, physical exercise is no longer limited to the daily monotonous walk which was thought all-sufficient in old-fashioned schools and houses. In spite of these undeniable facts, Dr. Maudsley charges the reformers with having neglected the physical requirements of girls, in order to stimulate their mental activity. 'It is quite evident,' he says, 'that many of those who are foremost in their zeal for raising the education of women, have not given proper consideration to the nature of her organization.' In another place he blames them for having neglected physical training and exercise. To those in a position to know the facts, such a charge as this seems peculiarly misplaced and unjust. It is no doubt true, that twenty years ago the physical training of girls was deplorably neglected, and that it still is so in homes and schools of the old-fashioned type. But the same people who during recent years have been trying to improve the mental training of girls, have continually been protesting in favour also of physical development, and to a great extent their protests have been successful. The schoolmistresses who asked that girls might share in the Oxford and Cambridge Local Examinations, were the first also to introduce gymnastics, active games, daily baths, and many other hygienic reforms sorely needed in girls' schools. . . .

But it may still be urged, that admitting the advantage to girls of assimilating their play-ground hours to those of boys, of substituting outdoor games for worsted work or crouching over the fire with a story-book, yet that when it comes to school work the case is different, and that to make girls work as hard as boys do, and especially to allow them to work for the same examinations, would be to press unfairly upon their powers. In answer to this, we must take note of some facts about boys.

It must not be overlooked, that the difficulties which attend the period of rapid functional development are not confined to women, though they are expressed differently in the two sexes. Analogous changes take place in the constitution and organization of young men, and the period of immature manhood is frequently one of weakness, and one during which any severe strain upon the mental and nervous powers is productive of more mischief than it is in later life. It is possible that the physiological demand thus made is lighter than that made upon young women at the corresponding age, but on the other hand it is certain that, in many other ways unknown to women, young men still further tax their strength, *e.g.* by drinking, smoking, unduly severe physical exercise, and frequently by late hours and dissipation generally. Whether, regard being had to all these varying influences, young

men are much less hindered than young women in intellectual work by
the demands made upon their physical and nervous strength during the
period of development, it is probably impossible to determine. All that
we wish to show is that the difficulties which attend development are
not entirely confined to women, and that in point of fact great
allowance ought to be made, and has already been made, for them in
deciding what may reasonably be expected in the way of intellectual
attainment from young men.

[64] A Teacher's View of Alleged Over-Pressure in Girls' Schools

S. Bryant, *Over-Work from the Teacher's Point of View with Special
Reference to the Work in Schools for Girls* (1885) pp. 3–17. Sophie Bryant
was the first woman to gain a doctorate (in Moral Sciences) at
London University and became headmistress of North London
Collegiate School.

In the early days of the over-work panic, when some members of the
medical profession first made against the scholastic profession the
charge of general over-pressure, and the public mind became alarmed,
and worked itself into an attitude of terror at every passing shadow of
fatigue, like that of a nervous child who fears familiar objects in the
dark, the sanguine amongst us hoped – and I was one of them – that this
panic, like others, would rise to a critical height, and then subside to the
quiet level of a reasonable caution which is neither fear nor rashness.
We were therefore content to defend ourselves merely at special points
when attacked, and were particularly slow to bring forward the
counter-charges against our friends the doctors, which nevertheless
have been in our minds all along. . . .

We believe that we see aspects of the question which the doctor, as
doctor merely, could hardly be expected to imagine; and we found our
opinions on a knowledge of children who are well, no less than of
children who are ill, whereas the medical man knows only the
latter. . . .

Assuming, then, normal physical health, we also, *as a first approximation to the solution of our problem*, assume a normal balance of mental
tendencies, a due appreciation of active and passive enjoyments, of
exercise physical, intellectual, and emotional, of play and of rest. In
other words, we assume such a degree of mental health in our pupils as
shall fairly guarantee them from over-balancing themselves in the

intellectual direction, unless we push them unduly in that direction. We assume that they are not, in general, morbidly intellectual, and apportion to them work which they can reasonably do with a due, and not excessive, amount of effort, supposing always that they are not morbidly something else. Our scheme, whether we carry it out or not, is to plan our work for the child who is normally healthy in body and in mind, and has average ability. . . .

But do the medical men who charge the teachers with over-pressure draw their examples from this normal class? Certainly, I think not, and my opinion is grounded on the fact that, with a fairly large experience, I have never known one instance of this kind on which the brief verdict of 'over-worked' has been passed. In other words, I never knew a *school-girl* whose natural tendencies were to a reasonable enjoyment of work and play and rest in fair proportion if left alone, who took to headaches or other forms of suffering, went under medical treatment, and was labelled 'over-worked.' I have known women and men, but not school-girls, of this description, and in all these cases, which are very few, there were other causes than intellectual work, such as severe emotional suffering, at work.

But, in the other classes, patients real and imaginary are to be found. . . .

Doctors, I believe, scarcely ever say: 'Your daughter is too much given to emotional excitement and, without being aware of it, has exhausted herself by indulging in morbid extravagances of sensationalism and emotionalism, and, what is still more serious, has laid and is still further laying the foundations of a most injurious habit. You must put a stop to everything that feeds this tendency – no novels, no dissipating amusements, no excitement, no encouragement to an excessive indulgence of feeling. Surround her with quiet influences and, above all things, give her some definite steady work which will keep her mind fully occupied. When she gets stronger, as probably she soon will, increase the work, and take every means to promote the development of her intellectual activity in the most purely intellectual way.' . . .

Now, the intellectually over-wrought patient is to be found, I think, chiefly in Universities, among tutors and lecturers and the cream of the undergraduates. . . .

In the world at large, however, and therefore at schools, there is not much of this kind, while there is, I believe, a good deal of the other kind, of thing; and therefore, as teachers, we ask the doctors to make some inquiries and observations, with a view to the diagnosis of moral as well as physical character in the cases of over-work that come before them.

But the doctors have other patients besides these, who are also 'over-worked.' The largest number comes, I believe, from that class of school-girls who are thoroughly idle and do habitually an amount of work which is beneath contempt. This, at least, is our experience: – 'A. B. is suffering from headaches, and the doctor says the cause is over-work and that she must have rest.' Enquiry is made into A. B.'s school history, and it is frequently found that she is a person who never, so far as known, or scarcely ever, made a mental effort in her life. This is the most common case, and the facts which it reveals are very remarkable. We know that the one thing necessary for the girl's moral and, in the end, physical health is that she should be induced to work somehow; and, if there was any support on the side of home, we could almost certainly succeed in finally getting her to make an effort. But there is no support; she does not really work even when in the working atmosphere of school; she and her surroundings become thoroughly inharmonious; she has a headache, and it grows by being extravagantly attended to; the possibility of escape from even the appearance of work suggests itself semi-consciously; the headache increases; the doctor is called in, the mother tells the tale of over-work, and the doctor, just seeing that in a general way absence from worry is a very good thing, enquires and looks no further, agrees to the over-work idea, and prescribes rest. Something like this is, I believe, the history of a surprisingly large number of cases, though not probably the cases which are brought before the public as 'awful warnings.' The awful warnings come from the classes already described as over-intellectual and over-emotional respectively; and our general opinion is therefore, that the first set are not typical, but require to be watched as *exceptions*, while the other set are much more common, though not typical either, and are, as we teachers plainly see, made worse rather than better by the simple physiological prescription of rest. Their case is psychological no less than physiological, and must primarily be cured by measures which take effect on the psychological aspect of the case.

I have made careful enquiries among my fellow-workers, and have carefully searched my own memory for cases of supposed over-pressure, and in our experience *the number of imaginary cases bears to the number of real cases a very large proportion.*

[65] Girls' Schools Do not Manufacture Pedants

D. Beale, 'Girls' Schools Past and Present', *Nineteenth Century*, XXIII (1888) 541–53. Dorothea Beale was appointed Headmistress of Cheltenham Ladies' College in 1858. She was replying to Miss Sewell's article 'The Reign of Pedantry in Girls' Schools'.

Miss Sewell has, with great candour, admitted that she criticises with 'hesitation,' because she 'cannot feel' that she has a 'sufficient acquaintance with facts to justify an absolute conviction of the truth' of her 'impressions.' I venture therefore to supplement her interesting article by wider and more varied recollections. Mine do not date as far back as hers, but I can go back a long way. My experience as Principal of the Cheltenham Ladies' College since 1858 enables me to speak with some confidence of the later educational developments. . . .

This College was the first Proprietary Girls' School, and now they are innumerable; it was one of the first to send in pupils for University examinations. . . .

I wished this to be a school and college combined; the mistresses to do the work which they could best do, thoroughly correcting exercises and giving the girls the womanly training which is so necessary for their characters; but I hoped that in time we should get the advantage for the elder ones of lectures from men who were masters of their subjects. When I came, only modern languages were taught – no science, no mathematics. I have always approved of beginning with modern languages, so I was content to wait for the classics. I did wish much to introduce geometry, for the sake of the help it gives in teaching girls to form clear ideas, and to set out their thoughts in order; but had I done so, many of the remaining pupils would have been frightened away, and I might have been the death of the college; so I had to wait for the tide. I was always hearing that girls would be turned into boys by studying the same subjects. I began my innovations with the introduction of scientific teaching, and under the name of physical geography I was able to teach a good deal. This subject was unobjectionable, as few boys learnt geography. Then we got lectures from a distinguished geologist who lived here, and spared no pains to interest the girls, taking them out for lectures and explorations on the hills. . . .

Let me now try to show why I disagree in some respects with Miss Sewell as regards the methods and aims of teaching, though feeling more acutely than those who look at schools only from without how much we have still to amend; the orbit of human progress is not a geometric curve, but one distorted by aberration.

Miss Sewell is certainly right in warning us that 'in avoiding ignorance based on superficiality there is always danger of ignorance based on narrowness.' Let me take the subject on which she has dwelt most at length, the teaching of history, both because she and I attach great importance to it, and because I have paid more attention to the teaching of this subject than to any other except one. She complains that certain periods only are brought into the light, but others remain shrouded in utter darkness; whereas she would have a general knowledge of the whole course of history and historical mythology, obtained from epitomes, &c., with such further illustrations as an intelligent teacher could give. She would have dates learned, either by simply committing them to memory, or perhaps by some system of *memoria technica*.

Now what is the *raison d'être* of historical teaching for school girls? I am sure Miss Sewell does herself injustice when she seems to say it is to enable girls to join intelligently in conversation. I know she would give a hearty assent to the statement that education has failed of its purpose, if it has merely added a grace or an ornament; we have to keep steadily before us, that the only worthy object is to make our pupils better, wiser, abler; then we may safely trust that their duties will be done faithfully, that their ways and conversation will not be 'pedantic' but intelligent, and that, whether married or single, they will prove themselves helps meet for those to whom God has given them. . . .

I do therefore think that we should take a short period, and go into it thoroughly: a year is not too much to spend on the reign of Charles the First and the Commonwealth; and those who have, so to speak, lived through this era, will know how to set about getting a real knowledge of another (including their own).

Besides, individual life is too short for us to read the life of humanity: what is best then to be done is surely to take a few typical eras, to make these real, to connect them by a background more faintly outlined. We must teach history as we do geography, bring into prominence the great mountain chains and chief rivers, not try to mark in everything in the map of the world. . . .

I regret the inadequate treatment by Miss Sewell of other subjects of study. As regards the teaching of literature I am heartily with her when she condemns 'the modern fashion of treating noble thoughts, feelings, and principles set forth in prose and verse merely as the material' for teaching grammar and etymology, when she calls this a kind of 'intellectual vivisection.' Still I do think it is better to master a few great works than to be always traversing the fields of literature, and I could scarcely find any book more admirable for developing the mind and character, and stimulating thought, than one she thinks unsuitable, viz. the *Areopagitica*. But I agree with her, that there is ground for complaint when examiners annotate books which have no educational value, and then force the sale by prescribing them for some University examination. I have had twice to protest against volumes which were worse than worthless, and they have been changed.

Language-study too is surely not to be valued chiefly for its conversational uses; we learn other tongues that our thoughts may be enriched by varied expression, and our sympathies enlarged by a new literature. Miss Sewell asks whether grammatical analysis does more than enable us to affix technical names; but is not this 'giving names essential if we would recognise and fix in the mind distinctions'? She sees this when she writes of architecture, 'Technical terms must be understood.'

Lastly, I must regret that Miss Sewell repeats the popular cry that women are to be 'educated for the home' by learning 'cookery and needlework and arithmetic enough for accounts.' These home arts are easily acquired by those whose minds are well trained, and the place for them to be learned is home, though they may and should be encouraged at school. But can it possibly be thought that such things can compare in importance with studies to which Miss Sewell does not even allude – elementary physiology and the laws of health – and those which open the eyes to see the wonders of the material universe, to

> Find tongues in trees, books in the running brooks,
> Sermons in stones, and good in everything?

Besides, is it a sufficient objection to 'classics and mathematics' that they 'do not tell in society'? Is it true that they do not 'prepare girls for home and social life'? Surely they enable a mother to take an interest in the work of schoolboy sons, and to know whether they are being well taught; and the mythology to which Miss Sewell attaches so much importance as 'necessary at every turn,' if we would understand 'poetry and poets,' is worthless and dead if taken apart from the literature of antiquity. I am with her in deprecating the imitation of the curriculum of boys' schools; but if the classics, especially the Greek classics, are studied, not too early, and by those who have some taste for language, they can scarcely be overvalued. The want of intellectual and therefore of moral sympathy, the separation in everything that relates to intellectual life between the mothers and the sons, is felt, in countries where it exists, to be a great evil, especially in religious matters. For this reason it is good that the education of boys and girls should run on parallel lines. Still I agree with Miss Sewell that a wide culture, offering many points of sympathy, is of greater importance for women than for men. Women ought to be more adaptive, and I deeply regret the great specialisation which the present system of University life favours in both men and women. It certainly makes women less valuable as educators, when they are trained only as specialists: men *unius libri* may be able to accomplish great works in the world of Nature, but seldom in that of Mind. I do not want girls' education to be what that of boys is now, but that both should move on together to a higher ideal, not as yet realised by either; and perhaps it may be even given to the girls, 'the weak things of the earth,' to improve the boys.

[66] A Headmistress's View of the Woman Teacher's Vocation

L. Soulsby, 'The Moral Side of Education', in D. Beale, L. H. M. Soulsby, F. Dove (eds), *Life and Work in Girls' Schools* (1898) pp. 374–80, 395. Lucy Soulsby was headmistress of the Oxford High School.

Many girls leave college with a vague idea that they had better take up teaching, because it is the only way of earning a livelihood for which they are in the least prepared. Unfortunately their preparation, too often, consists merely in having been taught themselves. Having eaten dinners is some preparation for the career of a cook, but not much; and these young teachers may perhaps find an educational cookery-book useful! The comparison does not hold good altogether, for almost every woman has the instinct of motherhood in her, which makes her more or less a born teacher, while it is only a few who are born cooks. Still, every young woman finds help in talking to an older one, who has had the same work, made probably the same mistakes, and has found a practical way out of them. We all value practical experience; what else is training but practical experience systematised? But it is not every young teacher who has an experienced friend at hand, or who can afford to be regularly trained. It is hoped that this book may be, in printed form, such talk as she would welcome had she an experienced friend at hand. . . .

The moral thoughtfulness, which Dr. Arnold demanded of his VI. Form, is the main requisite for a true teacher: no dexterity in imparting knowledge will make her an educator if this is lacking. . . .

Nothing can replace in a teacher the study of individual peculiarities of character: the motives, the special hindrances, the growth of each child in her class must be studied and individually met, if she is to rise to the true level of her work.

This is assuming that the teacher feels the full responsibility of being put in a position where, by the way in which she teaches French, or mathematics, she can help or hinder the spiritual growth of each of her pupils. But even supposing that this overruling underlying motive of every true educator be put aside for the moment, and we consider only the smaller question of more or less success in imparting knowledge – still, this very success (other things being equal) will lie with that teacher who has the insight into the peculiar disposition of each child, who can bring to bear on each nature the motives which appeal to it and who can foresee and obviate the difficulties, which vary in each child, according to its mental, moral and physical equipment. In all ways scholastic success is furthered by seeking first something higher still. A great educator used to say: 'If you teach one boy arithmetic only and another boy arithmetic and religion, other things being equal, the second boy will beat the first in arithmetic, because his nature is more widely developed'.

But it may be thought that this is asking more of teachers than can be fairly expected. A girl who has taken life from the outside, with a comfortable, one might almost say, 'wholesome' disregard of motives and such-like complications, who looks forward to giving her lesson in a special subject, and to then being free to be as untouched by the 'malady of thought,' as absorbed in games and the amusements of life, as was rightfully her state at fifteen, may well feel that she is not prepared to enter on teaching as a career combining the responsibility of doctor and clergyman. If so, let her consider carefully before she adopts the teaching profession. . . .

For, no matter how large the class, the true teacher must study and respect the individuality of each member of it. Though her class may pass a most successful examination, yet, in examining herself, she must mark down (against herself), as a failure, the name of each child who has remained to her merely one of the crowd. The eyesight, the hearing, the spine, the headaches, the home surrounding of each child, should be known to its teacher, and should modify the demands made upon that child.

Curvature of the mind is far more common than curvature of the spine, and the teacher must have keen intellectual sympathy with each child's individual mental tangles. She must clear the ground of harmful stumbling-blocks, and yet leave enough to exercise the mental muscles. Surely if the difficulty of a task can fire enthusiasm, the teacher should burn with zeal.

The moral temperament of each child is an even more complex study than the mental peculiarities; praise, for instance, is a tonic for one and poison for another. The teacher must have presence of mind to criticise on the spur of the moment, with due regard to the child's moral digestion, to the abstract question of justice in the class as a whole, and to maintaining a high, and yet not depressing, standard of work. One child requires to be repressed and one to be encouraged to do itself justice. One child has thoughtful difficulties which need sympathetic unravelling; another suffers from mere inattention, and requires decisive pulling together.

It stands to reason that, to appreciate all these shades of character and to satisfy the needs of each, in such a manner as not to waste the time of the class (and not to sin against the code of rough and ready justice, to which the childish mind, quite rightly, owns allegiance), is a very delicate task, and involves much of that moral thoughtfulness which is the foundation of a good teacher.

One reason for the supreme importance of this quality is that it not only means insight into others, but also involves self-mastery without which no *educative* control of others is possible . . .

To sum up shortly, the following are the main points I would seek to impress on a young teacher, in considering the moral side of education. First and foremost the heavy responsibility attached to the teacher's office – an office which combines the functions of clergyman, doctor and instructor. Next, the personal qualifications required of the teacher, holiness, serenity, insight into character, knowledge of the world; then the aims of the teacher's work, the building up a sound mind in a sound body, by the help of the good habits arising from right conditions of school life, most of all by the help of the Bible lesson, which must be the inspiration of the whole school course.

[67] Gender Roles in the Elementary School

'How We Kept House', an essay written in 1890 by Annie Jones aged twelve, and reproduced in E. B. Sargant (ed.), *School Field Magazine 1890–4* (1894). The book consists of lithographic reproductions of children's work from an elementary school in South Hackney. Annie Jones later became a pupil teacher at the school.

It was in the middle of August that mother thought she would like to take a holiday. 'Now be sure', said she, 'if the tax-collector calls tell him to call again in three weeks, and then I'll tell him when to call again.' So saying she departed. Directly she was gone the boys began to grumble. 'I wish you would take a turn at our work,' said they. 'How would you like to dig up weeds till your back aches.' 'Oh! I wish you would try ours,' said the girls, 'First there are a dozen pairs of stockings to mend, then the bed-rooms to scrub, and heaps more things.'

'Well,' said the boys, 'suppose we change.' No sooner said than agreed. Jack said he would scrub, so he fetched his pail of water. Before he had done half, he heard a noise, and on turning round to see what was the matter, he kicked his pail, and over went the water. Before he had time to get it up, it had gone all through the drawing-room ceiling, which had just been white-washed. We will now leave him, and go to the other, who was cook. He thought, 'I'll put the joint in early, so that it will be well done.' Before he had cobbled one stocking, he heard a noise, and on going to the kitchen, he found that the cat had upset the joint which was cooking before the fire. Down it fell among the cinders and was spoilt. He picked it up as well as he could, put it before the fire, and returned to his cobbling again.

When the girls returned they at once smelt the burning meat. They rushed to the rescue, but the meal was burned to a cinder. 'Oh! I thought you boys were going to do such wonders, why you don't know how much we've done. Just by the side of the stile, the weeds were innumerable.' 'Why goodness gracious me, they are the new turnips, set just a week ago,' said the boys. 'Well, how did we know,' replied the girls, 'you should have told us.'

'And somehow or other, I've upset a pail of water, and it has gone all through the drawing-room ceiling,' said Jack. 'I think I shall take a day's holiday, to give mother time to get over the shock.'

'Well you're very clever, I thought you boys were going to do such wonders, but hush! here comes mamma.'

I will not attempt to describe the scene that followed. I only know that we never tried to do one another's work again.

[68] The Little Cooks: Domestic Science for Pupils of the London School Board

C. Morley, *Studies in Board Schools* (1897) pp. 122–4. One of a series of sketches that appeared in the *Daily News*.

Every week after they have arrived at years of discretion – that is, about nine – they get an admirable lesson in cooking and kitchenwork for nothing at all. If they are good little girls they will be worth much more than their salt when they are thirteen or fourteen in many a middle-class household. Mistresses would compete for their services. But even if they despise the modest cap and apron, and prefer the factory with freedom, fringes, and feathers, they will be all the more likely to make home – sweet home. And many a home is broken up by bad housekeeping.

This spacious room is one of the Cookery Centres which are dotted about London. The first object that strikes you as you enter is the cheerful fire in the corner burning clear and bright as good cooks love to see it. That is the open fireplace. In the other corner is the more convenient but less attractive range, fully equipped with stewpans and other accessories. Against the wall stands the cupboard, above which rises shelf after shelf of plates, cups and saucers, cullenders, graters, dishes, and other utensils. Between you and them runs the long dresser, in the centre of which is a gas stove, such as is now to be found in many poor dwellings. Thus you see that the pupil is at once initiated into the three classes of fireplaces which are now in general use – the open, the close, and the gas. In the far corner is a store cupboard, a working scullery with sink, hot and cold water taps, plate and dish rack; and there is also a cloakroom where the little cooks keep their aprons (supplied by the school), and wash their hands from time to time. Teachers are most particular about this cleanliness – for in cooking especially is it not indeed next to godliness? Over and over again during the two hours that the lesson lasted did I hear, 'Jane Joyce, let me look at your hands,' 'Mary Johnson, your nails; go and take the dirt out at once.'

The chief beauty of this lesson, it seemed to me, was that everything was real and practical. A mere book lesson in cookery we have already heard. But here the neck of mutton – a very small one, I don't mind telling you – baking in the oven was very real. The delicious fragrance of it saluted every nostril. Eggs for a Yorkshire pudding lay neatly ranged on the snow-white dresser – there was no doubt about *them*. They were no conjuror's *simulacra* of wood or plaster of Paris. The flour in the neat little wooden bins was real. The scales and the weights were real. And above all the fire was real, and gave forth a most acceptable warmth on this raw winter afternoon. There was just one drawback to all this reality – namely, the pale and hungry faces of many of the little cooks.

[69] Differentiation Between Girls and Boys in Elementary Science Lessons

T. A. Spalding, *The Work of the London School Board* (1900) pp. 209–10.

This science teaching, which is being gradually introduced into the schools, both in the boys' and girls' departments, is known by the name of 'Experimental Science.' Huxley, when addressing a large audience at Manchester, is reported to have said: 'That the education which precedes that of the workshop should be devoted to the cultivation of the intelligence, and especially to the imbuing of the mind with a broad and clear view of the laws of that natural world with the components of which the handicraftsman will have to deal.'

By way of beginning, measurements are performed by the children – viz., linear, superficial and cubical, preferably in the metric system, using very simple objects that fall within the reach of most children. It must be admitted that those who enjoy such advantages would afterwards enter upon practical life with a distinct and ineffaceable experience of scientific methods. They would observe, measure, and reason in a different way for the future.

Next they are taught the use of the balance and the art of weighing correctly. A splendid course of exercises can here be introduced, dealing with the relative densities of solids and liquids. For girls this knowledge is useful when testing the purity of many liquids used in the household, and for boys in the detection of the alloying of metals. The course proceeds to deal with the general effects of heat upon matter. The girl here obtains, from very simple experiments, a correct idea of the principles of ventilation, the construction and use of clinical and household thermometers; and the boy can learn at what period of the frost his father's water-pipe bursts.

The girls then study the difference between conduction, convection, and radiation of heat. From a simple experiment, which they themselves perform, they can tell you why a cotton fabric is to be preferred to a woollen one in the summer; why the water in the boiler behind the kitchener rises to the cistern in the bath room; or whether water boils more quickly in a kettle covered with soot than in one new and polished. The boy can explain why ice is packed in flannel or felt in summer, and why it is necessary, when descending into mines, that the safety-lamp should be surrounded by a gauze of close mesh.

Boys and girls are then encouraged to take up the questions of evaporation, of distillation, and of filtration, as a means whereby liquids may be separated from any impurities which they contain. Where possible, daily readings are taken of the weight of a bag of sea-weed, previously moistened with water, so as to ascertain the loss in weight by evaporation. Opportunities are afforded of explaining such instruments as the hygrometer, and its use in preparing weather charts. The girls, at the same time, can be taught to observe the most favourable condition of the atmosphere as regards moisture, for drying and airing clothes. They are next instructed in the question of the composition and weight of the air, bringing in the use of the barometer as a means for measuring the heights of mountains, for observing the distance of a balloon from the earth, and likewise in foretelling the weather for the next twenty-four hours.

[70] A Different Curriculum for Boys and Girls: (i) Kidsgrove National School, Staffordshire (ii) Fleet Road Senior Mixed School, Hampstead

National Society Monthly Paper (November 1851). *Second Report of the Royal Commission Appointed to Inquire into the Working of the Elementary Education Acts, P.P.* (1887) XXIX, p. 1016.

TIME-TABLE FOR A MIXED SCHOOL

Kidsgrove, Newcastle-under-Lyne, 9th September, 1851.
SIR, – At the request of the Secretary of the National School Society, who did me the honour some time since to visit my school, I have the pleasure to enclose a copy of our time-table.

I am not aware that it will present any peculiar excellence or novelty; all that I can say in its favour is, that it appears to work well, and to keep

TIME-TABLE

Prayers – Inspect for Cleanliness

Chant a Grace before meat, and dismiss at 11¼

CLASS	9¾	10	10¾	11¼
I	Hearing Lessons and revising Exercises got up at home. Mon. Wed. and Fri.: Dictation. Tuesday: Geography. Thursday: English History.	Mon. Wed. and Fri.: Reading–Holy Bible. Tuesday, Thursday: General Reading; with questioning, and parsing a sentence from the Lesson.	Mon. Tues. and Wed.: Slate Arithmetic. Thursday: Mental Arithmetic and Tables. Friday: Catechising.	
II	Hearing Lessons, &c., as in first class. Mon. Wed. and Fri.: Dictation. Tuesday, Thursday: Geography of the British Empire and Europe.	Writing in Copy-Books.	Monday, Wednesday: Reading–Holy Bible. Tuesday, Thursday: Genral Reading, &c. and the Parts of Speech. Friday: Catechising.	
III	Writing in Copy-Books.	Hearing Lessons learnt at home. Mon. Wed. and Fri.: Dictation. Tuesday, Thursday: Elementary Geography, and that of the British Isles.	Mon. Tues. and Wed.: Slate Arithmetic. Thursday: Mental Arithmetic and Tables. Friday: Catechising.	

[continued-over]

Prayers, &c. Dismiss

Assigning work to be done at home

Friday: a Gallery Lesson for all the Boys

| | 1 | 1½ | 2½ | 3½ 3¾ 4 |

Tuesday, Thursday:
Reading—Holy Bible.
Monday, Wednesday:
Arithmetic, including
Mensuration of plain
figures.

2d and 3d Class boys
united.
Monday, Wednesday:
Bible Lessons.
Tuesday:
Tables and Mental
Arithmetic.
Thursday:
English History.

Boys and Girls dismissed to their respective play-grounds for 10 minutes

Girls employed in Sewing, Knitting, &c.

Tuesday, Thursday:
Dictation.
Monday, Wednesday:
Geography.
Friday:
English History.

2d and 3d Class boys
united.
Tuesday, Thursday:
Dictation.
Mon. Wed. and Fri.:
General Reading, &c.

Writing in Copy-Book.

Mon. Tues. and Wed.:
Slate Arithmetic.
Thursday:
Mental Arithmetic and
Tables.
Friday:
Reading—Holy Bible.

Mon. Wed. and Fri.:
Reading—Holy Bible.
Tuesday, Thursday:
General Reading, &c.,
and pointing out Parts
of Speech.

Chant Grace after meat.— Inspect for Cleanliness

I

II

III

the teachers and scholars constantly employed. The work we require to be done at home is an essential element in our system, and embraces catechism, texts, hymns, English history, geography, grammar, spelling, tables, arithmetic, and English composition.

The boys and girls work together until the hour for sewing arrives; then a separation takes place, the boys working higher rules in arithmetic than we require of the girls.

In our mining district the boys go very early to work, and hence it is necessary that at the same age they should be more advanced than the girls. . . .

The accompanying time-table is for the advanced department of our school; we have another for the junior branch, but it is on the same system.

After now having had experience of the working of *Mixed Schools* for some time, I have no hesitation in stating, that for the generality of our country villages they have some advantages. They are the cheapest, for you can provide a superior master to superintend the mental training, a seamstress being sufficient for the sewing, &c.

The manners of the boys are softened by association with the girls, and the girls' minds strengthened by coming in contact with the stronger intellect of the boys.

Separate play-grounds will in all instances be required, and the watchful eye of a vigilant and pains-taking teacher. All my experience fails to supply me with a solitary illustration for those of my brethren who apprehend evils as likely to arise from the mixed system. – I remain, &c.

FREDERICK WADE

FLEET ROAD SENIOR SCHOOL, HAMPSTEAD, N.W.
ANALYSIS OF TIME TABLE, BOYS AND GIRLS

EX. VII

	Boys	*Girls*
	H. M.	H. M.
Grammar	1 0	1 45
Arithmetic	3 45	3 45
Shorthand	1 30	1 30
Letter writing	0 45	0 45
Book-keeping	1 30	1 30
Latin	2 15	—
Drawing	1 30	1 30
Map drawing	0 45	0 45
Recapitulation	1 0	1 0
Geography	0 30	0 30
Mensuration	1 45	—
Algebra	1 45	—
Reading	1 0	1 0
French	1 15	—
History	1 0	—
Needlework	—	2 30
Scripture	3 45	3 30

TIME TABLE FOR EX. VII

	Morning					2 to 2.15	2.15 to 3	Afternoon	
	9 to 9.45	9.45 to 10	10 to 10.30	10.30 to 11.15	11.35 to 12			3 to 3.45	3.45 to 4.30
Monday	Scripture	Register	Grammar Analysis Parsing, &c.	Arithmetic	Shorthand	Registers closed	Arithmetic	Letter writing	Book-keeping
Tuesday			Recapitulation. Standard work	*Boys,* Latin *Girls,* History	Drawing		*Boys,* Mensuration *Girls,* Needlework	3 to 4 *Boys,* Mensuration *Girls,* Needlework	4.0 to 4.30 Reading Colonies
Wednesday			Geography	Shorthand	Arithmetic		*Boys,* Algebra *Girls,* Needlework	3 to 4 *Boys,* Algebra. *Girls,* Needlework	4.10 to 4.30 Reading History
Thursday			Recapitulation Standard work	*Boys,* Latin *Girls,* History	Map drawing		Arithmetic	Book-keeping	*Boys,* Latin *Girls,* Grammar
Friday			Grammar	Arithmetic	Drawing		*Boys,* French *Girls,* Geography	3.0 to 3.30 *Boys,* French. *Girls,* Geography	3.30 to 4.30 History

[71] 'The Flesh of the Rhinocerous is Esteemed by the Hottentots'

Minnie Bulmer's Home and School Lesson Book (1877–8), St Maurice's Elementary School, York (Castle Museum, York). Transcription, 'The flesh of the rhinocerous', Composition, 'Wisdom Rewarded', Analysis of poem, 'We are Seven'. The second piece was given eight out of ten marks and the third piece of work nine out of ten.

Ruminating Grazing Carnivorous. Feeding on flesh Amphibious Living in two different elements.

Transcription

The flesh of the rhinocerous is esteemed by the Hottentots but it has a musky flavour. The flesh of the lion is coarse & tough, yet the negroes & Algerines eat it with great avidity. The tiger furnishes a rich feast in a Hottentot village & to the negroes of Guinea who also eat the flesh of the leopard. Cats are eaten without disrelish by various people both civilized & uncivilized. Otter's flesh is eaten by the Laplanders & by the American Indians, & that of the sea otter is considered delicate

TRANSCRIPTION

The flesh of the rhinocerous is esteemed by the Hottentots but it has a musky flavour. The flesh of the lion is coarse and tough, yet the negroes and Algerines eat it with great avidity. The tiger furnishes a rich feast in a Hottentot village and to the negroes of Guinea who also eat the flesh of the leopard. Cats are eaten without disrelish by various people both civilized and uncivilized. Otter's flesh is eaten by the Laplanders and by the American Indians, and that of the sea otter is considered delicate.

Wordsworth.

We are seven or a child's notion of death.

A simple child
That lightly draws its breath
And feels its life in every limb
What should it know of death.

I met a little cottage girl
She was eight years old; she said
Her hair was thick with many a curl
That clustered round her head.

She had a rustic woodland air
And she was wildly clad etc..

Subject	Predicate	Completion	Extension
A simple child	draws	its breath	that lightly
"	feels	its life	in every limb
it	should	"	
"	know	"	What of death
I	met	a little cottage girl	"
She	was	eight years old.	"
She	said		a curl
Her hair	was	thick	(with many)
(Curls)	clustered		round her head
She	had	a rustic woodland	"
She	was	"	&
"	clad		wildly

HOME LESSONS

WE ARE SEVEN OR A CHILD'S NOTION OF DEATH

A simple child
That lightly draws its breath
And feels its life in every limb
What should it know of death

I met a little cottage girl
She was eight years old; she said
Her hair was thick with many a curl
That clustered round her head

She had a rustic woodland air
And she was wildly clad etc.

Subject	Predicate	Completion	Extension
A simple child	draws ,,	its breath ,,	that lightly ,,
It	feels	its life	in every limb
it ,,	should know	,, ,,	,, What of death
I ,,	met ,,	a little cottage girl	,, ,,
She	was	eight years old	,,
She	said		a curl
Her hair	was	thick	(with many)
(Curls)	clustered		round her head
She	had	(air) a rustic woodland	,,
She ,,	was clad	,,	and wildly

COMPOSITION

WISDOM REWARDED

An Emperor was going for a walk one day when he saw an old man, planting a walnut tree. He went up to the man and asked him how old he was. The old man answered 'Sir, I am four years old.' The gentleman Emperor rebuked him for his absurdity. When the old man replied. It was very true for he had only served his God four years and the other part of his life was spent in folly and he did not reckon those. The Emperor then said did he expect those trees to grow and he said yes for he said that others had and if those did not they would do for someone else. The Emperor then gave the man one thousand pieces of gold.

Minnie Bulmer
St Maurices School.
Aged 10 years 1878

Standard V

Composition
Wisdom Rewarded.

An Emperor was going for a walk one day when
he saw an old man, planting a walnut tree.
He went up to the man & asked him how old
he was. The old man answered "Sir, I am four
years old." The Emperor rebuked him for his
absurdity. When the old man replied. It was very
true for he had only proved his life was four years.
& that other part of his life was spent in folly
& he did not reckon those. The Emperor then
said did he expect those trees to grow & he said
Yes, for he said that others had & if those had not
they would do for someone else.

[72] Coeducation: A Sympathetic View by a Workhouse School-master

Walsingham Guardians' Minutes, 26 December 1838 (Norfolk County Record Office).

DOWNHAM UNION 6 OCT. 1838

SIR,

In answer to your question, whether I have seen the plan of educating boys and girls in the same school extensively tried. It may not be out of place to state my own personal experience, I taught a school in my native parish upwards of eleven years on the above-mentioned plan and during that time I never had the smallest occasion to reprimand a boy for any indecent or improper conduct towards a girl. I then had above one hundred children committed to my charge. And the same plan is pursued in the Glasgow Normal Seminary where I was a student seven months previous to my coming to England where in the juvenile department there were upwards of four hundred children and in fact according to our system it is indispensably necessary that they be educated together. If the boys and girls were to be educated separately it would be injurious to both because it would deprive the girls of the benefit of the concentrated answers produced by the stronger minds of the boys; and it would deprive the boys of the quick perception and sometimes strong feeling evinced even by very little girls, particularly when scripture narratives are under consideration.

The boys require to be educated with girls in order to soften the boisterous manners consequent on their exuberant animal spirits; and the girls require to be educated with boys, in order that they may set more value on intellectual and moral qualifications, and less on frivolous show – Female instructors alone have been tried before now, but the schools conducted by them have never succeeded, any more than they would do without them – The voice alone of the Master commands the attention of the giddy; there is a formality in all schools conducted by females alone, which is totally destructive of the liberty so essential towards the development of the infant mind.

In the hands of a woman the reins of discipline cannot be loosened because she feels the effort of again curbing them would be beyond her physical powers. . . .

I am, Sir, Your most obt. Servt.

ARCHD. DUNLOP

24464

46 EDUCATION AND GIRLS

[73] Coeducation at Bedales

J. H. Badley, 'Some Problems of Government in a Mixed School', in
A. Woods (ed.), *Co-education* (1903).

It is all, of course, a question of degree; we do not want a girl to become
merely a copy, and an inferior copy, of a boy. She needs to be taught to
feel that it is as fine a thing to be a girl as to be a boy – a fact which, in the
first delight of freedom, she is apt to lose sight of in the desire to be all
that a boy is. She has to learn that all that is best in the boy, – strength of
purpose, fearlessness, uprightness, independence, – these things are to
be her aim no less than his; but that roughness of manner is no real part
of manliness nor one of the qualities that she feels to be admirable in him
or in herself. This lesson needs to be enforced upon the girl, just as the
boy needs to be made to feel that gentleness and manliness, so far from
being contradictory, are most truly admirable in conjunction. . . .

What we want is some approximation of the two hitherto contradictory standards of behaviour, at once to strengthen the girl and to
refine the boy. We do not want an exaggerated quietness on the part of
the girl, or an exaggerated politeness on the part of the boy, tending
only to produce affectation on the one side and contempt on the other.
Both alike must be taught good manners towards their elders, and good
temper and consideration towards each other, the soil in which courtesy
is a natural growth. It is no doubt always easier to lay down a set of rules
to which all must be required to conform; but real training requires
more freedom of action to encourage self-activity, and this means that
we must fall back upon the living contact of personal influence rather
than the dead pressure of external rule. We cannot ever hope to
dispense with rules entirely, but where public opinion is most active and
the common tone healthiest, rules are least needed and press most
lightly. And these are the conditions of the truest growth.

A word in conclusion on the freedom of intercourse allowed here
between girls and boys. From what has already been said it will be plain
that no mere formalities of speech or manner are interposed. With us it
has become the custom to address boys by their surnames, girls by their
christian names or by both, and this they do amongst themselves. In the
intervals between the set tasks of the day (which as above pointed out,
are shared in common) they can mix together quite freely. Only in this
way, we think, by the removal of the formal barriers can we attain our
aim of establishing mutual understanding between the sexes, a bond of
sympathy growing from the interests and occupations of a common life.

Such a course we believe, so far from being a source of sentimentality, to be its surest prevention. And for the same reason we do not taboo friendship between boy and girl as a thing which cannot be sensible and good for both. Only it must be simple and frank. Secrets and silliness must not be allowed to root, and can soon be weeded out when the good feeling of the community is against them. A sense of humour is a great thing in a school, and especially amongst girls, as an antidote to the poison of sentimentality.

[74] A 'Progressive Curriculum for Boys and Girls at Bedales School, working with Cecil Reddie at Abbotsholme, Badley founded

BEDALES SCHOOL

	MORNING						
	7 a.m.	8	9	10	11	12 noon	1 p.m.
MONDAY						Clothes Inspection	
TUESDAY	DRESSING · MORNING RUN	BREAKFAST · BED-MAKING &c	CLASS WORK (MILK AND BISCUITS)			DRILL (IN SUMMER BATHING) · DINNER INSPECTION	DINNER
WEDNESDAY	DRESSING · MORNING RUN	BREAKFAST · BED-MAKING &c	CLASS WORK (MILK AND BISCUITS)			DRILL (IN SUMMER BATHING) · DINNER INSPECTION	DINNER
THURSDAY	DRESSING · MORNING RUN	BREAKFAST · BED-MAKING &c	{ Language[1] Mathematics Science	BREAK FOR LUNCH	{ Language[1] Mathematics Science	DRILL (IN SUMMER BATHING) · DINNER INSPECTION	DINNER
FRIDAY	DRESSING · MORNING RUN	BREAKFAST · BED-MAKING &c		BREAK FOR LUNCH			
SATURDAY						Clothes Inspection	
SUNDAY		Dressing Prayers	Breakfast / Letter-writing	Bed-making	Singing practice	F R E E	

J. B. Hadley, *Bedales School. Outline of its Aims and System* (1900). After Bedales School.

GENERAL ARRANGEMENT OF THE DAY

Columns: (AF)TERNOON | EVENING — times 3, 4, 5, 6, 7, 8, 9

(left)	3	4	5	6	7	8	9
hop	G A M E S²					Preparation / { Carving, Book-Binding, Stuffing &c }	
g &c	{ Gardening. Farm-work. Dairy 3 }				READING	Preparation | Sewing	
alf	Matches. Expeditions	Games. Nat. History &c		CLASS WORK	READING FOR TIME / SINGING / CHANGING	Concert / Debate or / Recitations	SUPPER (MILK AND BISCUITS) / PRAYERS / BATHS AND DORMITORY INSPECTION
hop	G A M E S	(CHANGING)	TEA	{ History, Literature }	QUIET TIME / SINGING	Preparation / { Carving, Book-Binding, Stuffing &c }	
ng &c	{ Gardening. Farm-work. Dairy }					Preparation / Dancing	
Half	Matches. Expeditions	Games. Nat. History &c				L E C T U R E	SUPPER
	Walk			Reading	Service		SUPPER

...guage includes Latin, French or German
...ls play lacrosse or hockey instead of football
...ls do dairying instead of farming

INDEX

Lyttelton, Alfred   23
Lyttelton, Edward   40, 104–7

Maclaren, Archibald   205–7
Mann, Horace   29
mark, attestation by   3
Marlborough   141
marriage and education   48–9
mass education, civilising power
  of   7
Maudsley, Dr   219–21
middle class: female education   207;
  plea for better educational opportunities for   127–30; schools   11,
  13
    coeducation in   53
    social grading of   11
    social regeneration by   24–7
    upbringing   74
mixed schools   53–4, 197, 245–9;
  curriculum in   234–40, 248–9
model school   16
Moffatt's Pupil-Teachers' Course   177–
  9
monitorial school, work and discipline in   153–8
moral agent, state as   73, 84–90;
  limits on   87–90
moral education   73, 114–16; headmaster's views on   104–9; religion
  and   73–109; teachers' responsibility for   185–6, 228–30;
  young teacher's views on   79–81
More, Hannah   46, 75–7
Morley, C.   232–3

National Education League   9
National Education Union   9
National Society for Promoting
  the Education of the Poor in
  the Principles of the Church of
  England   6, 14, 15, 17, 24, 81–3

monthly paper   190–2, 234–40
Nonconformity   15, 16–19
North London Collegiate School
  210–12, 222

object lessons   34, 36, 159–63
Owen, Robert   35

pagan beliefs   19
parents: influence of, inspector's
  views on   119–21; responsibilities
  of   96–8, 104–7; school discipline
  and   167–8; social elevation of,
  needed   122
Plumptre, Fellow of Eton   102–4
poor children, education of   6, 7, 14,
  27, 75–8, 89, 110, 112, 116, 122–5;
  see also charity schools; workhouse
  education
Potter's Academy   132–6
poverty, schooling sacrificed because
  of   29, 31, 110, 121–3
private schools: percentage of pupils
  in   5; run by working-class intellectual   182–5; schoolmaster's
  position in society   190–92; self-
  financing   5
proprietary schools   11, 39; for
  girls   48, 52, 196, 210–14, 225–8
Protestantism   84; interdenominational   74; working-class children and   19
public schools   11–12, 39, 107–8,
  111, 128, 130–32; curriculum
  137–42; devotional life in   21; religious instruction in   21–3; science in   140–2; tepid Christianity
  in   101–4
Public Schools' Commission   131,
  137; *see also* Clarendon Commission
pupil-teacher   34, 41, 155–6, 177–9;
  inspector on life as   179–82; in